Community Care
and Inclusion
*for People with an
Intellectual Disability*

Community Care
and Inclusion
for People with an
Intellectual Disability

Edited by Robin Jackson and Maria Lyons

Floris
Books

In memory of
Professor Nils Christie

1928–2015

Nils was to have contributed a chapter to this book, but sadly was killed in a traffic accident. He was Professor of Criminology in the Faculty of Law, University of Oslo, and wrote what many consider to be the most insightful description of the role of Camphill communities: *Beyond Loneliness and Institutions: Communes for Extraordinary People* (1989).

First published in 2016 by Floris Books
© 2016 Floris Books
The authors have asserted their right under the
Copyright, Designs and Patent Act 1988 to be
identified as the authors of this work

Also available
as an eBook

MIX
Paper from
responsible sources
FSC® C007785

British Library CIP data available
ISBN 978-178250-333-0
Printed in Great Britain
by Bell & Bain, Ltd

Foreword

I don't think there is anyone who mourns the closing of the large institutions that excluded people with serious disabilities from the rest of society. But that doesn't mean that the current forms of provision that replaced them should be exempt from critical examination. Can we be sure that the policy of 'care in the community' hasn't led to care in isolation? In the search for independent living have we lost the social and shared experience of living together? Has this emphasis on independent living merely led to greater exclusion? Increasingly I feel that in many cases 'care' has become something done to someone, not done with them. In the debate around welfare reform and how we should empower and support people with disabilities, the voice of those with an intellectual disability is frequently lost. The chapters in this book make a significant contribution to the debate on how best we can offer care.

Dame Anne Begg

Dame Anne Begg was Member of Parliament for Aberdeen South (1997–2015) and chaired the House of Commons Work and Pensions Select Committee (2010–2015). Dame Anne was the first permanent wheelchair user to sit in the House of Commons since 1880 and has long been a forthright advocate for the rights of people with disabilities.

Acknowledgements

This book would not have been possible without the enthusiastic response given by the contributors, all of whom were agreed that the topic of community care and inclusion for people with an intellectual disability was a vital one that merited urgent attention. We are immensely grateful to Eleanor Collins, Leah McDowell, Suzanne Kennedy and Jen Bowden of Floris Books for the wholehearted encouragement and invaluable professional advice and guidance offered to us in the production of this book from its inception to final publication.

Contents

Chapter Summaries

Introduction
Robin Jackson
Visiting Research Fellow, Centre for Learning Disability Studies, University of Hertfordshire, UK
Community care is a concept that has shaped government policy, provision and practice for people with an intellectual disability for four decades. Jackson introduces three key concepts, 'community', 'community care' and 'inclusion' and explores how discussion of innovative forms of social care provision – including intentional supportive communities of different kinds – can bring about the fundamental changes required to enhance the quality of life for people with an intellectual disability.

The History of Intellectual Disability: Inclusion or Exclusion?
Simon Jarrett
Wellcome Trust doctoral researcher, Department of History, Classics and Archaeology, Birkbeck, University of London, UK
Jarrett challenges the portrayal of the history of people with an intellectual disability as one of exclusion, neglect and abuse. He argues that exclusion is not the historical norm for people with intellectual disabilities, and is in fact an anomaly that has been in place for the last 150 years: a relatively short period in historical terms.

At Society's Pleasure: The Rise and Fall of Services to People with an Intellectual Disability
Robert Cummins
Emeritus Professor of Psychology, Faculty of Health, Deakin University, Australia
Cummins traces the historical path of service provision for people with an intellectual disability in the UK and Australia and

describes in detail the National Disability Insurance Scheme, one of the most important social reforms in recent Australian history.

Realities of Social Life and their Implications for Social Inclusion

Robin Dunbar

Professor of Evolutionary Psychology, Department of Experimental Psychology, University of Oxford, UK

Dunbar argues that over the last two centuries we have moved from care in the community to care in institutions and back. Using recent research in social psychology and neuroscience, he questions whether these changes have had in mind the real interests of those for whom they were intended and examines evidence regarding the suitability of small residences within the wider community.

Making a Space for the Lost Stories of Inclusion

Paul Milner

Senior Researcher, Donald Beasley Institute, New Zealand

Brigit Mirfin-Veitch

Director, Donald Beasley Institute, New Zealand

Focusing on New Zealand's vision of a more inclusive society, Milner and Mirfin-Veitch explore the limited ways in which people with an intellectual disability have had the opportunity to author their place in the social historical record. They argue that people with an intellectual disability have been written out of the research canon, and that until these people are heard we cannot claim as a society to be meeting our human rights obligations.

Affordances and Challenges of Virtual Communities for People with an Intellectual Disability

Judith Molka-Danielsen

Professor in Information Systems, Molde University College, Norway

Susan Balandin

Professor in Disability and Inclusion, Deakin University, Australia

The chapter highlights the affordances and challenges of virtual communities in the lives of people with an intellectual disability. It contends that ongoing research is needed into barriers to using virtual communities. Longitudinal studies are needed to learn more about the potential benefits of inclusion and involvement of people with an intellectual disability in the virtual communities of their choice.

Social Exclusion of People with an Intellectual Disability: A Psychotherapist's Perspective
Alan Corbett
Trustee, Institute of Psychotherapy and Disability, London, UK

Corbett suggests that the social exclusion of people with an intellectual disability is determined by two layers of psychological functioning: the individual and social unconscious. By placing people with an intellectual disability on the margins of society, we unconsciously hope that we have distanced ourselves safely from our own deficits and failures in thinking.

Community Health Care for People with an Intellectual Disability: A Pharmacist's Perspective
Bernadette Flood
Pharmacist, The Daughters of Charity Disability Support Services, Dublin, Ireland

Whilst equal outcomes in health care are important for people with an intellectual disability, the evidence of what forms of intervention are effective is sparse. The development of health literacy skills in this population will impact the health status of the population and medication use. In particular, community and pharmacy resources and services should be targeted at this vulnerable population, in which there is a high level of medication use.

Citizenship and Community: The Challenge of Camphill
Dan McKanan
Emerson Chair of Divinity, Harvard Divinity School, Harvard University, USA

McKanan argues that intentional communities, in which people with and without intellectual disabilities live and work together, have a vital role to play in addressing current challenges to democracy. The Camphill model is singled out by the author as one which succeeds in empowering persons with intellectual disabilities and treating them as full citizens of the communities in which they live and not merely as recipients of services.

The Widening Impact of an Intentional Supportive Community

Diedra Heitzman

Executive Director, Camphill Village Kimberton Hills, Pennsylvania, USA

Heitzman provides a description of the mission and operation of Camphill Village Kimberton Hills in Pennsylvania, where community members live alongside each other and work together to create a valid and useful life. The author argues that by uniting people from diverse backgrounds, ages and abilities in reciprocal and authentic relationships, it is possible to create together what otherwise would be difficult to achieve - a genuinely inclusive and widely interconnected community.

Re-thinking Work in Relation to Community Inclusion

Maria Lyons

Founder, Camphill Research Network, UK

In this chapter, access to employment is seen as a key component in strategies to improve levels of community participation and inclusion for people with intellectual disabilities. The author describes the thinking lying behind this objective and some of the obstacles to its realisation. It examines an alternative approach to disability and work where the pecuniary aspect is de-emphasised and the qualities of service and personal fulfilment are celebrated.

Employment Services for People with an Intellectual Disability: Building Connections in Vermont

Bryan Dague

Research Associate, Center for Disability and Community Inclusion, University of Vermont, USA

This chapter outlines the background to introducing supported employment programmes in the open community for people with an intellectual disability in Vermont, USA. The chapter also provides a description of an innovative and inclusive programme recently developed at the University of Vermont for students with intellectual disabilities: the Think College Vermont programme. This two-year course, which has succeeded in achieving a 90 per cent employment rate for participants, is now to be replicated in other Vermont colleges.

Community Living, Inclusion and Disability in China
Chris Walter
Tutor (BA Social Pedagogy), Camphill School Aberdeen, UK
Walter describes his experience of participating in a residential programme with children with an intellectual disability and their families in China. He notes that the Confucian emphasis on consensus and harmony can lead to conformity and an unwillingness to risk social disapproval. He draws attention to the notion of 'affiliate stigma', the negative perception resulting from being related to someone with an intellectual disability. Such a perception, which is widely prevalent in Chinese society, makes successful community acceptance and inclusion more problematic.

Gross National Happiness as an Alternative Development Paradigm, and its Relevance for Community Wellbeing
Ha Vinh Tho
Program Director, Gross National Happiness Centre, Bhutan
The author outlines his initial work in special education and the way in which this led on to an interest in general education, ecology, community building and social entrepreneurship. He then describes establishing the Peaceful Bamboo Family, an intentional working and learning community, in Vietnam. Finally, he presents the case for substituting Gross National Happiness for Gross National Product as a developmental paradigm if more equitable, sustainable and inclusive societies are to be created.

Longing for Virtuous Community
Michael Kendrick
Founder, Kendrick Consulting, Massachusetts, USA
According to Kendrick 'community' is a term that is constantly heard in regards to matters related to disability. A lack of precision in how community is defined and interpreted makes assessment of communities quite difficult. Community as an automatic source of the 'good life' may be quite a wishful, if not naïve, understanding of how communities actually work.

Introduction

A number of factors have prompted the publication of this book. First and foremost, that people with an intellectual disability – those with significant limitations in both intellectual functioning and adaptive behaviour – have become an invisible population. The Chief Executive of the National Development Team for Inclusion in the UK recently observed that people with an intellectual disability have achieved little or no profile for the last twenty years (Greig 2015). He highlighted an informal conversation that he had had with a senior government official who told him that any attempt to seek radical improvements in provision for people with an intellectual disability would fail, as the numbers were too small to warrant government action. But it is estimated that there are at least 1.2 million people with an intellectual disability in England (Emerson et al. 2012). When one adds those directly involved in the support of people with an intellectual disability, including family members and care staff, that figure is significantly increased.

A further reason for this book is that there continues to be a widespread lack of understanding of three key concepts, 'community', 'community care' and 'inclusion', which have shaped the policy, provision and practice of educational and social care over the past thirty years. This book challenges many of the common assumptions that lie behind these concepts.

Ideology

In examining developments in the field of intellectual disability, we must carefully examine the ideologies and beliefs to which people subscribe. Practitioners and researchers in the field continue to publish evidence that the needs of people with intellectual disabilities are not being met due to the influence of current ideologies (Gates & Atherton 2001). One argument that frequently emerges in disability studies is that the term 'disability' has been socially constructed often for what Lester (2012) has described as 'sinister (bourgeois) class reasons'.

The sociological literature of the 1980s portrayed special educational provision for pupils with an intellectual disability in a very negative light (Barton & Tomlinson 1981, Tomlinson 1982, Booth & Potts 1983), and pupils attending special schools were represented as victims of the class system. A significant feature of this literature was the total absence of any supportive empirical research.

Lester counters this understanding of 'disability' as constructed for 'sinister (bourgeois) class reasons', suggesting that over the years, valuable insights from the 1970s, including ideas such as 'normalisation' and 'social role valorisation', have become ossified into a disability dogma that is difficult to dislodge. He draws attention to the fact that there isn't much opposition to this output 'in literature on disability studies'. Anyone questioning these arguments is often represented as heartless and may risk professional and personal ostracism.

When society is replete with dogmas that are based on ideology rather than empirical research, political correctness flourishes. Political correctness is defined here 'as a canon of orthodoxies and prohibitions and as a set of claims that society today does not readily allow to be questioned' (Klatt 2000). Psychiatrists in the intellectual disability field have expressed concern about the impact of political correctness on their way of working. This was made clear at a conference of the Royal College of Psychiatry's Faculty of Learning Disability where the house proposed that 'Political correctness is laying waste to learning disability services' (Royal College of Psychiatrists 2007).

Kavale and Forness have described what happens when political, ideological and philosophical considerations count for more than logical, objective and rational study (1998). The fear is that, for some people with an intellectual disability, we may have replaced one oppressive living arrangement with another.

Many people who lived in the closed regimes of an institution had minimal opportunity to be accorded dignity and function independently. Now, some people with an intellectual disability are suffering similar restrictions in contemporary society by being located in densely populated urban areas where it is not safe to venture out alone, and where unskilled, under-resourced and stressed staff offer the only available interaction (Williams 2010a, 2010b). In the UK, there is considerable evidence to suggest that intellectual disability service provision has been made more difficult, complicated and expensive to deliver because of the intrusion of ideological factors (Jackson & Irvine 2013).

Thirty years ago, Zigler and Hall (1986) argued that we should avoid adopting an all-or-nothing attitude in any debate about providing appropriate services for people with intellectual disabilities. They noted that there are many forces at work that depict issues as being either/or choices, thus driving out the middle-ground. In their analysis, anyone who polarises the debate by promoting one solution to the total exclusion of all others, does that situation and its complexity a disservice. What is required is an approach that is open, evidenced and respectful.

Early on, Wolfensberger (2003) expressed concern at the ideological radicalisation of advocacy movements that purported to represent people with an intellectual disability, but which, because of their confrontational stance and strident tone, antagonised and alienated those professional workers whose support was vital if appropriate services were to be developed.

The case for the intentional supportive community

The policy of placing people with an intellectual disability in the open 'community' is based on the assumption that those communities will be welcoming and supportive. But research undertaken by Lemos and Crane, together with the Foundation for People with a Learning Disability, found that people with an intellectual disability living 'independently in the community' frequently experience a disturbing range of incidents often characterised by cruelty, such as crime, abuse and harassment (Gravell 2012).

A survey by Turning Point, a leading health and social care provider, found that more than half of those questioned believed that people with an intellectual disability were the group that experienced the most discrimination in society (Williams 2010c). Growing public concern at the vulnerability of disabled people, in particular their greater risk of experiencing violence or hostility, led the Equality and Human Rights Commission to examine the issue. The findings of the Commission were subsequently published in the report *Promoting the Safety and Security of Disabled People* (EHRC 2009).

In contrast to the risks of the open community, there is a strong case for broadening the range of options for people with an intellectual disability to include the *intentional supportive community*. The focus of such a community is to provide an environment where adults with and without an intellectual disability can live and work together in a climate of mutual respect. There are six qualities that can usually be found in intentional supportive communities: mutuality, rhythmicity, wellbeing, tranquility, ecological sensitivity, and economic sustainability (Jackson 2013). These six qualities are of great benefit to everyone, but particularly people with intellectual disabilities, and are much more difficult, indeed sometimes impossible, to find in the wider community. I will expand on each below.

(1) Mutuality

The relationship between the carer and the person with an intellectual disability in intentional supportive communities is characterised by mutuality, defined here as respectful give and take between and among persons. Mutuality is not merely a technique or attitude; it is a practice that embodies the value of interaction and understanding, in contrast to isolation and alienation. This life-sharing aspect of living in an intentional community is one of its defining features, and it ensures that the principles of dignity, value, and mutual respect can be meaningfully translated into practice.

The daily process of learning across difference and inequality is vital, for it transforms the basic attitudes of caregivers toward difference. Furthermore, the negotiation of power sharing among unequal persons makes a reality of the rhetoric of empowerment, because such an approach requires the power to come from, and be given up by, someone else, namely the caregiver. What we are talking about here is the establishment of an affective relationship that is unconditional. Mutual friendship provides the cohesive force that binds together the different elements of a community; it is the mortar without which any communal edifice would collapse.

(2) Rhythmicity

Rhythmicity is a potent force not only in linking people, but also in creating a sense of internal togetherness. Life comprises a wide range of natural rhythms, from the regularity of the heartbeat to the change from day to night. Rhythmicity is an essential ingredient in human communication and development. In attempting to communicate effectively with an individual, the carer has to fall into step with that person so they both dance to the same tune. The individual and the caregiver then search for ways to establish and maintain that joint rhythm in a process that is mutually inclusive. A sensitivity to rhythmic engagement can help carers pace their interactions with the individual, and interact and speak *with*, rather than *to*, this person. It is important for carers to learn to listen, to look, and to freshly explore the pulse of groups they work with. Only by living one's work in a community can one become fully sensitised to these rhythms and thus respond appropriately.

(3) Wellbeing

Attention to the wellbeing of the individual is an integral part of life in intentional communities. Wellbeing, which may have everything or nothing to do with religious belief and observance, can be defined as a sense of good health about oneself as a human being and as a unique individual. It occurs when people are fulfilling their potential, are aware of their own dignity and value, enjoy themselves and have direction, can recognise this quality in others and consequently respect and relate positively to them, and are at ease with the world around them. Wellbeing does not result from the acquisition and application of a series of techniques and skills, it comes from sharing together and learning together, addressing questions that relate to the value and meaning of life.

(4) Tranquility

A further feature of many intentional communities is the tranquility of the environment in which many are set. This contrasts with the location of many 'homes in the community' in busy, noisy and atmospherically polluted town and city centres. Most visitors to an intentional community quickly become aware of this distinct quality. But what do we mean by tranquility?

Too often, tranquility is simply equated with silence or an absence of noise, but tranquility is a quality that has to be created. It can be defined as a state of inner emotional and intellectual peace. While many recognise its general importance, few understand its specific benefits. Tranquility can help individuals overcome feelings of anger, nervousness, and fear that are often part of daily life. It brings enhanced levels of emotional and mental calm that enable the individual to feel mentally stable and grounded. By keeping the mind clear and constant, tranquility can help improve judgement and make the future appear bright and positive. This in turn helps to maintain a person's good physical health by keeping the body strong and resistant to illness. Thus there is a sense in which tranquility is healing or curative.

(5) Ecological sensitivity

Most intentional supportive communities attach particular importance to ecological sensitivity and a wide range of their activities enhance the quality of the natural environment. This is done through:

- using natural fertilisers and banning chemical herbicides and pesticides;
- employing organic and/or biodynamic practices in agriculture and horticulture;
- constructing installations that harness solar, wind and geothermal energy, to reduce the need for external power supplies;
- recycling materials and minimising waste;
- and constructing buildings from natural materials that are in harmony with their surroundings.

(6) Economic sustainability

In her chapter in this book, Heitzman points to research that estimates the cost for adults with disabilities in intentional supportive communities is between one half and one sixth the cost of state-funded or other private options (Larson 2010). This cost efficiency is achieved by a variety of means, including:

- no incremental salary structures;
- opportunities for collective budgeting;
- selling community-made products;
- self-sufficiency, for example, communities producing their own fruit, vegetables, dairy products, bread;
- minimising waste;
- using economic power sources;
- keeping the construction and maintenance of buildings and equipment 'in house';
- and renting community facilities to external groups.

The meaning of 'institution'

Some critics of the intentional supportive community model claim that it is a form of institutionalisation (Collins 2000). But that argument does not withstand close inspection. Erving Goffman (1961) identified what he saw as the essential characteristics of 'a total institution' as:

- the progressive loss by individual residents of their sense of identity;
- the imposition of constraints on basic liberties of residents (i.e. freedom of movement, speech and action);
- the development of professional hierarchies that lose sight of, and work against, the realisation of an institution's therapeutic and rehabilitative aims;
- the increasingly routinised and closely regulated nature of institutional life;
- staff seeking to create and maintain a social distance between themselves and residents.

But the intentional supportive community is the antithesis of the 'total institution' when one looks at its main features:

- 'staff' who live alongside residents;
- a generally low 'staff' turnover;
- an absence of shift work;
- no managerial hierarchies;
- engagement in meaningful work;
- location in a congenial and safe environment;
- handy access to the local neighbourhood for residents;
- convenient access by members of the public to the community (for example, the community shop);
- availability of a range of creative, social and recreational activities;
- and the perception of the intentional community as a local asset by the surrounding neighbourhood.

The effectiveness of intentional supportive communities (village communities) has been demonstrated in research sponsored by the Department of Health and undertaken by the Hester Adrian Research Centre (HARC) at Manchester University (Emerson et al. 1999). A curious feature of this research is that the selection of the three types of organisation surveyed – village communities, NHS residential campuses, and community-based dispersed housing schemes – was based on second-hand reports that they were exemplars of 'good practice'. In other words, the village communities were not being compared with a representative cross-section of 'homes in the community' for people with an intellectual disability. Nevertheless the results clearly demonstrated that in all the areas examined, the village communities did as well as, or better than, the dispersed housing schemes. Whilst reference continues to be made to this research by government departments, little or no attention is paid to the performance of the village communities. It's interesting to note how Collins (2000) transforms the benefits of living in intentional supportive communities (village communities), found in the HARC research, into 'disbenefits'. Most of the areas rated highly in this study reflect, in her opinion, the nature of the 'village community', which by definition is more structured, organised and enclosed than ordinary life. Collins states that an intentional supportive community, a 'village community', is not community in the ordinary sense of the word: it exists and operates as an institution. While it may have a more relaxed and homely style than the word 'institution' tends to suggest, its numbers, situation and focus underline its separation from mainstream life. Collins goes on to claim that people who live in institutions (including 'village communities') are inevitably denied the spontaneity and informality of real life experiences, and subsequently the risks and challenges they bring with them (Coe et al. 2001). Yet as discussed, when we look at the characteristics of Goffman's 'total institution' they are the antithesis of an intentional supportive community. Collins' rejection of any structure for communal living risks leaving people with intellectual disabilities isolated and unsupported.

It is telling that the cartoon accompanying Collins' article, depicts a 'village community' as a prison surrounded by high walls and barbed wire. The historic inference would not be lost on those working in Camphill settings, given that Camphill owes its origin to the flight from Central Europe of a small group of men and women escaping almost certain death in concentration camps – the ultimate total institution.

But intentional supportive communities can only survive if their work:

- is grounded in everyday reality and is not anchored to some mythical past;
- is operationally transparent to funders and users;
- is outwardly orientated and not insular in its philosophy and practice;
- possesses a clearly articulated philosophical purpose;
- and has policies and practices that are conceptually clear and not opaque.

I am not arguing here that the policy of placing adults with an intellectual disability in 'homes in the community' should be discontinued. I am proposing that a range of options should be available, including intentional supportive communities, so that people with intellectual disabilities are offered genuine choice – a right to which they are morally and legally entitled. For that to happen, we must first counter the invisibility of this population in the eyes of government.

Conclusion

As well as challenging some of the common and misleading assumptions that surround the concepts of 'community', 'community care' and 'inclusion', this book provides examples of innovative professional practice from Vermont, USA to Vietnam. A number of chapters make reference to Camphill intentional supportive (village) communities where great emphasis is placed on the importance of personal development within a framework of community living, and where the traditional boundaries between professional disciplines are dissolved. This transdisciplinary approach is holistic in character and embraces educational, therapeutic and medical activities, aspects of care, and the use of crafts and creative arts (Jackson 2011). However, more widespread acceptance of a holistic approach would necessitate not only a radical transformation in the character of educational and social care, but also fundamental changes in the nature and purpose of professional training for those working in such settings. As those who have made reference to the Camphill model will freely concede, there are other forms of intentional supportive communities that merit serious examination. While arguing for a stronger awareness of the benefits of Camphill communities, I do not envisage that these communities will ever form more than a minority of residential settings for people with an intellectual disability.

This leads to the key question of whether there is any inclination on the part of governments to create communities whose characteristics challenge current orthodoxies. It may well be the case that the only way to meet the needs of people with an intellectual disability is through adopting the kind of socio-political revolution described in the chapter here by Ha Vinh Tho, where countries are no longer in thrall to the Gross National

Product. He indicates a growing tension between an old economic model based on narrow financial metrics and an emerging developmental paradigm based on happiness and wellbeing – a tension that manifests itself in the field of educational and social care, and especially in the field of intellectual disability.

However if this kind of revolution is to be achieved in the UK, we would need to dismantle a powerful corporatist state where democratic institutions have been colonised by commercial and financial interests (Milne 2013). Ten years ago the possibility of such a challenge being mounted would have been unthinkable; now however, particularly among the young, there is an upsurge of the opinion that the present system of public governance in Western countries is not fit for purpose (Stevenson 2011).

Whilst the primary purpose of this book is to encourage the reader to look more closely and critically at the key concepts of 'community', 'community care' and 'inclusion' and to explore innovative forms of social care provision for people with an intellectual disability, it is the authors' hope that readers arrive at an understanding that real improvements in quality of life would require fundamental changes in the nature of our society.

Robin Jackson

References

Barton, L. & Tomlinson, S. (eds.) (1981) *Special Education: Policy, practices and social issues.* London: Harper & Row.

Booth, T. & Potts, P. (1983) *Integrating Special Education.* Oxford: Blackwell.

Coe, D., Haldane, C. & Jackson, R. (2001) 'Village communities: Time for an informed debate?', *Community Living,* 14(3): 22–24.

Collins, J. (2000) 'Are villages really 'a suitable option?', *Community Living,* 13(3): 24–25.

Emerson, E., Robertson, J., Gregory, N. & Hatton, C., et al. (1999) *Quality and Costs of Residential Supports for People with Learning Disabilities: A comparative analysis of quality and costs in village communities, residential campuses and dispersed housing schemes.* Manchester: Hester Adrian Research Centre.

Emerson, E., Hatton, C., Robertson, J., Roberts, H., Baines, S., Evison, F. & Glover, G. (2012) *People with Learning Disabilities in England 2011: Services & Supports.* Improving Health and Lives: Learning Disabilities Observatory.

Equality and Human Rights Commission (2009) *Promoting the Safety and Security of Disabled People.*

Gates, B. & Atherton, H. (2001) 'The challenge of evidence-based practice for learning disabilities', *British Journal of Learning Disabilities*, 10: 517–522.

Goffman, E. (1961) *Asylums: Essays on the social situations of mental patients and other inmates*. London: Penguin Books.

Gravell, C. (2012) *Loneliness and Cruelty: People with learning disabilities and their experience of harassment, abuse and related crime in the community*. London: Lemos&Crane.

Greig, R. (2015) 'The policy construct behind community care', *International Journal of Developmental Disabilities*, 61(2): 61–67.

Jackson, R. (2011) 'The origin of Camphill and the social pedagogic impulse', *Educational Review*, 63(1): 95–104.

— (2013) 'The Austrian provenance of the worldwide Camphill Movement', *Journal of Austrian Studies*, 46(4): 23–40.

Jackson, R. & Irvine, H. (2012) 'The impact of ideology on provision of services for people with an intellectual disability', *International Journal of Developmental Disabilities*, 59(1): 20–34.

Kavale, K. & Forness, S. (1998) 'The politics of learning disabilities', *Learning Disability Quarterly*, 21: 245–273.

Klatt, H. (2000) *Psychology and Ideology – the study of political correctness*. London: University of Western Ontario. http://www.safs.ca/september2001/psy383e.html.

Larson, S., Ryan, A., Salmi, P., Smith, D. & Wuorio, A. (2010) *Residential Services for Persons with Developmental Disabilities: Status and trends through 2010*. Minneapolis: University of Minnesota, Research and Training Center on Community Living, Institute on Community Integration.

Lester, J. (2012) 'The disability studies industry'. *Libertarian Alliance*, 26 September. http://www.la-articles.org.uk/dsi.pdf.

Milne, S. (2013) 'Corporate power has turned Britain into a corrupt state'. *Guardian*. http://www.theguardian.com/commentisfree/2013/jun/04/corporate-britain-corrupt-lobbying-revolving-door.

Royal College of Psychiatrists (2007) Programme for this conference held in Belfast on 4–5 October. http://www.rcpsych.ac.uk/PDF/ProvProgLD07.pdf.

Stevenson, A. (2013) 'New voters like politics, not politicians', *politics.co.uk*. http://www.politics.co.uk/news/2011/09/15/new-voters-like-politics-not-politicians.

Tomlinson, S. (1982) *A Sociology of Special Education*. London: Routledge & Kegan Paul.

Williams, R. (2010a) 'Poll reveals widespread discrimination against people with learning disabilities'. *Guardian*. http://www.guardian.co.uk/society/2010/jul/14/discrimination-learning-disabilities/. Accessed 4 Dec. 2014.

— (2010b) '"Mate crime" fears for people with learning disabilities', *Guardian*. http://www.guardian.co.uk/society/2010/sep/14/learning-disabilities-mate-crime. Accessed 4 Dec. 2014.

— (2010c) 'Poll reveals widespread discrimination against people with learning disabilities', *Guardian*. https://www.theguardian.com/society/2010/jul/14/discrimination-learning-disabilities.

Wolfensberger, W. (2003) *The Future of Children with Significant Impairments: What parents fear and want and what they and others may be able to do about it*. Syracuse, New York: Training Institute for Human Service Planning, Leadership and Change Agentry.

Zigler, E. & Hall, N. (1986) 'Mainstreaming and the philosophy of normalisation'. In: C. Meisel, (ed.), *Mainstreaming Handicapped Children: Outcomes, controversies and new directions*. New Jersey: Lawrence Erlbaum Associates Inc., pp. 1–10.

The History of Intellectual Disability: Inclusion or Exclusion?

SIMON JARRETT

'The idiot', wrote Dr Martin Barr in *Mental Defectives: Their history, treatment and training* (1904), is a form of human who 'sees nothing, feels nothing, hears nothing, does nothing and knows nothing'. Barr was the medical superintendent of the Pennsylvania Training School for Feeble-Minded Children and also the president of the American Association for the Study of Feeblemindedness. This was the first attempt to write a comprehensive history of the group of people whom Barr knew as 'mental defectives' or 'the feeble-minded', who in the past had been known as 'idiots' and 'imbeciles', and who in the future would become known, at different times, as 'the mentally deficient', 'morons', 'mentally handicapped', 'learning disabled' and 'intellectually disabled'.

It is frequently claimed that history belongs to the victors, and there is certainly the sense in Barr's writing of the medical profession planting their flag on this newly conquered territory of feeblemindedness. They now claimed this territory as theirs to identify, treat and manage. According to Barr, the 'idiot' and the 'imbecile' had been a 'despised and neglected class' until the medical profession came to their aid. (From this point, 'idiot' and 'imbecile' will no longer be set in quotation marks. The terms are used for historical accuracy; the offensive power they have acquired over time is still recognised.) A new era, argued Barr, began in nineteenth-century Europe and America, when hitherto cruelly abused idiots were kindly treated in the new network of segregated asylums. Here they were educated in the few skills they could master and led purposeful, but very separate, lives under medical supervision. The public, Barr explained, had become aware of the 'evil in its midst' and allowed medical men to take on the burden of the idiot class. Using their skill and knowledge, these medical men had transformed the life of the idiot from one of pitiable misery to a story of admirable improvement and contentment.

How could Barr write a history of people who could not, in his opinion, see, feel, hear, do or know anything? In truth, his history was not about them at all, but was in fact the heroic story, as he told it, of how the medical profession had rescued and rehabilitated the idiot class. For Barr, there was no history for this permanently excluded group, other than brutal treatment and abuse by the rest of society, until the medical profession intervened. Idiots only came into historical focus once the system of specialist medical asylums was established to treat and care for them in the mid-nineteenth century. Thus the history of the idiot is that of medical treatment and the asylum. But how accurate is this medical account of history?

There is a growing body of work on the history of intellectual disability, which paints a very different picture to Barr's shocking story of exclusion, neglect and abuse. Before the asylum era, evidence indicates that people with intellectual disabilities had been very much part of their communities. In common with most people, they had not necessarily led easy lives, and some had been mistreated or at times dehumanised; yet, for the majority, life had been lived amongst families, social networks and communities, largely accepted and included.

There are of course pitfalls for the historian when trying to identify this group in the past. When people talked about 'idiots' and 'imbeciles' at different times in history, were they talking about a group synonymous with those we call people with intellectual disabilities today? Did those whom Barr labelled as the feebleminded in 1904 occupy the same social position and have the same characteristics as those described as the mentally handicapped from the 1950s onwards? The answer to both questions is a qualified 'no'. Those we describe as having intellectual disabilities today are not some fixed, universal, unchanging, ahistorical grouping that is immediately recognisable in any age, but whose name just happens to have changed (with alarming regularity) over time. The concept of who is an 'idiot' or a 'mentally disabled' person, while retaining some continuity, expands and contracts with the values, priorities and preoccupations of different societies. In the medieval period, the vast majority of people could not read or write, nor did they need to in order to fulfil their allotted functions. The elite classes saw the labouring and poorer classes as idiotic; such a term was so general as to be almost meaningless (Goodey 2011). It was only in the nineteenth century that so-called idiots and imbeciles became a medical category. At this point the medical profession acquired the right to determine who should be included in such categories, and who should not. Until then medical practitioners, who were paid to make people better, weren't interested in those with a lifelong, chronic, stable condition.

By the early twentieth century, when Barr was writing his history, thinking had changed. Idiots had acquired new names and definitions – feebleminded or defective – and were seen as dangerous, sexually incontinent beings who would pollute the human race and cause degeneration. They obstructed progress, as they were unable to read, write, or understand social rules and expectations. It was the job of doctors and psychiatrists to protect society from the threat they posed.

In more recent times the 'problem' of what used to be called idiocy has come to be seen as one of learning, adaptation and the perceptions of others. New terms such as learning difficulty and learning disability have been introduced, and advocates have campaigned for a 'new' culture of rights and inclusion. This 'problem' has become, again, a non-medical matter. Each time terminology changes, so does the membership of the group it defines, sometimes expanding, sometimes decreasing. Perceptions change also: sometimes more hostile, sometimes more accepting.

This is how the history of intellectual disability has unfolded: as a succession of claims by the victors to define, understand and be responsible for those perceived as lacking intellectual capacity. Historians therefore have to be careful to 'avoid trans-historical assumptions about what constitutes intellectual disability, otherwise they will simply find themselves "chasing shadows"' (Stainton & McDonagh 2001). Who, then, have they been over time, these changing groups of idiots and defectives, mentally handicapped and intellectually disabled? To what extent have they been included or excluded from mainstream society?

In the medieval period, there was a relatively clear distinction between the two terms. An idiot was someone with a lifelong condition of impaired mental faculties, while a lunatic would have been born with their mental faculties intact but then suffered a permanent or temporary loss of reason.

A thirteenth-century document, the *Prerogativa Regis* (*King's Prerogative*) gave the Crown the right to take custody of those judged to lack mental capacity, and to acquire their land and revenues. When doing this, the King also had a duty to protect and provide for the idiots (or 'natural fools') who had been deprived of their lands and assets, ensuring that they had at least the necessities of daily living (Neugebauer 1996). According to *Prerogativa Regis* the lunatic could recover their lands if deemed to have regained their capacity, something which the idiot was seen as incapable of doing. These monarchical rights were claimed on the grounds that idiots were childlike and the monarch therefore 'owned' them as they had 'not... reason to govern themselves and also they are not able to do service to the realm' (McGlynn 2005, Bell 1953).

Idiot incapacity was seen as a legal problem with implications for property rather than a pathological condition. For the vast majority of the labouring poor, with no property to maintain or bestow and no finances to manage, their mental capacity was simply not an issue. For those with wealth it was a legal rather than a medical matter. Legal enquiries into a person's capacity would be conducted by laypersons such as parishioners, state officials and lawyers. They consisted of very practical questioning about matters such as the value of money, the days of the week and family relationships (Neugebauer 1978, McGlynn 2005). This method was aimed at understanding a person's ability to function in the everyday world, their capacity to resist exploitation, distinguish family from enemies and safeguard their assets. There was no attempt to describe or understand any interior mental condition, and at no point was there any suggestion that incapacity should entail institutionalisation or separation from community.

There was an overwhelming social and familial expectation in the medieval period that the locus of care resided in the family. There was some institutional provision for people deemed unable to care for themselves, virtually all of it in monasteries and convents providing an early form of hospital care. However this care focused on particular groups who, for one reason or another, had no system of family support – the aged infirm, blind ex-monks and nuns, and lepers – and who were unable to work or to function in their communities, so needed a permanent place of rest. Idiots were not seen in this way. People with any sort of intellectual impairment were almost entirely absent from these institutions. They were not seen as a medical or psychological problem and in an agrarian, labour-intensive, largely non-literate society, functioned within their communities without being seen as particularly disabled in the modern sense (Stainton 2001). Institutional care might rarely occur as the result of the breakdown of family care through death or poverty, but never through any conscious process of institutionalisation.

Idiots were, then, integral members of their communities in the medieval period, slowness of mind and illiteracy were not obstacles to life in the agrarian and labouring, family-based world to which they belonged. The state only intervened if a person held family wealth they were deemed incapable of managing, and in these cases a system of guardianship and confiscation applied. This remained the case in the sixteenth and seventeenth centuries. Institutional provision in the sixteenth century actually declined as, under Henry VIII, the monasteries, the main providers of care for the infirm, were dissolved and stripped of their assets in his dispute with the Church of Rome. Institutional provision would not recover until the seventeenth century, when a programme of secular almshouse and hospital building began, funded by charitable largesse (Jordan 1960). Yet for the idiot population, this was all irrelevant. They were seen as neither physically frail nor sick. Their characteristics may have made them appear odd and somewhat limited, but they were not a matter for medical or charitable attention and certainly did not need special care. Poor Law records over the sixteenth and seventeenth centuries show only very limited and occasional granting of relief funds to idiots or their families. Parish authorities intervened and provided relief for idiots only when there were secondary problems, such as ill health or death of family carers, or the wider family collapsed into extreme poverty. Even then, relief came in the form of small amounts of money to meet the person's basic clothing and food needs. In extreme cases a local male 'keeper' or female 'nurse' might be paid to look after the person in their home. But these were not 'nurses' in our modern sense of the word, but local women, often widows, who carried out such tasks as a means of subsistence (Rushton 1996, Andrews 1996). The public policy focus, such as it existed, was always based on the assumption that idiots were a part of communities and should remain so, either within families or within neighbourly networks. Institutionalisation and separation were not significant options, however 'differently' idiots were perceived.

Under Henry VIII the loose guidance of the medieval *Prerogativa Regis* was formalised into the powerful legal institution of the Court of Wards in 1540. This court oversaw the process of collecting revenues from the estates of idiots and others who had come under the 'protection' of the king. The court, through to its demise in the 1640s (after which its role passed to the Court of Chancery), consolidated and shaped the conventions and practices of the legal treatment of those deemed incapacitated into a form that persisted through the eighteenth and nineteenth centuries. These practices survive, in somewhat moderated form, even today in the Court of Protection.

Despite some improvements in the legal protection afforded to those deemed idiots, the enhanced role of first the Court of Wards and then the Court of Chancery signalled that idiots, certainly those with any sort of wealth or assets, had come more firmly under the gaze of the state. In 1628 the jurist Lord Coke expanded the definition of those who, under the law, lacked the capacity to look after themselves or their assets because of impaired mental faculties. To the category of the 'Idiota… from his nativitie [birth], by a perpetuall infirmitie' he added 'all other persons, who from natural imbecility… are incapable of managing their own affairs' (Coke 1628, Collinson 1812). This represented a significant widening of those the law, and therefore the state, recognised as lacking sufficient mental capacity to look after themselves, introducing a new category of 'natural imbecile'. While the idiot, and this new class of imbecile, remained very much part of mainstream communities, increased legal attention was a sign that this position might become precarious.

In the eighteenth century the idiot and imbecile class continued to be seen as natural members of communities to whom families and neighbourly networks had obligations of support. There were growing numbers of charitably funded hospitals for the poor, some of which provided long-term relief, and workhouses which provided transitory relief for those who had fallen into absolute poverty or distress. However a survey of these has shown not only that idiots were present in extremely small numbers in such institutions, but that in some cases they were actively excluded from them (Andrews 1998a, 1998b). The prevailing belief that idiocy was not something that required medical intervention or institutionalisation persisted. Instead it was the obligation of families and neighbours to provide support when needed.

There is much evidence that those characterised as idiots at this time lived highly integrated lives. Eighteenth-century trial records from the Old Bailey, London's criminal court, show defendants who were clearly characterised as idiotic or of extremely low intelligence by witnesses and family members. The majority were living with their families or sometimes even married, working and well known in their communities. Many were clearly part of strong social networks, with workmates and family members pleading on their behalf and testifying to their good character (Jarrett 2015). Idiots were a pervasive presence in eighteenth-century society, characterised in slang terms such as 'nockie' and 'ninnie' (Grose 1788), the butt of jokes in the popular jest books of the time and appearing as characters in novels, such as John Cleland's *Fanny Hill* (1750/51) and Fanny Burney's *Camilla* (1796). While some of the language used to describe them appears harsh, and the humour cruel, to modern ears, it is indisputable that idiots in the eighteenth century lived at the heart of their communities, were deeply entrenched in networks of family, neighbourhood and work, and were an accepted part of daily life.

All this began to change from the early nineteenth century. There was a discernible shift in attitude towards idiots and imbeciles, whereby they became perceived as people unfit to live in communities, who needed the exclusionary environment of the closed asylum. A number of factors converged to bring about this change in perception.

Firstly, the idiot started to attract the attention and interest of the medical profession. In France in particular, medical practitioners who were also medico-legal theorists, such as Francois Emanuel Fodéré and Etienne-Jean Georget, began to promote the idea that the idiot and imbecile population were the domain of the medical man to identify, treat and manage. Fodéré and Georget began a process of clinical codification of idiocy. Their classifications ranged from what they called the first degree of absolute thoughtless idiocy, to the higher degree of the clever but 'mischievous' imbecile who could parrot words but not understand the moral meanings and responsibilities that went with them (Fodéré 1813, Georget 1820, 1826). Writing in the wake of the French Revolution, these theorists reflected Enlightenment ideas that 'scientific' approaches could solve all the 'problems' of mankind. Their work influenced medical theorists in Britain, such as John Haslam, who wrote *Medical Jurisprudence as it Relates to Insanity* in 1817, in which he created new graded medical categories of idiots and imbeciles. Gradually the concept of the idiot as a person needing medical segregation and treatment seeped into British legal and medical thought. Pinel, Seguin and other French 'alienists' (the early word for psychiatrists) were engaging in educational work with idiots in the huge Parisian Salpêtrière and Bicêtre asylums. This work garnered a growing reputation, fuelling the belief that institutionalised segregation was the modern, scientific way to respond to idiocy.

Secondly, growing medical interest coincided with wider changes in social and cultural attitudes. From the early nineteenth century there was a general reaction against the laissez faire individualism of the eighteenth century and a drive to 'clean up' society by reforming the manners and behaviours of 'deviant' groups. Driven by social reformers and a vigorously revived evangelical Christian movement, this general 'cleansing process', sustained by 'a deepening wish to control, moralise and pathologise those who defied that process' (Gattrell 2006, p.432), was bad news for the idiot population, who would inevitably struggle to understand and conform to complex new expectations of social behaviour and internal restraint. 'Deviant' populations of lunatics, prostitutes, criminals, drunks and idiots were increasingly exposed to the gaze of the reforming movements, and action to control them was inevitable.

Finally, a growing early nineteenth-century state apparatus of government both influenced, and was influenced by, these social movements and cultural changes. Rejecting the parish localism of the previous century, they sought to impose order by extending the boundaries of state intervention and building an institutional response. In 1808 the County Asylums Act was passed, enabling the building of Britain's first public hospitals to house idiots and lunatics. In 1845 the Lunacy Act made admission of these categories compulsory, while under the 1834 Poor Law Act, a network of punitive workhouses for the poor and 'impotent' was built at twenty-mile intervals across Britain. The idiot population began to transfer from an inclusive space in mainstream communities to a segregated space in asylums and workhouses. Many were included amongst the lunatic population of the new asylums, probably numbering about 1,000 out of 15,000 by 1850, while larger numbers, as many as 10,000, were soon in workhouses following the introduction of the 1834 Poor Law Act (Wright 2001, p.19).

Concerns grew about the presence of idiots in asylums and workhouses. Because idiocy was a lifelong condition that did not change substantively, idiots were perceived as clogging up what was intended to be a dynamic asylum system of admission, treatment, improvement and discharge. Workhouses were intended either to be the final resting place of the elderly infirm in absolute poverty, or an unpleasant temporary shock for the so-called feckless unemployed. They were not meant to be permanent homes for 'unimprovable' idiots.

In 1845, John Conolly, medical superintendent of the first Middlesex County Lunatic Asylum at Hanwell, started a programme for the small population of idiots in his asylum, after visiting the Bicêtre in Paris to study French physician Edouard Seguin's pioneering treatment and educational approaches to idiocy (Conolly 1849). Conolly and other physicians who had visited the Bicêtre pressed for the establishment of a separate asylum for idiots in England. He joined forces with a group of wealthy charitable donors and, after experiments from 1847 with small institutions in Highgate and Colchester, established the Earlswood Asylum in Surrey in 1855. With 500 beds, this was the world's first purpose-built asylum for idiot children, built and run entirely on charitable subscriptions.

In the following years a number of medically supervised, charitable idiot asylums opened across the country, covering the eastern, western and northern counties, and the Midlands (Wright 2004, p.96). By the 1870s, the idiot, who until recently had been seen as someone who lived, worked and eventually died in their community, had become someone who needed medical supervision in a specialist institution. A convergence of medical, social and political factors had placed them there.

The community of idiots now became a separately maintained and observed construct of the science of medicine, bearing no resemblance to the communities in which they had previously lived. In 1862, for example, Earlswood Idiot Asylum, under its dynamic young superintendent John Langdon Down, hosted the annual meeting of the British Association for the Advancement of Science (Earlswood 1863). Drawing on the anthropological beliefs of the time, Down claimed he had discovered that the 'five races of man' (Caucasian, Ethiopic, Aztec, Malay and Mongolian) could be found, through a process of evolutionary regression, in the idiot population. This was the basis of his 'discovery' of Mongolian imbecility, later to be known as Down's syndrome (Down 1867). Down referred to his patients as a 'family' or 'community', but this was a closed community that existed only within the walls of the asylum. They became a matter of scientific interest to a curious world; the very world of which the idiot had been a natural and accepted part only several decades earlier.

Earlswood and its regional counterparts were private, charitable idiot asylums and therefore mostly available to the sons and daughters of the middle classes. However they were seen as models of idiot care and transformation and many campaigners, including Charles Dickens, expressed the hope that the state would build specialist asylums to cater for the idiot offspring of poor families (Dickens 1853). Their wishes were granted with the building, under the Metropolitan Asylums Board, of the huge Caterham and Leavesden imbecile asylums in 1870 and Darenth in 1880. Thousands of Londoners labelled idiots and imbeciles were transferred there, and the pattern was repeated across the country (Thompson 1998, p.13).

From the 1880s the eugenic doctrine of degeneration, propagated by Francis Galton and other social theorists, criminalised the idiot and imbecile population, now perceived as a dangerous threat to racial health (Rafter 1997). New professional perceptions and claims regarding management and treatment brought new terminology; 'idiots' and 'imbeciles' now became 'mental defectives'. The 1913 Mental Deficiency Act specified that defectives must either be closely supervised in the community or maintained in new mental deficiency colonies, providing lifelong settlement in isolated rural environments. Close control and supervision in the community meant that people with intellectual disabilities were simultaneously part of, yet outside, the community in which they lived. The Central Association for Mental Welfare, reporting to a new Board of Control, sent volunteers and officials to identify defectives and visit them under statutory supervision, a particular concern being the prevention of sexual relationships and marriage (Walmsley et al. 1999).

The new mental deficiency colonies aimed to remove the mental defective from the sight, consciousness and memory of mainstream communities. The aim was to allow defective breeds to disappear, sterile and unproductive, in these closed, walled, self-sufficient communities. Each was a small, self-contained world with up to 1,500 people living in detached 'villas' housing up to sixty people, grouped around a central administrative block. The block always formed a barrier between male and female villas, as separation of the sexes was deemed essential (Board of Control 1930).

This was a community whose aim was to eradicate those who comprised it, to ensure that the class of defectives would wither away and die in isolation. The colonies would live on until the

1990s, re-named as mental handicap hospitals. It was from these and other institutions that the great community resettlement programme of the 1980s took place. 'Mental defectives' became first the 'mentally handicapped', then the 'learning disabled' or 'intellectually disabled'. Clinical and social care professionals tried to throw off the past and create a bright new beginning of inclusion in the community.

However, the past never would go away. The stigma of 150 years of institutionalisation in asylums always lurked. The libel of criminality and degeneration perpetrated against people with intellectual disabilities in the eugenics era lingered. New community provision was established, including care homes, group homes, sheltered workshops, day centres, social work teams and community nurses. Some hospitals reinvented themselves as assessment and treatment centres or specialist treatment units. Inclusion was offered, but in a watered-down version and at a price. People with intellectual disabilities moved into communities from their hospitals, but many remained encircled by a protective, and excluding, bureaucratic and professional wall.

Even as the asylum movement swung into action in the mid nineteenth century there were always alternatives. Many people with intellectual disabilities managed to evade the institution and live with their families, or even independently. There was always a range of social care support, including residential provision and 'boarding out'. After the Second World War, village communities such as the Camphill movement emerged, offering alternative lifestyles in communal settings. However, the fundamental effect of the asylum movement was to alter the position that intellectually disabled people occupied in public consciousness. A mentality formed that they were people who needed separation, either through exclusion in separate buildings or through being under special care. They became objects of medical treatment and control, despite not being ill. In this process they transformed from a group perceived as limited but harmless and largely included, to an outsider group, carrying a threat of dangerousness and menace. It is from this disadvantageous position that people with intellectual disabilities today seek to reclaim not only the rightful, included place in society that they used to occupy, but also their identity as respected humans.

Exclusion is not the historical norm for people with intellectual disabilities. It is in fact an anomaly that has been in place for the last 150 years: a short period in historical terms. Modernity and progress have not been friendly to this group.

References

Andrews, J. (1996) 'Identifying and providing for the mentally disabled in early modern London'. In: A. Digby & D. Wright (eds.), *From Idiocy to Mental Deficiency*. London: Routledge, pp. 65–92.

— (1998a) 'Begging the Question of Idiocy: The definition and socio-cultural meaning of idiocy in early-modern Britain', *History of Psychiatry*, 9(33): 65–95.

— (1998b) 'Begging the Question of Idiocy: The definition and socio-cultural meaning of idiocy in early-modern Britain', *History of Psychiatry*, 9(34): 179–200.

Barr, M. (1904) *Mental Defectives: Their history, treatment and training*. Philadelphia: Blakiston.

Bell, H. (1953) *An Introduction to the History and Records of the Court of Wards and Liveries*. Cambridge: Cambridge University Press.

Board of Control (1930). Committee on Mental Deficiency Colonies. *Hedley Report*. The National Archives (TNA) MH 58/97.

Coke, E. (1628) *Institutes of the laws of England*. In: G. Collinson (1812) *A Treatise on the Law Concerning Idiots, Lunatics, and Other Persons non compotes mentis*. London: W. Reed.

Collinson, G. (1812) *A Treatise on the Law Concerning Idiots, Lunatics, and Other Persons non compotes mentis*. London: W. Reed.

Conolly, J. (1849) 'On the management of Hanwell Lunatic Asylum', *Journal of Psychological Medicine and Mental Pathology*, 2: 424–427.

Dickens, C. (1853) 'Idiots', *Household Words*, June, vii: 167.

Down, J. (1867) 'Observations on an ethnic classification of idiots', *Journal of Mental Science*, 13: 121–122.

Earlswood, (1863) *Earlswood Annual Report 1863*. SRO 392/1/1. Surrey: SRO.

Fodéré, F. (1813) *Traité de Médecine Légale et d'Hygiène Publique ou de Police de Santé: Tome premier*. (Second edition) Paris: Mame.

Gattrell, V. (2006) *City of Laughter: Sex and satire in eighteenth-century London*. London: Atlantic Books.

Georget, E.J. (1820) *De la Folie: Considérations sur cette maladie*. Paris: Crevot.

— (1826) *Discussion médico-légale sur la folie ou aliénation mentale*. Paris.

Goodey, C. (2011) *A History of Intelligence and 'Intellectual Disability': The shaping of psychology in early modern Europe*. Farnham: Ashgate.

Grose, F. (1788) *A Classical Dictionary of the Vulgar Tongue*. (Second edition) London: S. Hooper.

Jarrett, S. (2015) 'The meaning of 'community' in the lives of people with intellectual disabilities: An historical perspective', *International Journal of Developmental Disabilities*, 61(2): 107–112.

Jordan, W. (1960) *The Charities of London, 1480–1660: The aspirations and the achievements of the urban society.* London: Allen and Unwin.

McGlynn, M. (2005) 'Idiots, lunatics and the royal prerogative in early Tudor England', *Journal of Legal History*, 26(1): 1–20.

Neugebauer, R. (1978) 'Treatment of the mentally ill in medieval and early modern England: A reappraisal', *Journal of the History of the Behavioural Sciences*, 14: 158–169.

— (1996) 'Mental handicap in medieval and early modern England: Criteria, measurement and care'. In: A. Digby & D. Wright (eds.), *From Idiocy to Mental Deficiency*. London: Routledge, pp. 22–43.

Rafter, N. (1997) *Creating Born Criminals.* Chicago: University of Illinois Press.

Rushton, P. (1996) 'Idiocy, the family and community in early modern north-east England'. In: A. Digby & D. Wright (eds.), *From Idiocy to Mental Deficiency*. London: Routledge, pp. 44–64.

Stainton, T. (2001) 'Medieval charitable institutions and intellectual impairment c. 1066–1600', *Journal on Developmental Disabilities*, 8: 19–29.

Stainton, T. & McDonagh, P. (2001) 'Chasing shadows: the historical construction of developmental disability', *Journal on Developmental Disabilities*, 8(2): ix–xvi.

Thompson, M. (1998) *The Problem of Mental Deficiency: Eugenics, democracy and social policy in Britain, c. 1870–1958*. Oxford: Oxford University Press.

Walmsley, J., Atkinson, D. & Rolph, S. (1999) 'Community Care and Mental Deficiency 1913–1945'. In: P. Bartlett & D. Wright, *Outside the Walls of the Asylum: The history of care in the community 1750–2000*. London: Athlone Press.

Wright, D. (2001) *Mental Disability in Victorian England*. Oxford: Oxford University Press.

— (2004) 'Mongols in our midst: John Langdon Down and the ethnic classification of idiocy, 1858–1924'. In: S. Noll & J. Trent Jr. (eds.), *Mental Retardation in America: A historical reader*. New York: New York University Press, pp. 92–119.

At Society's Pleasure:
The Rise and Fall of Services to People with an Intellectual Disability

ROBERT CUMMINS

Introduction

The objective of this chapter is to trace an historical path of publicly funded service provision to people with an intellectual disability. The theme I will develop is that such public expenditure is hostage to popular opinion, especially to the public's perception of what constitutes necessity. As a result, government funding over the past few centuries changes with the changing mood of the times: there are wild oscillations in both the amount and purpose of allocations. I will examine this theme using a structure of six historical phases, and follow the examination with descriptions of the contemporary situation in publicly funded service provision for people with an intellectual disability in both the UK and Australia.

Phase one: Early public attitudes

In pre-institutional times, people with significant disability rarely survived childhood. 'Infanticide has been practiced on every continent and by people on every level of cultural complexity, from hunters and gatherers to high civilisations, including our own ancestors. Rather than being an exception, then, it has been the rule' (Williamson 1978). There have been many reasons for selective infanticide, but the basic underlying cause is conservation of resources for survival. For early societies, and even some today, the struggle for survival means there are no spare resources. Each person must contribute positively to their family, and to the community, or the group will not survive. The most easily predicted non-contributors were newborns with a disability.

Of course, a few people with significant disability did survive. Their lot was to become objects of public ridicule or, for a very few, to be maintained for private entertainment. In ancient Rome (753 BC–476 AD) some disabled people were kept as 'fools' by the wealthy for amusement. This practice continued for at least the next six centuries, into the courts of medieval nobility (Horsfield 1940), such as the court of Philip IV of Spain (1605–1665).

In the USA, British settlement in 1607 was dominated by the Puritans. Following the teachings of both Martin Luther (1483–1546) and John Calvin (1509–1564), the Puritans believed that deviant human conditions originated from Satan, and the only moral response was to purge deviants from the community (Baumeister 1970). Thus, people with a disability were, at best, considered the 'town fool' (Wolfensberger 1976, p.45) and at worst subjected to exorcism or torture.

Phase one summary
Early public opinion regarding disability was negative and exploitative.

Phase two: Institutional beginnings

By the late Middle Ages (eleventh to thirteenth centuries) there are records of unwanted children left at the door of religious institutions in the expectation that the clergy would raise the child. Such practice gave rise to the first orphanages. Religious concerns at this time also underpinned assistance given to destitute adults. From the tenth century in England, almshouses attached to monasteries provided accommodation for poor, old and distressed people. These almshouses usually incorporated a chapel, benefiting the soul of the founder and his family, with their upkeep funded by parishioners through Christian charity. However, the Protestant Reformation, initiated by Martin Luther in 1517, closed monasteries and their almshouses under an act of 1547.

These closures substantially increased the number of people living in poverty and threatened social order. In order to regain control, a series of 'Poor Laws' were passed in the Tudor period that were designed to control public behaviour, such as begging, and to raise alms through parish taxes and also, in 1576, to establish workhouses. While these workhouses provided free food and lodging, life was made deliberately harsh to ensure that only people who were truly destitute would enter. Workhouses were also commonly run at a profit by utilising the free labour of their inmates, who were employed on tasks such as breaking stones, crushing bones to produce fertiliser, or picking oakum.

With the establishment of more populated and stable towns in the eighteenth century, together with improved public resources and economic conditions, community attitudes moved towards the belief that deviants should be segregated from the rest of society (an excellent account of early institutions in the USA is provided by Baumeister (1970)). Most institutions founded in this period were custodial, serving as crowded, communal dumping grounds, where people with an intellectual disability were congregated with the destitute and mentally ill. At that time, the term 'degenerates' served as a collective noun for all people who did not fit the mould of regular society. Thus when the first house of corrections was built in the American colonies, in Connecticut in 1722, people with all forms of 'degeneracy' were housed together. Through this inclusion, people with an intellectual disability became categorised as just a normal part of society's fringe, especially since illiteracy and poverty were so common.

Phase two summary
Six hundred years of religious charity was followed by public funding to segregate 'degenerates' from the rest of society.

Phase three: Institutional education

Jacob Rodrigues Pereira (1715–1780) is credited with pioneering the teaching of deaf mutes and the creation of sign language (Josué 2004). Pereira believed that the sense of touch was the basis of 'physiological training' through which the faculty of thinking could be brought about in all intellectually disabled people, including deaf-mutes who, at that time, were also included in this group.

Almost two decades after Pereira's death a child, 'Victor', was discovered living wild in the woods of Averyon in 1798. Victor had no speech and only 'the most feeble indications of intelligence' (Deutsch 1949). He was delivered to the National Institute of Deaf and Dumb in Paris where Jean Itard, the chief medical officer, devoted himself to educating the boy.

In Itard's view, idiocy was understood as a deficiency of nutrition. This lack of sustenence was believed to have caused the cessation of 'foetal progress' resulting in 'a soul shut up in imperfect organs, an innocent' (Seguin 1907, Section 87). Thus, a combination of enhanced nutrition and physiological training would recapitulate the missing growth sequences and 'treat' the disability. This idea appealed to physicians as a logical approach to education.

Despite his considerable efforts, Itard could not educate Victor to the level of 'normality', but he did demonstrate that Victor was trainable. This was recognised as a great achievement and heralded a new era in which developing the limited potentialities of 'the feebleminded' became a worthy scientific and societal goal.

These activities ushered in the era of 'moral treatment', practiced by luminaries such as the French physician Philippe Pinel (1745–1826) and the English Quaker philanthropist Samuel Tuke (1784–1857), among others. As described by Menninger (1963), this treatment was moral, not in the sense of opposing immorality, but rather in creating a favourable environment in which spontaneous recovery could take place. This setting involved individualised care with exercises, amusements, kind treatment, and a repudiation of mechanical restraint.

These advances engendered optimism among educators that people with a disability could be trained and returned to society as self-supporting citizens (Baumeister 1970). Moreover, this period coincided with increasing public recognition of intellectual disability (Little & Johnson 1932) and growing concern with the problem of their care.

Between 1846 and 1860, several US state legislatures voted for funds to be made available for trial classes based on the beneficent effect of Seguin's physiological education. Thus, these institutions resembled schools built for education, rather than hospitals for sick people or prisons for criminals. The sense of optimism was palpable. Seguin describes the excitement generated by laying the cornerstone of the first US school to be built expressly for idiots in Syracuse, New York on September 8, 1854 (1907, sections 4–12).

Phase three summary
By 1850 in the USA, public funds were being directed to the education of people with an intellectual disability.

Phase four: Segregation

The promise of education was that the 'students' would be discharged from 'schools' ready to assume independent living. However, over the next few decades, serious charges of misreported discharge rates were made public. Doubts set in among professionals and administrators, support for 'moral treatment' evaporated, pessimistic predictions became the order of the day, and intellectual disability came to be once again regarded as 'incurable'. The benign public mood to educational funding changed.

By the turn of the twentieth century it was clear that institutions for people with an intellectual disability were being used primarily for custodial care. Moreover, the number of people housed in such institutions was continually increasing (Little & Johnson 1932). As such institutions multiplied and the drain on the public purse intensified, sinister ideologies gathered strength. They had their distant beginnings in 1859 with the publication of Darwin's *Origin of Species* (Darwin and Bynum 2009) which, among other things, advanced the theories of 'natural selection' and 'survival of the fittest'.

These themes were elaborated in 1865 by Francis Galton, whose publications dovetailed with contemporary research interest in the reasons for intellectual disability. Practically every conceivable cause for disability was championed, but the greatest impact came from linking these ideas to the new science of genetics. This was reinforced by Dugdale's 1877 publication tracing the history of a family called Jukes and concluding that intellectual disability in that family was hereditary. Despite the methodological weakness of this study, the time was right for influential people to conclude that intellectual disability was inherited.

These ideas gave rise to 'eugenics', which was based on the belief that degenerate parents produced degenerate children. Worse, such parents were more fecund, thereby increasing that proportion of the population. The most authoritative voice promoting eugenics was Henry Herbert Goddard, whose (1912) account provides a harrowing description of poverty and intellectual disability for people living in the society of that time. Thus the public was persuaded that the 'feebleminded' were helpless, hopeless and too dangerous to be at large (Packard & Laveck 1976, Deutsch 1949).

The solution was to prevent their procreation through sterilization or institutionalization. The first institution specifically for feebleminded women of childbearing age was opened in 1878, at Newark, New York. Freshly minted legislation in the USA promoted compulsory sterilization. This was made possible through the infamous Supreme Court decision by Justice Holmes, who analogised sterilization to compulsory vaccination, and declared, 'Three generations of imbeciles are enough' (Buck v. Bell, 1927). As an example of the consequences, from 1910 to 1962, Nebraska (USA) law prohibited the discharge of institution residents with an intellectual disability unless they were sterilised or were beyond reproductive age (Kurtz & Wolfensberger 1969).

Phase four summary

In the century prior to 1950, the public view of people with an intellectual disability moved from optimistic − educational to pessimistic − dangerous, with public funding shifting from schools to institutions.

Phase five: Normalisation

In the early 1970s, a seismic shift in attitude caused the dismantling of institutions. The seeds had been sown much earlier by Bank-Mikkelsen, who described normalisation as 'letting the mentally retarded obtain an existence as close to the normal as possible'. He was instrumental in having this principle written into Danish law of 1959 governing services to people with an intellectual disability (Wolfensberger 1972), with Swedish law following suit in 1968 (Nirje 1969).

However, a decade passed before Bank–Mikkelsen's insight was systematically presented in the literature by Bengt Nirje (1969), executive director of the Swedish Association for Retarded Children. Nirje himself described normalisation as 'making available to all mentally retarded people patterns and conditions of everyday living which are as close as possible to the regular circumstances and ways of life or society' (Nirje 1985, p.67). The first description in British literature of the normalisation principle was in the December 1970 issue of the *Journal of Mental Subnormality* (Gunzburg 1970, Nirje 1970, Zarfas 1970).

Shortly after these publications, Wolfensberger (Wolfensberger 1972, Wolfensberger and Glenn 1973, Wolfensberger and Glenn 1975) successfully proselytised the ideology. His 1972 manifesto was published in the USA, and the principle of normalisation swept through the world of intellectual disability. Deinstitutionalisation legislation was passed, but at different times in different countries: in Britain in 1971 (UK Department of Health 2001), Canada in 1981 (Griffiths & Curtis 1984), and Australia in 1986 (Victorian Government 1986). The rate of deinstitutionalisation also varied markedly by location (for USA, see Scheerenberger 1976). Effectively, however, by about 1990, the great majority of people with an intellectual disability throughout the Western world had been relocated out of institutions and into share-homes of some description.

Over the intervening years, the principle of normalisation has been developed and interpreted from several different perspectives. Griffiths & Curtis (1984) have provided a 'rights' interpretation, founded in the belief that people who are disabled have 'a legitimate right to participate in the mainstream of society and that as closely as possible the conditions of their everyday life should reflect the normal rhythm of daily existence' (p.259). In these terms, life quality for the resident would be measured by the extent to which such rights have been recognised.

Jones (1986) has provided an 'age-appropriate' measure of share-home success, requiring that the lifestyle of residents closely approximates the lifestyle expected of non-disabled people of the same age. This, then, forms a criterion for objective life quality. In his most recent work, Wolfensberger (1983) describes his conception of 'social role valorisation'. He proposes that the ultimate aim of normalisation must be the creation and support of valued social roles for people who are at risk of societal devaluation.

Phase five summary
The impact of normalisation has been, once again, to shift the focus of public funding away from segregation and towards supporting an ordinary life for people with an intellectual disability in general society.

Phase six: Now what?

It is now some forty years since the evangelical fervour of normalisation initiated the mass relocation of people out of institutions in Western nations. Considerable public moneys have been spent on this exercise and it is timely to take stock, and to speculate on what may lie ahead.

The five previous phases documented oscillating public opinion during the preceding 1,000 years, varying from complete indifference to the allocation of substantial public resources. Now, the considerable positive energy created by normalisation is spent, and societal indifference again dominates. This is predictable. Officials and politicians responsible for funding allocation in the public sector will ensure that the given resources are as low as possible for areas deemed of low public interest. Moreover, available funding will be managed most efficiently through agencies, which develop increasing control and autonomy. Unless this momentum can be turned around, the re-establishment of congregate care is the most likely outcome.

A new 'spark' is required to resurrect public interest in disability. The following sections contrast the UK and Australia, countries that twenty years ago were much on the same page, but now their paths have diverged.

The United Kingdom
Early reviews of deinstitutionalisation in England reported systematic misadministration within carehomes, as documented

in the White Paper on intellectual disability (Department of Health 2001). This paper also set out a programme for change, but seemingly to little avail. In 2005, an investigation of small group homes in Cornwall reported entrenched institutional practices of physical, emotional and environmental abuse (Health Care Commission and the Commission for Social Care Inspection 2006). More recently, an evaluation of two residential homes for people with intellectual disabilities, established in the 1980s, revealed long-standing mental, sexual and physical abuse of the residents (Collins 2015).

But perhaps the most damning report is one of the most recent. The Comptroller and Auditor General (2015) describes systematic abuse of patients with intellectual disabilities in a private hospital opened in 2006. The government responded with a pledge to meet 63 transforming care commitments, but the initiative failed due to administrative errors.

In his appraisal of this scene, Jackson writes: 'Unthinkingly, we are slipping into the same institutional practices that were common at the beginning of the twentieth century, although now in a more modern guise' (2015). He suggests many contributory reasons for this, such as ideas like inclusion or normalisation having been 'interpreted in an overly simplistic manner by policy makers'. Charities, who society expects to protect the interests of people with intellectual disabilities, are now largely service providers, and increasingly passive in the face of pressure from central or local government. Regulation is seen as the primary method for ensuring appropriate service delivery. For example, The Mansell Report, commissioned and first published by the Department of Health in 1993, then revised in 2007, states '... the factors that make for good services are relatively well-understood and there are many examples of good practice. The key to the difference between good and indifferent community services lies not in resources, but in the quality of management...' (Mansell 2007). In Jackson's view, the government focus on regulation has led to an increasingly bureaucratic and destructive mentality that corrodes human relationships (Jackson 2015). The dependence on private-sector care homes, which are often reliant on highly leveraged debt, makes it likely that many private services will collapse as the economy continues to falter and as social care continues to be cut. This unhappy picture has been reinforced by Duffy who states, '... in the UK, between 2009 and 2014, social care has been cut by 30 per cent, with 500,000 people losing social care – and this has happened without any significant public outcry' (2015, p.5).

All in all, observers convey a dismal view of contemporary service delivery in the UK. As a final bleak comment, Collins writes, 'Many residential services, from large residential homes to small group homes, claim to provide community care yet replicate the oppressive and controlling institutional culture of the old long-stay hospitals...' (2015, p.76).

Australia

Mirroring the UK, there has been common knowledge in the Australian care industry of widespread and systematic abuse of people with disabilities in care facilities. In early 2015, a letter calling for an urgent enquiry was sent to the Prime Minister, endorsed by over 95 state- and territory-based disability organisations and with a petition of over 11,000 signatories. The response was an inquiry and report by the Senate Community Affairs References Committee (2015) that confirmed the petitioners' claims. Further confirmation of system failure comes from a review of current models of health service delivery in both the UK and Australia, by Giuntoli et al. (2015). The authors conclude, 'it seems to be increasingly accepted that generic models of health care for people with an intellectual disability are not resourced sufficiently to appropriately meet their needs' (p.31).

Enter the National Disability Insurance Scheme (NDIS), possibly the most important social reform in recent Australian history. It is based on the principle of the right to personal choice and control, as opposed to the traditional Australian paternalistic welfare model that has dominated the delivery of disability services. It is remarkable, not least for the fact that all political parties agreed to fund it from the introduction of a new universal tax of 0.5 per cent added to the national medical insurance scheme (Griffiths 2014).

The NDIS was legislated in 2014 (National Disability Insurance Scheme Act 2013, 2014) and requires the National Disability

Insurance Agency (NDIA) to provide support and assistance to eligible participants. It creates a uniform system of disability services across Australia 'based on individual aspiration and choice'.

Among other things the Act has the objectives of:

- supporting the independence, and social and economic participation of people with a disability; and
- enabling people with a disability to exercise choice and control in the pursuit of their goals, and in the planning and delivery of their supports.

Crucially, NDIS payments are not made to organisations, but directly to either the participant or to the person managing their funding. Four NDIS trial sites commenced on July 1, 2013, with the full national roll-out of the scheme having commenced in July 2016 and be completed by July 2018. The support providers are mainly small/medium enterprises. The second report of the Joint Standing Committee (National Disability Insurance Scheme 2015) for November 2015, states that:

- participant satisfaction was measured at 90.8 points. Of course there are also many issues and problems to be addressed, but these are frankly presented in the report and solutions suggested;
- the top two primary disabilities listed are Autism and Intellectual Disability; and
- the overall cost of the scheme was in line with expectations.

Certainly the NDIS does not suit everyone, especially the larger extant operatives with expensive programmes. No longer will they receive block funding, but they will need to attract customers who have chosen between alternatives. A full chapter in the November report of the National Disability Insurance Scheme (2015) concerns the preparedness of providers to transition into a fee-for-service market.

Conclusions

Undoubtedly, the NDIS has outstanding positive features. Perhaps foremost, it has normalised disability because, as funding is linked to a universal tax, all Australians directly contribute to this form of insurance. Thus, the NDIS has created a shared conceptual space where drawing on the NDIS resource is as socially acceptable as claiming any other form of personal insurance. Funding for disability does not diminish public moneys for other purposes. Neither can the need to fund for other purposes diminish funding for the NDIS.

Perhaps this has broken the oscillating cycle of funding described in the six phases above. Because funding is no longer dependent on societal whim, and because all citizens benefit, the funding source is likely to continue. Disability can strike any family at any time, and the NDIS will provide the support they need. Importantly, the NDIS does not discriminate between disability types, with a model of funding allocation based simply on demonstrated need. And since each funded person chooses their own service provider, this will surely diminish systematic abuse within the service agencies.

The NDIS has also cleverly avoided the pitfall created by the philosophy (Wolfensberger 1972) that demands complete societal integration to meet the standard of normalisation. While high-level integration should rightly be regarded as aspirational for some individuals, to have this as an aspirational norm creates an impossible task, for reasons understood for about seventy years (see Allport 1958). As noted in 2001 by the UK Department of Health, 'helping people sustain friendships is consistently shown as being one of the greatest challenges faced by learning disability services'.

Instead of 'integration', the NDIS legislation and documentation aims for 'inclusion'. This may be defined as 'the belief that all people should feel that they are included in society, even if they lack some advantages' (Macmillan English Dictionary 2014). Perhaps, by extension, we should consider the wisdom of Nirje (1985). He considered the principle of normalisation to be based on recognition of a person's integrity, 'meaning to be yourself among others – to be able and be allowed to be yourself among others' (p. 67). This aim does not require that the 'others' are non-disabled people. Coupled with NDIS funding, such an approach could realistically provide people with an intellectual disability the same level of inclusion as normally experienced by members of society.

Acknowledgements:

I thank Dr. Christine Baxter for her insightful comments on an earlier draft of this manuscript.

This work was supported by the National Research Foundation of Korea Grant funded by the Korean Government (NRF-2013S1A3A2054622).

References

Allport, G. (1958) *The Nature of Prejudice*. New York: Doubleday Press.

Baumeister, A. (1970) 'The American residential institution: Its history and character'. In: A. Baumeister & E. Butterfield (eds.), *Residential Facilities for The Mentally Retarded*. Chicago: Aldine.

Bell, B. (1927) *Buck v. Bell*, 274 US 200.

Collins, J. (2015) 'From hospital to home: The drive to support people with intellectual disabilities in the community', *International Journal of Developmental Disabilities*, 61: 76–82.

Community Affairs References Committee (2015) *Violence, Abuse and Neglect against People with Disability in Institutional and Residential Settings*. Canberra: Parliament House.

Comptroller and Auditor General (2015) *Care Services for People with Learning Disabilities and Challenging Behaviour*. London: Department of Health.

Darwin, C. & Bynum, W. (2009) *The Origin of Species by Means of Natural Selection: Or, The Preservation of Favoured Races in the Struggle for Life*. New York: A. L. Burt Company.

Department of Health (2001) *Valuing People: A new strategy for learning disability for the 21st century*. London: The Stationery Office.

Deutsch, A. (1949) *The Mentally Ill in America*. New York: Columbia University Press.

Duffy, S. (2015) 'Foreword'. In: R. Jackson. *Who Cares? The impact of ideology, regulation and marketisation on the quality of life of people with an intellectual disability*. Sheffield: Centre for Welfare Reform.

Giuntoli, G., Newton, B. & Fisher, K. (2015) *Current Models of Health Service Delivery for People with Intellectual Disability: Literature review*. Sydney: Social Policy Research Centre.

Goddard, H. (1912) *The Kallikak family: A study in the heredity of feeblemindedness*. New York: MacMillan.

Griffiths, E. (2014) 'Federal budget feels pain as savings measures slated for July 1 delayed by Senate', *ABC News (Australian Broadcasting Corporation)*. http://www.abc.net.au/news/2014-07-01/budget-hole-as-savings-measures-delayed-by-senate/5561118.

Griffiths, J. & Curtis, C. (1984) 'Integrating deinstitutionalised persons into the community', *British Columbia Journal of Special Education*, 8: 257–266.

Gunzburg, H. (1970) 'II – The hospital as a normalizing training environment', *British Journal of Mental Subnormality*, 16: 71–83.

Health Care Commission and Commission for Social Care Inspection (2006) *Joint Investigation into the Provision of Services for People with Learning Disabilities at Cornwall Partnership NHS Trust*. London: Commission for Health Care Audit and Inspection.

Horsfield, E. (1940) 'Mental defectives at the court of Philip IV of Spain as portrayed by the great court painter Velasquez', *American Journal of Mental Deficiency*, 45: 152–157.

Jackson, R. (2015) *Who Cares? The impact of ideology, regulation and marketisation on the quality of life of people with an intellectual disability*. Sheffield: The Centre for Welfare Reform.

Jones, M. (1986) 'An examination of the lifestyle of residents of a group home', *Journal of Intellectual and Developmental Disability*, 12: 133–137.

Josué, N. (2004) *Jacob Rodrigues Pereira*, Judeus Portugueses. http://ruadajudiaria.com/index.php?p=248.

Kurtz, R. & Wolfensberger, W. (1969) 'Separation experiences of residents in an institution for the mentally retarded: 1910–1959', *American Journal of Mental Deficiency*, 74: 389–396.

Little, A. & Johnson, B. (1932) 'A study of the social and economic adjustments of one hundred thirteen discharged parolees from Laconia State School', *Proceedings of the Fifty-sixth Annual Session of the American Association for the Study of the Feeble-minded, Philadelphia, PA*, 37: 233–248.

Macmillan English Dictionary (2014) Melbourne, Australia: Macmillan Education. http://www.macmillandictionary.com/dictionary.

Mansell, J. (2007) *Services for People with Learning Disabilities and Challenging Behaviour or Mental Health Needs*. (Revised edition) London: Department of Health.

Menninger, K. (1963) *The Vital Balance*. New York: Viking.

National Disability Insurance Scheme (2015) *Joint Standing Committee: Second Progress report on the implementation and administration of the NDIS*. Canberra: Parliament House.

National Disability Insurance Scheme (2014) *Act 2013, 2014*. Includes amendments up to *Act No. 62*. Canberra, Australia: Office of Parliamentary Counsel.

Nirje, B. (1969) 'The normalization principle and its human management implications'. In: R. Kugel & W. Wolfensberger (eds.), *Changing Patterns in Residential Services for the Mentally Retarded*. Washington: President's Committee on Mental Retardation.

— (1970) 'I – The Normalization Principle: Implications and comments', *British Journal of Mental Subnormality*, 16: 62–70.

— (1985) 'The basis and logic of the normalization principle', *Australia and New Zealand Journal of Developmental Disabilities*, 11: 65–68.

Packard, K. & Laveck, B. (1976) 'Public Attitudes'. In: United States President's Committee on Mental Retardation (ed.), *Mental Retardation: Century of Decision*. Washington, D.C.: President's Committee on Mental Retardation.

Scheerenberger, R. (1976) 'A study of public residential facilities', *Mental Retardation*, 14: 32–35.

Seguin, E. (1907) *Idiocy: And Its Treatment By The Physiological Method*. Columbia: Teachers' College, Columbia University.

UK Department of Health (2001) *Valuing People: A new strategy for learning disability for the 21st Century*. CM 5086. London: The Stationery Office.

Victorian Government (1986) *Intellectually Disabled Persons' Services Act*. Melbourne: Victorian Government.

Williamson, L. (1978) 'Infanticide: An anthropological analysis'. In: M. Kohl (ed.), *Infanticide and the Value of Life*. New York: Prometheus Books.

Wolfensberger, W. (1972) *The Principle of Normalization in Human Services*. Toronto: National Institute on Mental Retardation.

— (1976) 'The origin and nature of our institutional models'. In: R. Kugel & A. Shearer (eds.), *Changing Patterns in Residential Services for the Mentally Retarded*. Washington, D.C.: President's Committee on Mental Retardation.

— (1983) 'Social role valorization: A proposed new term for the principle of normalization', *Mental Retardation*, 21: 234–239.

Wolfensberger, W. & Glenn, L. (1973) *PASS: A method of the quantitative evaluation of human services (Handbook-Field Manual)*. Toronto: National Institute on Mental Retardation.

— (1975) *PASS 3: A method for the quantitative evaluation of human services*. Toronto: National Institute on Mental Retardation.

Zarfas, D. (1970) 'III – Moving toward the normalcy principle in a large government operated facility for the mentally retarded', *British Journal of Mental Subnormality*, 16: 84–92.

Realities of Social Life and their Implications for Social Inclusion

ROBIN DUNBAR

Introduction

Humans are, above all else, social creatures. Our capacity to live and prosper depends to a large extent on the fact that we are embedded in communities that provide support. That support is not unconditional. It is premised on an implicit social contract: we agree to provide mutual support mainly because of family ties or common interest. These two pillars of the social world underpin much of what we do, biologically, sociologically and psychologically. In this chapter, I want to explore this aspect of our sociality and ask what implications it has for the intellectually disabled. If we are to provide an appropriate social context for the intellectually disabled, we need to understand what motivates our own social life and then ask how this maps across onto their social world.

A great deal of ink has been spilled over the past several decades on the question of how we should best cater for those whose intellectual capacities make it difficult for them to cope with everyday life. Over the last two centuries we have moved from care in the community to care in institutions, and back to care in the community. Although much of this has been well meaning, it is a moot question as to whether each change has been ultimately motivated by the real interests of those whom it most affected. This is, perhaps, most conspicuous in the most recent manifestation, where there seems to have been a politically, if not financially, motivated view that the intellectually disabled will fare better if they are embedded in the wider community as members of the community. If this reflects an implicit desire to return to an historical past when the disabled lived in the community, it is important not to be too much in awe of a halcyon past when the world was kinder. Yes, often the disabled might at times have been treated with affection and protection, but by no means always.

Abandonment and infanticide were common ways of dealing with congenitally disabled (and even many perfectly normal, but unwanted) children in the historical past (Jackson 2002, Symonds 1997), and its frequency in Europe from medieval time through to eighteenth century led directly to the establishment of many orphanages, often associated with religious houses with their hole-in-the-wall babyhatches where a baby could be left anonymously for the nuns to collect. The situation has not improved a great deal since then. In an extensive review of infanticide and abuse in contemporary small-scale societies, Daly and Wilson (1985, 1988) noted that children born with deformities are disproportionately likely to be victims. Hill and Ball (1996) collated the reasons given for infanticide in ethnographic studies, and concluded that the most common reasons were associated with conditions that in our own societies are associated with a high risk of childhood morbidity and mortality. The bottom line is that, in mobile hunter-gatherer societies, a woman cannot afford to commit to a child who is unlikely to manage for itself by the time it is four or five years of age. Even in industrial societies, handicapped children are more likely to be abused at the hands of their parents than healthy children (Figure One). Detailed analysis of these kinds of data suggest that they are best explained by parental (often maternal) attempts to manage reproduction within constraints of limited resources (for a review, see Barrett et al. 2000, Chapter 7). Neither the past nor the present have been the kindly places we sometimes wish they were.

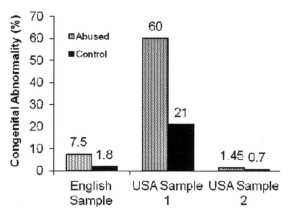

Figure One: Percentage of children admitted to hospital because of injuries who had congenital abnormalities, split by whether or not the accident was attributed to abuse or to accident (control group), in one UK and two USA samples. Source: Daly and Wilson (1985). Redrawn from Barrett et al. (2000).

The well-intentioned nineteenth-century movement to provide sheltered institutions for the disabled, and especially the intellectually disabled, arose in large part out of a recognition that such individuals were not always well treated in society at large. Had it been the case that Victorian communities treasured and looked after their disabled, there would have been no incentive to establish institutional care. Whatever its faults came to be, the Victorian solution did at least recognise, even if only implicitly, that gathering the intellectually disabled together might provide a form of community that was not especially evident for them in the wider world.

The question I want to address here, then, is the simple one of what social environment is most beneficial for those with an intellectual disability. The reason we need to consider this is that the human social world is extremely complex; social life is probably one of the most complex phenomena in the world. We take our social world for granted, though we often find it challenging. Indeed, we hardly give a second thought to the incredible sophistication of the cognitive processes that allow us to navigate our way through this world. What the human brain achieves in this domain far exceeds the cognitive demands of simple physical survival.

We should not underestimate just how challenging the social

world is, especially for those whose cognitive capacities are impaired. The classic case of this is, of course, autism. Though autism is a wide-spectrum condition, with a spread of disabilities that ranges from the mild (for example, Asperger syndrome) to the completely incapacitating, its central focus is a lack of theory of mind, or mentalising, that is, the capacity to understand other people's mind states. Most normal adults are able to cope with four other people's mind states as well as their own (conventionally referred to as 5th order mentalising to represent each of the minds involved, including your own), but autists typically can only correctly understand their own (formally, 1st order mentalising). One simple consequence of this is that autistic individuals do not understand metaphor, which is a major social problem, since much of how we use language is metaphorical. More generally, this means they simply do not understand why people behave the way they do; they are therefore likely to make social mistakes and easily become overwhelmed and disorientated in social situations whose subtleties they cannot fathom. As a result, they find it difficult to make friends, and indeed may even find the very concept of friendship difficult to comprehend.

To see why all this is so important in our lives, let me first give a brief overview of the nature of human community. I will then explore some of the psychological and social skills that underpin human communities as we live them. Finally, I will comment on how this impacts on the interests of those with an intellectual disability.

What's in a community?

Human communities have a natural size. This size is determined by the volume of key parts of our brain that manage our social relationships. Principally, this is the neocortex, but the frontal lobes of the neocortex seem to play an especially important role in this respect. This arises out of what has become known as the social brain hypothesis – the finding that, across monkeys and apes, the typical size of a species' social groups correlates with the size of its neocortex (Dunbar 1993, 1998a; Barton & Dunbar 1997). The typical size of communities in small-scale human societies (hunter gatherers, traditional horticulturalists, etc.) is around 150 individuals (Zhou et al. 2005, Hamilton et al. 2007), and is exactly what would be predicted for our brain size from the social brain relationship.

The personal social networks of normal adults (defined as the number of people whom you could ask a favour of, or with whom you have a meaningful, reciprocated relationship that has history) are also of this size (Hill & Dunbar 2003, Roberts et al. 2009), and have remained at this size despite the advent of internet social media (Dunbar 2016, Wolfram 2013). Indeed, neuroimaging has revealed that individual differences in the size of personal social networks correlate with individuals' distinct size of the volume of the frontal and temporal lobes (Lewis et al. 2011, Kanai et al. 2011, Powell et al. 2012). So this social brain effect is not just something to do with species but also applies within species at the level of the individual. It is important to appreciate that this constraint isn't simply a memory problem. The number of faces we can put names to is about 1,500 – an order of magnitude larger than the 150 individuals that make up my social network. The constraint seems to rise from the number of people with whom we can have meaningful relationships.

In small-scale societies, this 150 would be made up almost entirely of people related to you by genetic pedigree or by marriage (in-laws, or affines). In contemporary post-industrial societies with our lower birth rates, typically only half of this number is made up of extended family (including close in-laws) (Roberts et al. 2009). Roberts et al. (2009) showed that we prioritise family, such that people who come from large extended families typically have fewer non-family friends. There are, perhaps, good reasons for prioritising family: they are much more likely to come to your aid and provide help than are non-family friends (Madsen et al. 2007, Curry et al. 2013, Burton-Chellew & Dunbar 2015a).

The size of our personal social network is determined by how effectively we can manage relationships, and this turns out to be associated with our capacity for mentalising. Powell et al. (2012) have shown that the volume of core parts of the brain in the frontal and temporal lobes seem to determine mentalising skills, and mentalising skills in turn determine how many relationships we can manage. However, social cognition, unlike the more conventional aspects of cognition that make up IQ, also depends on considerable learning and experience and takes such a long time to develop that it doesn't reach its final adult state until the mid-twenties (Blakemore & Choudhury 2006, Dunbar 2013).

More importantly, perhaps, the number 150 is just one in a series of socially relevant numbers. In effect, our personal social networks consist of a series of inclusive layers that have very specific sizes: 5, 15, 50, 150, 500, and 1500, with each of these layers being inclusive of the layers within it (Figure Two). These layers (sometimes known as the circles of acquaintanceship) correspond roughly to what we might think of as intimate friends, best friends, good friends, friends, acquaintances and people we recognise by sight. These same numbers reappear all over the place, not only in social networks (Dunbar et al. 2015), but also in the way organisations are structured (Dunbar 2014). All modern armies are structured in this way, for example (Dunbar 2011).

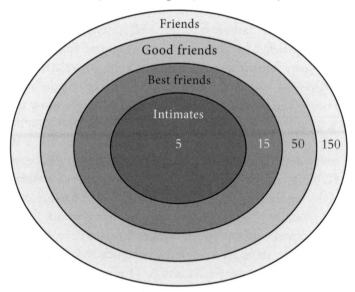

Figure Two: The circles of acquaintanceship. Each of us sits at the centre of a series of circles that increase in cumulative size, but decrease in average emotional intensity (as indicated by the labels attached to each layer). These circles have very distinct sizes (indicated for each layer), notwithstanding the fact that there is considerable variation between individuals. Family typically make up about half of each layer. (This figure is redrawn from Dunbar 2015).

The layers emerge out of the fact that relationships take time to create and service, and, since time is limited, we have to ration it across the individuals who are important to us (Miritello et al. 2013, Saramäki et al. 2014). Typically, we devote about 20 per cent of our day to social interaction (Dunbar 1998b). Since the quality of a relationship depends on the time invested in it, we distribute what time and effort we can afford (our social capital) amongst our family and friends in a very distinctive way. About 40 per cent of that social time is given to the five people in our innermost circle (our intimate friends and family), and a further 20 per cent to the next ten people that make up the second layer (the layer of 15 best friends and family) (Sutcliffe et al. 2012). This yields very specific frequencies of interaction: we see the individuals in our layer of five at least once a week, those in our layer of 15 at least once a month, those in the layer of 150 at least once a year. Failure to see a friend at the requisite frequency results in a very rapid weakening of the friendship – they will drop down through the layers on a scale of months rather than years. Family relationships are typically more robust to this effect, but friendships are not (Roberts & Dunbar 2011a).

These layers correspond not just to specific frequencies of interaction, but also to the degree of emotional closeness we feel to the individuals concerned. In fact, emotional closeness and frequency of contact correlate closely, even in family relationships (Roberts & Dunbar 2011b). We see most often the people we feel emotionally closest to – or it may be that the causal direction is the other way around – we feel emotionally close to those we see most often. In addition to emotional closeness, the layers differ consistently in how altruistic we are to the people in them. It seems that our willingness to help others is correlated with how emotionally close we feel to them, and this is true for both family and friends (though we are always more willing to help family than friends in the same layer) (Curry et al. 2013).

This raises a second important issue, namely the mechanisms that underpin the friendships that create these patterns. What makes a friendship?

Studies of friendship suggest that relationships are commonly characterised by similarity (the principle of homophily): the urban myth that opposites attract notwithstanding, friends are more likely than not to be similar in their interests and tastes (McPherson et al. 2001). Our studies suggest that friendships can be categorised in terms of six major dimensions: shared language, same place of origin, similar educational experience, common interests/hobbies (including musical tastes), similar world views (moral, religious and political attitudes) and shared sense of humour (Curry & Dunbar 2013). The more of these dimensions we share with someone, the warmer the quality of the relationship, and the closer they will sit to us in our circles of acquaintanceship, *and* the more likely we are to be altruistic towards them (Curry & Dunbar 2013, Launay & Dunbar 2015).

Similarity on these six dimensions marks us out as belonging to the same community. Indeed, several of them (same dialect, same natal location, same schools) specifically identify us as having come from the same local community. That is important for two reasons. First, it increases the likelihood that we are related, or at least have relatives in common by marriage. Kinship has a particularly strong hold on our behaviour. We are invariably more altruistic towards relatives than non-relatives (for example, Madsen et al. 2007), in part because of the influence of biological kin selection (a predisposition to favour close relatives over less closely related individuals) and in part because family networks are denser and more interconnected than non-family networks (creating a policing effect in which our behaviour is more likely to reach the ears of people who matter to us. See Roberts et al. 2009, Curry and Dunbar 2011). Second, the fact that we come from the same small community is more likely to mean that we have interests in common as well as psychological attitudes in common: we know how much we can trust each other, because we all know the rules of the game in the community. That makes it easier for us to manage the often unspoken give and take of relationships.

Implications for those with an intellectual disability

In thinking about the implications of these findings, there are three aspects to consider. One is the question of who is most likely to provide support for a disabled person. The second is the practical question relating to the natural size of community appropriate to someone with an intellectual disability. And the third is how this can best be provided.

Although we make a great deal of the importance of altruism and invariably extol individuals who act generously over and beyond the call of duty, we are in reality a great deal less generous as a species than we might sometimes wish to believe. Indeed, the very fact that we extol, and so often plead for, such behaviour ought to alert us to the fact that altruistic help is not a simple given. If it were, there would be no need to comment on it or encourage it. In reality, a huge literature indicates that help, when it is given, is much more likely to be given to relatives (and generally in rough proportion to the degree of relatedness: Madsen et al. 2007, Curry et al. 2013) or to people, such as prospective romantic partners, about whom we have ulterior motives. While help is often given generously and without expectation of return to relatives, it is typically given to unrelated individuals only on a strictly reciprocal basis: implicitly or explicitly, it is assumed that the favour will in due course be returned in kind (reviewed in Barrett et al. 2000, Chapter 4). This is not to undervalue the importance of altruism and generosity of behaviour, nor to encourage people to behave selfishly, it is simply an observation of fact. To borrow the moral philosophers' dictum of the naturalistic fallacy, 'is' does not mean 'ought', and equally 'ought' does not mean 'is'.

This observation has important implications for those with an intellectual disability: because disabled people are less likely to be able to enter into an agreement of reciprocity, never mind actually reciprocate, their most likely source of help by far will be close relatives, or very close friends of those relatives who will help out of a sense of personal obligation to the relative. If we isolate people with an intellectual disability from their family networks, we risk undermining their principal source of help. The only exception to this is highly religious people who may be willing to bear the costs of help (whether in time or money, but especially time) for reasons unrelated to the identity of the disabled person, purely as a form of charity. The number of people who fall into that category is very small (even among religious people), and, for most individuals, the willingness to behave in this way is probably not especially stable over time. Each of us is subject to time pressures and the demands of our other relationships.

The second issue concerns the size of social networks and communities. Normal adults have a natural size of community that varies somewhat around a figure of 150 (probably between about 100–250), being higher in extroverts and lower in introverts. This represents the number of individuals with whom we have meaningful relationships, and in that respect seems to represent the size of communities within which we feel most comfortable. Given this, what size of network might we expect individuals who have intellectual disabilities to have? So far, no one has tried to determine this, and it might in any case be quite challenging to do reliably. However, we can gain some insight into the question by noting that, in normal adults, the size of social networks is correlated with individuals' mentalising competences (Powell et al. 2012). The best guide for those whose mentalising competences lie outside the normal range (roughly 4–6 orders of mentalising) is the larger scale provided by primates in general, remembering that primate sociality is identical to our own. Though we do not have many data for mentalising competences in non-human primates, what data there are suggest a near-linear relationship between mentalising competence and typical social-group size across the span represented by a typical Old World monkey (rhesus macaque), an ape (chimpanzees) and humans (Figure Three). The sequence is pretty much what we see during child development, with 2nd order mentalising (formal theory of mind, the ability to understand someone else's mindstate) being the equivalent of a five–six year old, and 4th order the equivalent of a young teenager (Henzi et al. 2007).

Figure Three gives us a rough idea of what the size of natural personal networks might be as a function of an individual's mentalising competences. Someone with the mentalising competences of an autistic individual (equivalent to mentalising level 1) might be expected to be able to handle only about 35

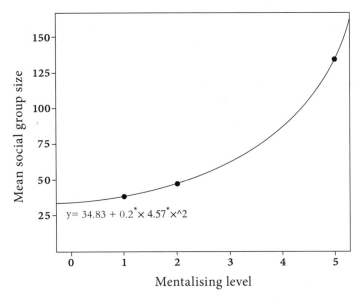

Figure Three: The relationship between mean social group size and mentalising skills for three Old World primates (left to right: rhesus macaques, chimpanzees and humans). Mentalising skills are indexed as the number of other individuals' mind states (including one's own) that can be handled simultaneously.

people in their entire network. Someone with the mentalising competences of a six year old (mentalising level 2) might manage 50–60 people in their network, while someone with the mentalising competences of a teenager (level 4, at the lower level of the natural variation in normal adults) might be expected to have a personal network of around 120 individuals. Bearing in mind that, on average, about half of our social network of 150 is made up of relatives (Roberts & Dunbar et al. 2009), and that this component of the network is a given, this tells us that if a disabled person is well-embedded within their family network, they are likely to have very little, if any, capacity for forming relationships with unrelated individuals. To do so, they would have to sacrifice family members – in other words, the very people we normally prioritise in our networks (Roberts et al. 2009) and the most likely sources of unstinting support and assistance (review in Barrett et al. 2000, Chapter 3). We would do well to be very careful when we scale the size of communities for the disabled.

An important corollary of Figure Three is that many of the

skills that enable us to cope with our social world correlate with mentalising skills, and may even be a component part of these. These include, for example, the ability to inhibit prepotent responses (i.e. to put off immediate gratification in expectation of greater benefits in the future, or in more prosaic terms simply to know when 'to hold our tongue'), a skill that is crucial to our ability to maintain functional social networks. Being able to mitigate immediate self-interest underpins our ability to ensure that everyone gets a fair share of the benefits of the group. Failure to share effectively has the effect of driving people away because we are commonly unwilling to give time to those who are unwilling to reciprocate.

This neatly brings us to the third issue: reciprocity. I suggested in the previous section that, in the normal course of life, our friendships are based on a principal of homophily. We choose as friends people who are most similar to us on a string of cultural traits. Most often, this concerns those things that we are intrinsically most engaged by (hobbies, interests, musical tastes, sense of humour, religion, political views, moral attitudes), all of which typically depend on the individuals concerned having the same language skills as we do. These traits provide the basis for our being willing to invest time in people. Since we invest most of our available social time in a very small circle of individuals – on average, 60 per cent of our social capital is devoted to the 15 people in the two innermost layers of the network (Sutcliffe et al. 2012) – being asked to include someone who does not (and maybe cannot) share many of these traits is a big stretch. It inevitably results in us devoting less time to someone else who might be important to us, and who would then be excluded from that magic circle. Since including someone who can't, or won't, reciprocate in our innermost circles would reduce the network that provides us with the moral, social and maybe financial help on which we depend throughout life, we would be bearing a significant cost.

We cannot assume that people will be willing to bear this cost. Nor can we assume that simply by asking people to do so they will start taking it on, or that offering them the opportunity to do so when we house the disabled among them will be effective.

The more demanding the recipient is in terms of our time and mental energy, the less willing we will be to make room for them. The only people we are usually prepared to bear such costs for are romantic partners (Burton-Chellew & Dunbar 2015b). Indeed, even relatives are not immune to the pressures imposed on them by very demanding relatives. In a study of close social networks, Roberts et al. (2008) found that women who scored high on the neuroticism personality scale (i.e. were not actually suffering from a definable clinical condition but showed a general propensity in that direction) had fewer female relatives in their social networks. This is most likely explained by the fact that the more demanding behaviour of these women had ostracised many of their female kin. In other words, even the one group of people who are usually most willing to continue offering support are likely to withdraw from contact with those who are very demanding. Help and support does not come for free, even from those most likely to offer it. Saints are rare in the real world, which is why their behaviour attracts comment and admiration. Most people have their own lives to lead, and have only a limited capacity to sacrifice this in the interests of those less fortunate than themselves.

Conclusions

Taken together, these observations suggest two important conclusions. First, placing people with an intellectual disability in small (i.e. conventional) dwellings within the wider community, however well intentioned that might be, may not be in their best interests. The kinds of argument for this, based mainly on freedom of choice and the individual's right to do as they wish, work only when the individual's social playing field is level and they can meaningfully exercise that choice. When that assumption does not hold, the argument is specious. The underlying assumption that people with an intellectual disability should be discouraged from forming friendships with other disabled people for their own good (Rhoades & Browning 1977) is at best misguided and at worst displays an astonishing lack of understanding of how friendships are formed in the real world.

The bottom line is that we cannot rely on the wider community being willing to form meaningful friendships with people with an intellectual disability, even if they are willing to act more tolerantly towards them and accept their presence in the community. The consequence of housing those with an intellectual disability in the community in small care homes, as has become increasingly fashionable, may, paradoxically, be increasing loneliness and a greater sense of isolation (McDevitt et al. 1978, Cummins & Kim 2015).

This raises the second point, namely whether, because of the homophily effect, it is important that the disabled have ready access to people at their own intellectual level with whom to form friendships and other relationships. In an ideal world, the answer might be no. But in the real everyday world in which we actually live, the answer is almost certainly yes. Moreover, they need to have access to enough others of similar social and intellectual level to provide a choice of friends, because friendships do not last forever. The turnover on friendships is surprisingly high, perhaps as high as 30–40 per cent in network membership per year among twenty –year olds (Saramäki et al. 2014); indeed, even family relationships are not immune, with an estimated terminal collapse in a family relationship (often a very close family relationship) once every four and a half years (Dunbar & Machin 2014). This means that sufficient numbers of appropriate people need to be available to provide a pool from which new friendships can be developed as old ones fade or break.

The size of 'homes' that seem to be currently preferred in the dispersed model (those with no more than ten to fifteen clients, often less) is almost certainly too small. With so small a community, it is unlikely, unless the home operates a policy of very strict selection, that two or more individuals with sufficiently similar intellectual and social abilities to allow the formation of natural friendships will meet. Realistically, a community of around thirty to fifty individuals would probably be nearer the mark for an ideal size, but larger communities subdivided into smaller, partially self-contained sub-communities of this size between which it might be possible to move would probably have many advantages. Such communities do not, of course, need to be isolated from the wider world, and can still be embedded into the wider community if well designed. Size is not a bar to the public being involved in the activities of communities, and a large community is more likely to be able to put on events in which the wider public can be involved. There will, inevitably, always be an issue of safety and security for individuals who would put themselves at risk if left to wander out on their own, but that is an issue with which even smaller care homes have to contend.

References

Barrett, L., Dunbar, R. & Lycett, J. (2000) *Human Evolutionary Psychology*. Harmondsworth: Palgrave-Macmillan.

Barton, R. & Dunbar, R. (1997) 'Evolution of the social brain'. In: A. Whiten & R. Byrne (eds.), *Machiavellian Intelligence II*. Cambridge: Cambridge University Press, pp. 240–263.

Blakemore, S. & Choudhury, S. (2006) 'Development of the adolescent brain: Implications for executive function and social cognition', *Journal of Child Psychology and Psychiatry*, 47: 296–312.

Burton-Chellew, M. & Dunbar, R. (2015a) 'Hamilton's Rule predicts anticipated social support in humans', *Behavioral Ecology*, 26: 130–137.

— (2015b) 'Romance and reproduction are socially costly', *Evolutionary Behavioral Sciences*, 9: 229–241.

Cummins, R. & Kim, Y. (2015) 'The use and abuse of "community" and "neighbourhood" within disability research: An exposé, clarification, and recommendation', *International Journal of Developmental Disabilities*, 61: 68–75.

Curry, O. & Dunbar, R. (2011) 'Altruism in networks: The effect of connections', *Biology Letters*, 7: 651–653.

— (2013) 'Do birds of a feather flock together? The relationship between similarity and altruism in social networks', *Human Nature*, 24: 336–347.

Curry, O., Roberts, S. & Dunbar, R. (2013) 'Altruism in social networks: Evidence for a "kinship premium"', *British Journal of Psychology*, 104: 283–195.

Daly, M. & Wilson, M. (1985) 'Child abuse and other risks of not living with both parents', *Ethology and Sociobiology*, 6: 197–210.

— (1988) 'Evolutionary psychology and family homicide', *Science*, 242: 519–524.

Dunbar, R. (1993) 'Coevolution of neocortex size, group size and language in humans', *Behavioral and Brain Sciences*, 16: 681–735.

— (1998a) 'The social brain hypothesis', *Evolutionary Anthropology*, 6: 178–190.

— (1998b) 'Theory of mind and the evolution of language'. In: J. Hurford, M. Studdart-Kennedy & C. Knight (eds.), *Approaches to the Evolution of Language*. Cambridge: Cambridge University Press, pp. 92–110.

— (2011) 'Constraints on the evolution of social institutions and their implications for information flow', *Journal of Institutional Economics*, 7: 345–371.

— (2013) 'The social brain in developmental perspective: Neuro-evolution and implications for social cognitive development'. In: M. Legerstee, D. Haley & M. Bornstein (eds.), *The Infant Mind: Origins of the social brain*. Abingdon: Guildford Press, pp. 3–18.

— (2014) 'The Social Brain: Psychological underpinnings and implications for the structure of organizations', *Current Directions in Psychological Research*, 24: 109–114.

— (2015) 'Social networks and their implications for community living for people with a learning disability', *International Journal of Developmental Disabilities*, 61(2): 101–106.

— (2016) 'Do online social media cut through the constraints that limit the size of offline social networks?', *Royal Society Open Science*, 3: 150–292.

Dunbar, R. & Machin, A. (2014) 'Sex differences in relationship conflict and reconciliation', *Journal of Evolutionary Psychology*, 12: 109–133.

Dunbar, R., Arnaboldi, V., Conti, M. & Passarella, A. (2015) 'The structure of online social networks mirrors those in the offline world', *Social Networks*, 43: 39–47.

Hamilton, M., Milne, B., Walker, R., Burger, O. & Brown, J. (2007) 'The complex structure of hunter-gatherer social networks', *Proceedings of the Royal Society, London*, 274B: 2195–2202.

Henzi, S., de Sousa Pereira, L., Hawker-Bond, D., Stiller, J., Dunbar, R. & Barrett, L. (2007) 'Look who's talking: Developmental trends in the size of conversational cliques', *Evolution and Human Behavior*, 28: 66–74.

Hill, C. & Ball, H. (1996) 'Abnormal births and other "ill omens": The adaptive case of infanticide', *Human Nature*, 7: 381–401.

Hill, R. & Dunbar, R. (2003) 'Social network size in humans', *Human Nature*, 14: 53–72

Jackson, M. (2000) *Infanticide: Historical perspectives on child murder and concealment, 1550–2000*. London: Routledge.

Kanai, R., Bahrami, B., Roylance, R. & Rees, G. (2011) 'Online social network size is reflected in human brain structure', *Proceedings of the Royal Society, London*, 279B: 1327–1334.

Launay, J. & Dunbar, R. (2015) 'Playing with strangers: Which shared traits attract us most to new people?', *PLOS ONE*, 10(6): e0129688.

Lewis, P., Rezaie, R., Browne, R., Roberts, N. & Dunbar, R. (2011) 'Ventromedial prefrontal volume predicts understanding of others and social network size', *NeuroImage* 57: 1624–1629.

Madsen, E., Tunney, R., Fieldman, G., Plotkin, H., Dunbar, R., Richardson, J. & McFarland, D. (2007) 'Kinship and altruism: A cross-cultural experimental study', *British Journal of Psychology*, 98: 339–359.

McDevitt, S., Smith, P., Schmidt, D. & Rosen, M. (1978) 'The deinstitutionalized citizen: Adjustment and quality of life', *Mental Retardation*, 16: 22–24.

McPherson, M., Smith-Lovin, L. & Cook, J. (2001) 'Birds of a feather: Homophily in social networks', *Annual Review of Sociology*, 27: 415–444.

Miritello, G., Moro, E., Lara, R., Martínez-López, R., Belchamber, J., Roberts, S. & Dunbar, R. (2013) 'Time as a limited resource: Communication strategy in mobile phone networks', *Social Networks*, 35: 89–95.

Powell, J., Lewis, P., Roberts, N., García-Fiñana, M. & Dunbar, R. (2012) 'Orbital prefrontal cortex volume predicts social network size: An imaging study of individual differences in humans', *Proceedings of the Royal Society, London*, 279B: 2157–2162.

Rhoades, C. & Browning, P. (1977) 'Normalization at what price?', *Mental Retardation*, 15: 24.

Roberts, S. (2010) 'Constraints on social networks'. In: R. Dunbar, C. Gamble & J. Gowlett (eds.), *Social Brain, Distributed Mind*. Oxford: Oxford University Press, pp. 117–138.

Roberts, S. & Dunbar, R. (2011a) 'The costs of family and friends: An 18-month longitudinal study of relationship maintenance and decay', *Evolution and Human Behavior*, 32: 186–197.

— (2011b) 'Communication in social networks: Effects of kinship, network size and emotional closeness', *Personal Relationships*, 18: 439–452.

Roberts, S., Wilson, R., Fedurek, P. & Dunbar, R. (2008) 'Individual differences and personal social network size and structure', *Personality and Individual Differences*, 44: 954–964.

Roberts, S., Dunbar, R., Pollet, T. & Kuppens, T. (2009) 'Exploring variations in active network size: Constraints and ego characteristics', *Social Networks*, 31: 138–146.

Saramäki, J., Leicht, E., López, E., Roberts, S., Reed-Tsochas, F. & Dunbar, R. (2014) 'The persistence of social signatures in human communication', *Proceedings of the National Academy of Sciences, USA*, 111: 942–947.

Sutcliffe, A., Dunbar, R., Binder, J. & Arrow, H. (2012) 'Relationships and the social brain: Integrating psychological and evolutionary perspectives', *British Journal of Psychology*, 103: 149–168.

Symonds, D.A. (1997) *Weep Not for Me: Women, ballads, and infanticide in early modern Scotland*. Philadelphia: Pennsylvania State University Press.

Wolfram, S. (2013) 'Data science of the Facebook world'. http://blog. stephenwolfram.com/2013/04/data-science-of-the-facebook-world/#more-5350. Accessed 29 Aug. 2015.

Zhou, W-X., Sornette, D., Hill, R. & Dunbar, R. (2005) 'Discrete hierarchical organization of social group sizes', *Proceedings of the Royal Society, London*, 272B: 439–444.

Making a Space for the Lost Histories of Inclusion

PAUL MILNER & BRIGIT MIRFIN-VEITCH

Baron's Paradox

In writing about the humanising effect of storytelling within the legal context, Jane Baron famously observed that the people who most need to have their stories told are often those least able to tell them (Baron 1991, p.103). Writers have argued that 'seeing' and 'responding' to the human story has an ability to 'cut through' the (often self-protective) epistemologies of the institutions that shape our day-to-day lives (Baron 1999, Nussbaum 1995). 'Baron's Paradox' reminds us that although the moral thinking of a society is informed by the stories it comes to hear, the narratives of those who fall beyond the moral and legal protections of storied sameness are most likely to be excluded from our library of legitimate and instructive narration.

People understood as having high and complex support needs have had little opportunity to author their place in our historical record. They have also been 'written out' of the research canon, largely as a consequence of their subjectivity being thought to lie beyond the protocols of existing qualitative research methods. Theirs, according to Atkinson and Walmsley (1999), are the 'ultimate lost voices', still waiting to tell us how they read the 'ordinary places' within which their stories dwell (Atkinson & Walmsley 1999). However, until we hear from people with high and complex support needs, we can make no claim to have had a complete conversation about the progress nation states like New Zealand are making towards meeting their human rights obligations. This is especially true for rights that seek to redress the historical exclusions of disabled people because, in ways that echo 'Baron's Paradox', a proper assessment cannot be made if the voices of those most likely to be exposed to an abuse of rights continue to remain silent and unheard (Milner & Mirfin-Veitch 2012).

Searching for the meaning of inclusion

In 2003, CCS Disability Action commissioned research (Milner & Bray 2004) that sought to learn more about disabled people's understanding of the policy objective of 'community participation'. The project, which used a participatory action research design, was entitled the 'Community Participation Project'. CCS-Disability Action is a national disability support provider whose stated aim is to help 'create communities that include all people'. As a way of capturing some of the major research themes identified through the research, we invented 'Pamela', whose fictional life summarised recurrent motifs we detected across the participants' narratives (Milner & Kelly 2009).

Pamela was described as living a dichotomised life characterised by spending long hours 'hemmed' or 'stuck' in two service settings. Her community group home and vocational centre represented her cardinal spaces of social knowing, from which she was fleetingly liberated in an array of public community settings. In Pamela's vernacular these were 'out there' destinations. The least surprising finding was that when we located all of the ways Pamela was present in her community, her community map was devoid of the intermediary socio-spatial contexts between being 'stuck in' and having a transitory presence 'out there'. Pamela, like all of the 23 people who participated in the project, was described as having no access to the social worlds that pull other citizens into common community, such as full-time paid employment, continuing education, parenthood, neighbouring, or inclusive sport and recreation.

Drawing on the earlier work of geographer Yi-Fu Tuan, we suggested that being marginalised from these social worlds made it more difficult for Pamela to access the psychosocial attributes we all seek from feeling 'in place' within participatory contexts

75

that lie between the sacred and more private location of 'Home' (or, in the case of community group homes, perhaps Non-Home) and the excitement and recreative possibilities intrinsic to the unpredictable spaces of meeting and encounter (Tuan 1977).

Perhaps the most important lesson provided by the people who collaborated with us in the community participation project, and whose experiences were reflected in 'Pamela', was that they told us it was not so much *where* they were that mattered. It was *how* they were in a place that counted toward whether or not they felt a sense of belonging to their local communities. They told us that rather than looking to the literal spatial indicators of inclusion, privileged as service and social policy outcomes, we should explore instead relational markers, in particular five qualitative attributes of relationship that communicated a sense of belonging. The signposts they instructed us to look for were:

1. **Autobiographic** People were participating in ways that were autobiographic, not just in the sense that they were self-determined, but they were chosen because the particular participatory context spoke to how a person understood and wished to communicate their sense of self.
2. **Social identity** Within a social context, people had an acknowledged and affirmed social identity, found themselves represented in the social history of place as a member, and contributed to the way a community saw itself.
3. **Reciprocity** People were aware of, and strengthened, relationships through culturally specific systems of reciprocity, including acts of kindness and consideration that bind people one to another rather than money being the medium of social exchange.
4. **Insider** When in place, people experienced an insider's sense of psychological safety, including feeling 'off' rather than 'on stage'.
5. **Expectation** People were met by an expectation that they contributed to the wellbeing of other members and/or the wider community as a dynamic social entity (Milner & Bray 2004, Milner & Kelly 2009).

Slow progress towards
the (authorised) vision of an inclusive society

In a paper he wrote in 2005, Hall suggested that reducing the number of people experiencing exclusion from 'mainstream society' represented the unifying principle of social policy in the UK. He foregrounded the pervasiveness of principles espoused as instrumental to people living 'full and purposeful lives' in the *Valuing People* White Paper to make his point (Hall 2005). In New Zealand, the social policy equivalent to the White Paper is the New Zealand Disability Strategy (2001): it evokes the same language and intent. The vision at the heart of the strategy is to transform New Zealand from a 'disabling to a fully inclusive society', in which the experience of living 'valued lives' is similarly benchmarked against the participatory presence of disabled people in employment and other mainstream social spaces (Minister for Disability Issues 2001).

The Community Participation Project was commissioned at a time when disability providers like CCS Disability Action were attempting to translate the vision of the Disability Strategy into everyday service practice. Conducted in 2003–04, the research anticipated major shifts in the design and delivery of disability support, including;

- the closure of segregated day-bases and the rebranding of old sheltered workshops into business enterprises;
- the emergence of person-centred planning and individualised service delivery;
- and, from 2008 onwards, New Zealand's ratification of the UN Convention.

In 2012, almost a decade after commissioning the Community Participation Project, CCS Disability Action requested a second descriptive research project to make transparent the day-to-day lives of people with high and complex support needs. The research was to have a particular focus on the ability of such people to access rights codified in Article 19 of the UN Convention on the Rights of Persons with Disability (the Convention). The commission was CCS Disability Action's way of answering the conversations they were having with disabled people and their families, including growing disquiet that those most weakly connected to their community were also those whose stories had yet to inform the social practices of service delivery.

The Article 19 Project drew on the narrative tradition to create a space for twelve people with high and complex support needs to co-create and control the telling of their own stories. To title the research we appropriated the second half of the traditional Zulu greeting Sawubona – 'I am here' – itself derived from an older South African proverb 'a person is a person because of people'. Both the proverb and its articulation in the moment of meeting remind us that we co-author existence by seeing others in ways that allows us both to say: 'I am here'. In the process of seeking co-authorship through the Article 19 Project, we met Angela and Richard.

Angela's story:

http://www.donaldbeasley.org.nz/assets/Uploads/publications/
Angela-Griffin-story-for-email-AW2mp.pdf

Angela lived alone in a small flat that looked out towards the wide streets of Oamaru*. We met not long after Angela had moved into her new flat. It was, she said, the first place she could call 'home' after spending twenty of her first twenty-five years as a patient within the walled and dehumanising community of the Total Institution. Angela rented the flat from her sister and told us later that, 'No-one [could] ever move [her] out again!' There was, however, a cost to living alone and independently.

Disabled people in New Zealand draw on a range of different support contracts to meet their total support needs. Angela drew on personal care and domestic assistance and vocational support, which were provided as a way of promoting greater community participation. Choosing to live by herself meant that Angela

---

* Oamaru is the largest town in North Otago on the South Island of New Zealand.

received less vocational funding than she might otherwise have received had she been more mobile but lived in a residential (less 'independent') support context. For Angela this meant having to weigh the benefits of home ownership against the realities of having more limited access to her community and the social relationships that lay beyond her flat. Beyond the personal care and domestic assistance she received, Angela was exposed to the real risk of social isolation.

In the week that Angela diarised her community presence for the purposes of the research, she only managed to leave her flat for four hours. Every Sunday she went with her Dad to their family home for lunch. Every Thursday afternoon, a staff person chaperoned Angela to the supermarket to do her shopping. Angela's visual impairment meant that she needed someone to walk beside her, so they could both 'motor' the block that separated the flat from the supermarket.

The geography of Angela's life-space greatly impacted on her ability to generate a sense of community. None of the ways she was routinely present in her community offered her the prospect of encounters likely to seed new relationships. As a consequence, staff and family represented oases of intimacy in an otherwise desert of social knowing. But Angela's story was not the same as Richard's.

Richard's story:

http://www.donaldbeasley.org.nz/assets/Uploads/publications/
Richard-Beale-story-for-print-v1mp.pdf

Richard grew up in Hilderthorpe, a small rural community north of Oamaru. His family had lived there for four generations, breeding horses and raising chickens (Beale, Beale & Milner 2014). When we met, Richard was living in a community group home where he had been for ten years, having moved there when his then seventy-year-old mum became unwell. Hilderthorpe, though, remained the emotional and physical reference point in Richard's life. In many ways, the town and his community group home were antithetical social settings, separated experientially by differences that followed from being understood either as a member of a generation of horse breeders or a well-respected service user. At the time of the research, Richard noted that while he liked his flatmates, it was staff and family who also dominated his 'friendship field'.

Angela's flat and Richard's group home were separated by less than five kilometres, but they clearly lived in very different Oamarus. When we asked Angela how well she knew Oamaru, she told us she knew it 'very well'. Like Richard she was born there and her family had lived in Oamaru for three generations. But when we asked her how well Oamaru knew her, she said, 'Most places – absolutely no one knows me.'

The same could not be said for Richard. He was a highly visible member of his community. Richard could not travel a neighbourhood block in his motorized chair without someone greeting him, usually to ask questions that implied personal knowing, such as 'Are you off for your cappuccino?' or 'Would it be the egg sandwich or the cream cake this morning?' Or he would be teased about women.

Communities of a (disabled) type

If Richard had complete control of his narrative he would tell you that his life was great and that it was the cappuccinos, the egg sandwiches and the women that made it so. But Richard's community was one of a particular (disabled) type. With the exception of the people and places he was connected to through his family, Richard's life was restricted to the public spaces into which he ghosted in and out. His capacity to draw people to him meant he had succeeded in turning public encounters into contextually specific forms of social acknowledgement and he rightfully celebrated the transformation. However, within spaces like the pool, the café and the Two Dollar Shop, his 'relationships of place' tended to be characterised by the veneer of social knowing. The conversations he loved seldom strayed far from questions about coffee or egg sandwiches or a teasing about women.

Richard went to places that evoked the ordinary rituals of friendship: we have coffee with our friends, and swim or shop only with those we feel most comfortable being with. However, Richard did this with staff, not friends, whose very presence extinguished the possibility of seeding new relationships. Being present with staff also broadcast that being in a relationship with people with high and complex support needs was a skilled occupation.

Finally, Richard only had islands of social contact. The women from the Aquarobics class who coincided with his regular session at the local swimming pool never met Richard's 'bevy of beauties' at the coffee shop, and unlike his Hilderthorpe 'home', no one other than staff ever came 'over there'. (In a lexicon of about ten easily understood expressions, Richard used 'over there' to describe either his community group home or vocational service settings.) Just like Angela, almost all of the places he went to were difficult contexts in which to generate the kind of relationships with which he might repopulate his friendship field.

Stories we had heard before

Angela and Richard approached their stories from diametrically different life trajectories. As different as their lives were, however, the experiential geography of Angela and Richard's community, including the pool of people they could draw from as sites of participatory membership or belonging, looked remarkably similar.

In truth, though, theirs were stories we had heard before.

Just like Pamela's story ten years before, the participatory presence of the people we spoke to was characterised by their continued absence from the social contexts from which other (non-disabled) New Zealanders draw a sense of participatory citizenship. Of the twelve narratives that informed the Article 19 Project, no one belonged to a club or organisations that also included non-disabled members, and only one person had found employment, albeit very part-time and casual. Like Pamela before them, Angela, Richard and the other co-authors in the Article 19 Project tended to have a fleeting presence on the margins of daily community life. Theirs was a community largely defined and delineated by the horizons of traditional service practice, with life-spaces continuing to reflect their inability to draw people located in the social worlds of acknowledgement and encounter into more intimate (proximal) relationship. Beyond the sanctuary of the places they called 'home', Angela and Richard's lives continued to be lived out in a narrow range of public spaces, such as the supermarket, gym, swimming pool, boccia hall or tenpin bowling lane, the mall, public library and the Two Dollar Shop.

Angela and Richard's entrances and exits from these community spaces were almost always moderated by staff, whose presence was largely based on a service understanding of them as clients or service users. Staff also brought with them a belief that the arrow of inclusion only ever pointed away from people and places where Angela and Richard's stories resonated with self-authored social knowing, outwards towards the anomie and unpredictability of the cultural 'mainstream'. Few staff believed that non-disabled New Zealanders had any reciprocal obligation, or indeed might have something to gain, from making the return journey.

Beyond their relationships with staff and family, Angela and Richard struggled to populate their friendship field. Paradoxically, their migrations towards community tended to be steered towards places that offered them little prospect of seeding relationships likely to transcend mere acquaintance. But most importantly, Angela and Richard were largely absent from participatory contexts in which they were able to experience the (relational) markers of membership and inclusion that disabled peers identified as more appropriate metrics of inclusion.

What will be the drivers of inclusive social change?

For people with a learning disability, the major philosophical drivers of inclusive social policy have proved blunt as ideological instruments with which to dismantle the exclusionary organisation of 'mainstream' spaces. Normalisation and its reinvention as social role valorisation have had a significant influence in terms of shaping learning disability policy and practice. Both philosophies hold as axiomatic that the most effective way to remediate the personal costs that typically follow the social devaluing of more marginalised populations is to appropriate and then redefine what is culturally valued within the spaces and places of the dominant (non-disabled) cultural majority. Some authors attribute this lack of momentum to the assimilative assumptions underpinning these major philosophical constructs (Buell & Minnes 2006, Milner & Kelly 2009). They argue alongside Hall (2005, 2010) that support practices that seek to fit people into mainstream spaces leave largely untroubled the (non-disabled) socio-economic ordering of spaces that have always excluded people with a learning disability (Hall 2005, Hall 2010). Others point to the failure of the social model to adequately imagine bodies beyond a narrow disability trope, suggesting that whilst the social model has succeeded in prying the doors of inclusion ajar for a few, others like Angela and Richard have had to remain outside (Hall 2010, Rice, Chandler, Harrison, Liddiard & Ferrari 2015).

(Re)situating disablement has meant that we have tended to see the path towards a more inclusive society as being paved by non-disabled people transforming mainstream spaces into places that accommodate the diversity of embodied humanity. Richard and Angela's narrative, therefore, demonstrates the failure of those institutions to find any place for them.

This conceptualisation of disablement, however, also locates alternative imaginings of inclusion beyond the agency of people with a learning disability. Furthermore, understanding issues of (ex)inclusion as socio-political in origin runs the risk of ignoring the contribution everyday relational transactions make to shaping personal community. For example, the (atypical) geography of Angela and Richard's life-spaces owed as much to their experiences of the people and places of Oamaru through service activity as it did to more systemic forms of discrimination. And yet, the social practices of those who partner disabled people in the processes of providing or receiving support remain almost completely unexamined in academic literature.

More than a decade after the articulation of the transformative vision contained in the New Zealand Disability Strategy (2001), Angela and Richard continued to be present in their community in ways that made it difficult for them to draw places and people into more proximal relationship. Like Pamela, the intermediary social spaces between being stuck 'in there' and 'out there' remained uncolonised as a consequence of the unchanged way staff showed up to transact 'vocational support'.

Within these relationships, Angela and Richard experienced their community as programmed acts. Angela still described herself as being 'under CCS', locating herself by referencing the predictable timetabling of her 'community participation programme'. The support she received was almost always task-oriented and time constrained. 'How are we going for time?' was a constant refrain, with the press of purchased outcomes denying the time necessary for curiosity to flourish, or for moments of surprise to destabilise the dehumanising social constructions of 'service user' and 'staff member'. Few opportunities existed for those who provided or received support to follow the unanticipated lines of flight that can sometimes lead to self-discovery. But more troublingly, no time existed to talk about how people were experiencing their community, even in situations when being present was overtly oppressive. People habitually rode buses to nowhere, took van rides with people they wouldn't choose to be with, went to places where they could only ever be tourists, or were forced to weather the curious stares and 'social othering' that followed them during well-worn circumnavigations of the mall and other public spaces. Finally, Angela and Richard were only ever present in their community at times that were out of cadence with its social rhythms. It was difficult to get support on weekends or at night, which had the effect of transforming a range of outwardly inclusive settings into segregated social spaces. Richard bowled at his local bowling club, but only ever with disabled people and never on a Club Day.

Although our understandings of disability and disablement have altered with the shifting tides of paradigm change, the seemingly intractable social scripts of those most intimately engaged in the human exchanges of support have remained the same. In general terms, disability support staff have continued to 'show up' in much the same way as they always have, with professionally authored entrances, entrenched by systems of service delivery that make it difficult for staff to imagine disabled people in any other way than dissimilar.

Within the institutions of disability support, it has been professionals who have always determined the boundaries of (dis)similarity. For people with a learning disability, this has meant that they are culturally defined by their (professionally ascribed) functional limitations – an act that, Dan Goodley argues, both imagines and simultaneously limits their role to that of the 'other' (2007). Furthermore, by understanding people this way, services have unintentionally created and maintained social practices that further marginalise people with a learning disability within the very spaces in which men and women like Richard and Angela can spend much of their lives.

Whatever else may have been written about the social model of disability, one of its major accomplishments has been to cement an expectation that disabled people have the right to be present and active participants within the social spaces of a society. From here, it is a relatively small step to suggest that the degree to which disabled people experience a sense of belonging within community spaces will be contingent upon their ability to access the five qualitative attributes of relationship they asked us to adopt as more instructive metrics of inclusion (Milner & Kelly 2009).

What we struggle with, however, is the assumption that people with a learning disability may have an equivalent right to experience the same relational attributes of participatory citizenship within the relationships they draw on to realise their vision of inclusion. Few would say, for example, that 'service user' or 'client' were self-chosen or affirming social referents. Even fewer would suggest that people who provide and receive support are held in relationship by common and equitable systems of reciprocity. And no one would argue that being a service user was accompanied by an expectation that you contribute to the wellbeing of other people with whom you share a common (service) community.

One of the consequences of marginalising the voices of people with a learning disability in this way has been that services have also distanced themselves from stories that reimagine support in ways that liberate others from similarly disabling social scripts and moribund ways of 'showing up' to the support relationship.

Support staff –
the other lost voices of disability

The voices of those who partner disabled people in the complex and highly nuanced transactions of personal support have also been marginalised from the discourses of inclusion and service delivery.

Richard and Angela didn't readily discriminate between people with differently ascribed roles in their lives. Included in their respective circles of intimate relationships were:

- the community of family who listened, loved, respected and held aspirations for them;
- the community of disabled people who listened, loved, respected and held aspirations for each other; and
- staff who blurred the bright line of social distance by also daring to listen, love, respect and hold aspirations for the people with whom they shared their lives.

Angela and Richard both located a small number of staff at the very epicentre of their 'friendship fields'. The pre-eminence of staff within people's circle of more intimate relationships has always been negatively imagined as everything that is wrong with disabled lives. Except, that is, for people who regularly receive disability support. When Marquis and Jackson (2000) asked Australian service users how they experienced 'quality' service delivery, they said they were immediately directed to the relational context of their support. In the taxonomy of support experiences they developed together, it was staff who were described as providing support that had 'life sharing capacity' and thus sat atop their relational hierarchy. Like all other intimate relationships, disabled people described valuing support that included the humanising attributes of shared affection, respect and expectation. They called it 'sharing the inner circle', consistent with Furedi's (2004) observation that progress towards an inclusive society was contingent upon the 'colonisation of people's informal (social) lives'. The men and women Marquis and Jackson spoke to had worked hard to dissolve the bright line of (professionally authored) distance that separated them from the quintessential freedom to be and to belong with others.

Their narratives invite us to contemplate what alternative being and becomings might be possible should we dissolve the 'bright line of social distance' in ways that demand a renegotiation of the disabling social scripts of being either a provider or a receiver of disability support. Goodley (2007) invites us to contemplate a situation where no clear defining line exists between people who may be, at different moments, interchangeably either learner or educator, transformer or transformed, dependent or independent, disabled or able, friend or ally. A shift, he suggests, that takes us beyond the mere valuing of difference, to acknowledging and embedding a shared belief in the benefits that flow from recognising each other's humanity.

Progressing inclusion: 'Two people at a time.'

In the book she wrote with Marjorie Olney and Sue Lehr, Pat Fratangelo encouraged disability service providers to deconstruct residential facilities like the community group home Richard lived in, by moulding and reorganising support to fit the capacities and vulnerabilities of individuals 'one person at a time' (Fratangelo, Olney and Lehr 2001). The expression became a mantra that is still used today to guide service design and delivery. However, it is an axiom that continues to understand services and the allies of disabled people rather than disabled people themselves as agents of social change. After listening to the stories of Angela, Richard and all those who participated in the two projects we were involved in, it became clear that if we are to ever approximate the New Zealand Disability Strategy's vision of a more inclusive society, it will be transacted by disabled people who pull non-disabled New Zealanders across the bright line of social distance and into the inner circle of shared lives.

Embedded in this vision, however, is an obligation to revisit

'Baron's Paradox' by attending to the stories of all those we have failed to include in our library of legitimate and instructive narration. Fully acknowledging people's shared humanity can only occur when the power of the human story dissolves the defining line between people so that they might also interchangeably be story-teller or listener too. Whatever else inclusion might be, it is a process that can only happen 'two people at a time'.

References

Atkinson, D. & Walmsley, J. (1999) 'Using autobiographical approaches with people with learning difficulties', *Disability & Society*, 14(2): 203–216. http://doi.org/10.1080/09687599926271.

Baron, J. B. (1991) 'The many promises of storytelling in law', *Rutgers Law Journal*, 23: 79–105.

— (1999) 'Law, Literature, and the Problems of Interdisciplinarity', *The Yale Law Journal*, 108(5): 1059–1085. http://doi.org/10.2307/797370.

Beale, R., Beale, M. & Milner, P. (2014) *Full of Beans*. Wellington, New Zealand: CCS Disability Action. www.donaldbeasley.org.nz/assets/Uploads/publications/Richard-Beale-story-for-print-v1mp.pdf.

Buell, K. & Minnes, P. (2006) 'An acculturation perspective on deinstitutionalization and service delivery', *Journal on Developmental Disabilities*, OADD 20th Anniversary Issue, pp. 7–17.

Fratangelo, P., Olney, M. & Lehr, S. (2001) *One Person at a Time: How one agency changed from group to individualised services for people with disabilities*. Augustine, Florida: Training Resource Network Inc.

Furedi, F. (2004) *Where have all the Intellectuals Gone: Confronting 21st century philistinism*. London: Continuum.

Goodley, D. (2007) 'Towards socially just pedagogies: Deleuzoguattarian critical disability studies', *International Journal of Inclusive Education*, 11(3): 317–334. http://doi.org/10.1080/13603110701238769.

Hall, E. (2005) 'The entangled geographies of social exclusion/inclusion for people with learning disabilities', *Health & Place*, 11(2): 107–115. http://doi.org/10.1016/j.healthplace.2004.10.007.

— (2010) 'Spaces of social inclusion and belonging for people with intellectual disabilities', *Journal of Intellectual Disability Research*, 54: 48–57. http://doi.org/10.1111/j.1365-2788.2009.01237.x.

Marquis, R. & Jackson, R. (2000) 'Quality of life and quality of service relationships: Experiences of people with disabilities', *Disability & Society*, 15(3): 411–425. http://doi.org/10.1080/713661967.

Milner, P. & Bray, A. (2004) *Community Participation: People with disabilities finding their place. Report on the CCS Community Participation Project*. Wellington, New Zealand: CCS Disability Action.

Milner, P. & Kelly, B. (2009) 'Community participation and inclusion: People with disabilities defining their place', *Disability & Society*, 24(1): 47–62. http://doi.org/10.1080/09687590802535410.

Milner, P. & Mirfin-Veitch, B. (2012) *'I am here.' The Article 19 Project: Finding a place for the life stories of disabled people.* Wellington, New Zealand: CCS Disability Action.

Minister for Disability Issues (2001). *The New Zealand Disability Strategy: Making a World of Difference Whakanui Oranga.* Wellington, New Zealand: Ministry of Health.

Nussbaum, M. (1995) *Poetic Justice: The literary imagination of public life.* Boston, Mass.: Beacon Press.

Rice, C., Chandler, E., Harrison, E., Liddiard, K. & Ferrari, M. (2015) 'Project re-vision: Visibility at the edges of representation', *Disability & Society*, 30(4): 513–527. http://doi.org/10.1080/09687599.2015.1037950.

Tuan, Y.-F. (1977) *Space and Place: The perspective of experience.* London: Edward Arnold Publishers.

Affordances and Challenges of Virtual Communities for People with an Intellectual Disability

JUDITH MOLKA-DANIELSEN
& SUSAN BALANDIN

General implications of engagement in virtual communities

Virtual communities existed long before the current popular forms of online networks such as Facebook, Twitter and Instagram, and are supported in many forms of technology. For example, in the late nineteenth century some of the earliest virtual communities used Ham radio technology to communicate. Today, 'virtual communities' can be defined as 'online communities', whose members interact primarily without face-to-face contact, and commonly do so via the Internet. These person-to-person interactions can take place using a variety of modes of communication such as asynchronous text messages (for example, via email lists or discussion boards), synchronous text messages (chat rooms), voice and video (YouTube), photographs (Flickr, Instagram) via social networking sites (Facebook, Twitter), and recently through virtual games and virtual worlds (Second Life).

The technical limitations of using technology to support virtual communities for the general user varies across application platforms. Each technology enables community members to interact in different ways, for example writing short messages on Twitter or sharing photos on Flickr. Furthermore, some technologies are easier to use than others. This chapter considers some of the technical challenges that people with an intellectual disability may encounter when attempting to engage in virtual communities, and discusses the implications of these using case examples as illustrations.

Thinking beyond the 'technical' issues, we will identify some of the affordances and disadvantages to using virtual communities. One major advantage of virtual communities is that they have no geographic boundaries for participation, thus allowing users to communicate at a distance. Sawyerr and Pinkwart (2011) found that virtual communities reduced loneliness for a group of people with physical mobility limitations by increasing their social interactions. Other important affordances are that virtual communities may support learning through sharing of information (Molka-Danielsen & Brask 2011, 2014), offer a sense of presence, or 'being-there', with others of the community (Schultze & Leahy 2009, Schultze 2010), and offer opportunities for self-governance in that the users are self-empowered to interact with the community as they themselves decide (Stendal, Molka-Danielsen, Munkvold & Balandin 2011). These affordances can be shared by people with an intellectual disability and have the potential to increase social interaction, grow feelings of wellbeing and engender community inclusion for individuals who have been, and may still be, isolated, lonely and excluded (Balandin & Molka-Danielsen 2015).

Nevertheless, despite the positive affordances that virtual communities may offer, not all people with an intellectual disability are able to access the social media technology that supports virtual communities, for example in the case of virtual worlds. Furthermore, anyone who accesses a virtual community, regardless of abilities, needs to be aware of potential dangers. Some of the major dangers or disadvantages of participating in virtual communities are the potential for bullying, fraud or invasion of privacy. People with an intellectual disability may be at greater risk of experiencing these disadvantages unless specific efforts are made to ensure that, when faced with a difficult situation, they know what to do. This includes being aware of basic cyber-safety, such as not revealing bank account details or a home address.

Before we enter a detailed discussion on the challenges and affordances of virtual communities, it is useful to summarise the categories of main usage and special characteristics of some of the more popular forms of social media.

Virtual communities based on different types of social media

Virtual communities are based on, and expressed through, different types of social media technology platforms. Throughout this chapter we will use the term social media (SM) to refer to the use of technology and the description of technological characteristics. In this context, social media can be viewed as a container of the virtual community, and the virtual community as the substance. Space does not permit us to mention all types of social media, but the common examples listed in Table One are those forms that support social communication amongst members of virtual communities.

Table One

Commonly used forms of social media: A summary of usage and characteristics

Examples of social media	Main usage	Special characteristics
Facebook	Social connections: Individuals establish networks of 'friends' and communicate with them.	Text, image, audio, and video exchange supported. Global user community and popular across all ages.
Twitter	Short text-based exchanges between individuals and 'followers': Often used for individual-to-group communication, and a common source of information sharing.	Short text and images can be exchanged. Can establish 'hashtag' communities and Twitter networks (groups) of followers. Growing global adoption rates.
Flickr	Public or private posting of images and the creation of interest groups who can view those images.	Sharing, commenting on and browsing groups of photos.

Pinterest	Akin to an online scrapbook or pinboard: Browse categories of photos, tag ('pin') images, and follow individuals who collect categories of tagged images.	Possible to send messages to individuals, simple to use interface to 'pin', 'like' and 'see' followers and follow others.
Second Life	Multi-user, 3D, virtual space for social interaction: Personalised avatars represent users. Users can also exchange virtual objects, for example, clothing, cars, and buildings. Second Life belongs to the Massively Multiplayer Online Games (MMOG) category.	Accessed through a specialised desktop browser. Allows exchange of voice and text chat in real time. Individuals can add 'friends' and join 'groups'. They can chat with all members of a group simultaneously, regardless of their virtual proximity to each other. Asynchronous text-chat can be received.
Other Massively Multiplayer Online Games (MMOG) (for example, Clash of Clans, Boom Beach)	MMOG have specific game objectives and often support text chat and allow for communication with members of a player's own group (for example, their clan or task force).	Such games can have limited and simple objectives. Many support easy-to-use interfaces, allowing interactions through touchscreen devices such as tablets or smart phones.

As is evident in Table One, the characteristics of social media differ and therefore each medium presents different technical challenges. Thus social media are not 'one size fits all', rather it is important to be aware of the challenges and individual differences in order to match the person's ability to a platform and maximise successful media use.

Technical challenges

The technical challenges of using virtual communities differ depending on the technology interface between the intended user and the SM technology platform that supports the person-to-person community. The challenges of using social media may be distinguished by the available functionality of its interface that is often based on presumptions of the target user's abilities.

In Table Two, we present a list of common disabilities along with the interface challenges for social media in relation to individuals with that impairment, and the implications that follow for adopting of the SM technology platform. In doing this we acknowledge that there are some people who are unlikely to be able to use SM independently because of cognitive, sensory, and/or motor impairments.

Table Two

Interface challenges of social media by disability type

Disability	Interface Challenges of the Social Media (SM) for individuals with impairment of ability		Implications for SM adoption
	Text-based SM	**Image-based SM**	
Vision (sensory)	Standard interface (browser) must provide large text or alternative screen readers for use with Facebook, for example.	Standard interface (browser) and screen readers will not enhance value of SM that focuses on sharing images (such as Flickr). Alternative browsers are available for virtual worlds such as Second Life.	SM that have the main objective of sharing visual content such as objects and images, as on Snapchat or Flickr, may not be adopted. Screen readers may not work with many applications.
Hearing (sensory)	Standard browser works well with most popular social media (e.g. Twitter).	Users in the virtual world (e.g. Second Life) cannot depend on other users to use text based communication rather than chat (so text to voice conversion tools will not cover all in-world communication exchanges.)	Users may avoid use of virtual world for social interaction, as other SM may provide better control over the communication mode used in exchanges with other users.

Complex Communication Needs	Standard browser is adequate for social media that focus on exchange of text such as Twitter.	Standard interfaces are adequate for SM that focuses on exchange of images and where text chat is also supported such as Twitter, Flickr and Second Life.	SM provides opportunities for this group, but impaired language skills or poor literacy skills may be major barriers.
Motor	Access to tools, for interaction with SM applications may be problematic. Rate barriers could mean that it takes too long to type text for real-time conversation. Programmed shortcuts for specific applications such as Facebook may not be available.	Access to mouse or keyboards for moving user-avatars in virtual worlds may be too difficult. Special tools and hooks to virtual world browsers may not be developed for each medium.	Access barriers, including difficulty using small buttons, links or tabs. Alternative eye-gaze controls may not be developed for an application.
Limited Language and/ or Literacy skills	Limited language and/or literacy skills may prevent individuals from understanding how to use the interface or use text to communicate.	Image-based SM may provide greater incentive for use of visual object sharing; but the browser interface may prevent independent use of the format (for example Flickr, Second Life).	Picture-based instant messaging applications (such as SymbolChat) and other symbolic tools for self-expression are needed for those with limited literacy.
Limited computer skills	Text in SM often presents abstract concepts such as menus, files, and links that are difficult for a person with an intellectual disability to relate to concrete meanings and actions.	Multiple-step interfaces that require memory of logical steps and cognitive understanding of metaphors, such as a virtual classroom, may prevent use of virtual worlds as social meeting spaces.	Alternative touchscreen interfaces for intellectual disabilities may make it easier for individuals to see the connection between action and reaction

Besides technical barriers to use of SM, there are other significant barriers to use of virtual communities that have impact on disadvantaged people, in particular people with an intellectual disability. These include financial and economic barriers, negative societal attitudes, lack of access, lack of government policy for support, lack of educational or training support, and gatekeeping by services, support workers and families (Molka-Danielsen & Balandin 2009).

Economic barriers mean that many people with an intellectual disability cannot afford to purchase technology or internet connection. Regarding societal attitudes, families and support workers may not consider a range of technology, thus preventing access to it because they may make judgements about its suitability for the person with a disability. They may also have a negative view of a person with a disability's 'ability to learn' or the individual's wish to try new technology. An additional problem is that despite widespread use of social media, particularly among young people, family members and support workers may not be familiar with the SM technology that gives access to the virtual community and therefore will avoid using it with the family member/client who has a disability. The need for education and training in this subject is recognised (Chadwick et al. 2013), yet caregivers from family or support services have quoted lack of time to undertake training along with lack of expertise in support of ICT as reasons why they cannot undertake coaching on this issue.

Access issues are not always easy to solve. People who have limited access to specialised services, including those living in rural and remote areas, may not be able to try a range of options that might improve that level of access, such as wheelchair mounts for equipment, switches, and touch screens. If there are limited or no services and funding, then it is difficult for people to successfully access technology. Hence there is a difference between how people with a disability in the Scandinavian countries access technology, where the policies support equal access across the community, compared to those living in many other countries where individuals must purchase all services and technology themselves.

Gatekeeping arises where there is a common fear that adults with a disability are vulnerable to cyberbullying (Kowalski & Fedina 2011, Marzano, Lubkina & Rezekne 2013), and are at risk of predatory behaviour and sexual exploitation when using social media (Balandin & Molka-Danielsen 2015). Consequently it is important that people with an intellectual disability are given not only the choice to use SM but also the same practice as any other person in learning how to use these media.

It can be argued that being digitally connected is important to educational and economic wellbeing. For all the promises that the Internet holds, there is evidence that a 'digital divide' exists, that a greater percentage of people with an intellectual disability do not have access to the Internet in comparison to the non-disabled population; in the US in 2011, only 54 per cent of people with a disability had the Internet, compared to 81 per cent of people without a disability (Fox 2011). Regarding societal attitudes, Chadwick et al. (2013) point out that the needs of people with an intellectual disability have rarely been included in decisions of systems design. This argument may be extended to the design of human-to-computer (ICT) interfaces for virtual communities. Universal design principles may also be ignored in the design of private software platforms that form the basis of many virtual communities.

Thus, there is a need to ensure that people with an intellectual disability have access not only to education and training support around social media, but also that they have other people in their support networks who have the technical skills and expertise to use the technology to facilitate the inclusion of the person with a disability in social media of their choice. We would argue that competence in using SM technology in support of virtual communities should be a perquisite skill for support staff working with people with a disability, including those with an intellectual disability.

Affordances of virtual communities for people with a disability

Currently, the potential social benefits of virtual communities for people with a disability, in particular virtual communities such as those in virtual worlds like Second Life, are thought to be that they support inclusion, increase social networks, engender feelings of being part of a group, reduce loneliness, and offer the ability to share virtual objects with geographic and mobility independence. Furthermore the use of virtual communities provides meaningful activity that is accessible from home and is free. Nevertheless, to date there is limited research to support these claims of benefit. Most studies refer to the use, and impact of use, in the context of specific case examples of social media. Further longitudinal and cross-technology platform studies are needed.

Reducing loneliness

Two studies have indicated that virtual communities may have the potential to reduce feelings of loneliness for people with an intellectual disability (Kydland et al. 2012, Guo et al. 2005) but Cooper, Balandin and Trembath (2009) noted that a lack of quick responses to email, for example, can exacerbate feelings of loneliness and a sense of being devalued. There is also some suggestion that, as social media use by people with a disability is often strictly monitored and restricted to interaction with family members, it is unlikely to increase feelings of connectedness and wellbeing. Nevertheless, both Guo et al. (2005) and Stendal and Balandin (2015) suggested that people with a disability who are able to access the Internet experience improved quality and frequency of social interactions. Yet, as we have noted, gaining access to Internet is not always easy due to economic, access or knowledge barriers, and, in particular, fears about safety.

Greater autonomy and self-governance

Chadwick et al. (2013) gave a comprehensive overview of the factors that can impair and facilitate access to the Internet and social media for people with an intellectual disability. They described the constant societal tensions between offering protection and the individual's right to self-determination. Factors used to advocate social media access are the great potential of the Internet for self-expression, advocacy and for creating friendships. The researchers pointed out that online access gives people with an intellectual disability the opportunity to counter the oppression that they face frequently in their lives, such as labelling, stigma, discrimination and restriction on human rights. Further, the label of intellectual disability is often so strong that it overrides personal identities including both gender and sexuality.

At the same time, Löfgren-Mårtenson's (2008) study of young people in Sweden with an intellectual disability found that social media provides opportunities for a private life away from caregivers, and the freedom to communicate for both social and romantic purposes. The study pointed out that the perceived vulnerability of people with an intellectual disability has led to the creation of 'safer social networking websites'. However, reporting on the experiences of the study group, the author noted that people with an intellectual disability did not necessarily want to use the 'safe' websites restricted to those with an intellectual disability but preferred access to sites with a wider audience. Despite positive studies, some researchers have observed challenges for people with an intellectual disability in maintaining online relationships. Burke, Kraut and William (2010), in a study of sixteen high-functioning adults with autism, reported that participants in online communities reported difficulties around issues of trust, disclosure and maintaining perspective. Many have noted, however, that the group of people with an intellectual disability is very heterogeneous and will use social media to present and experience different challenges and opportunities.

A further study by Stendal and Balandin (2015) described a case study of a person with autism spectrum disorder. The authors pointed out that 'virtual worlds' may offer greater empowerment than the physical world. For example, a participant in this study noted that it was easy to leave threatening or unsafe situations by teleporting to another virtual location or turning off the computer, whereas in real life this is not possible, so real interactions can be more challenging. An added affordance noted by the participant was the ability to personalise the avatar to reveal whatever the player wished to divulge or emphasise about themselves, or the player could choose to remain anonymous behind the avatar†. Social media, such as virtual worlds or Twitter, allow a person with a disability to interact on a 'level playing field' without having to disclose that disability. Currently there is little, if any, research on the impact of social media on feelings of equality in social interactions, although anecdotally we know that some people with a physical disability, for example, will choose to use a wheelchair in virtual worlds if they use one in the real world. Thus there is scope for research on social media and feelings of identity in people with a disability.

Greater self-efficacy

Social media has the potential to provide new opportunities for people with a disability to obtain and share skills. Besides gaining access to a wider variety of online education, SM offers the opportunity to come into contact with communities of similar interest. One example is that of a social community within a virtual world; such as Virtual Ability Island in Second Life. Virtual Ability Inc. (VAI since 2008) was founded by A. Kruger (http://www.virtualability.org/) and is a not-for-profit corporation, whose mission is to support people with any disability (physical, intellectual, emotional, developmental, and sensory) as they come into, and learn to use, virtual worlds. VAI has almost 800 members, 75 per cent of whom have one or more disabilities. The remainder are parents, spouses, children, friends, caregivers, medical professionals, professors, researchers and anyone interested in disability issues. The term Virtual Ability

† Avatar: an icon or figure representing a particular person in a computer game or internet forum.

had been chosen as it focuses on people's ability, what they *can* do, and often its members contribute as lecturers and trainers for newcomers to the virtual world.

The case of Twitter

For people with adequate literacy skills, Twitter offers a range of opportunities for inclusion and access to information (Hemsley, Palmer & Balandin 2014, Hemsley, Dann, Palmer, Alan & Balandin 2015). The use of short 'Tweets' of no more than 140 characters are not so demanding for those who experience difficulty with typing. Additionally, because Tweeting is quick and immediate, it is a medium where poor grammar and spelling are well tolerated. Twitter users may choose to be active 'Tweeters' by participating in a range of forums or tweeting to friends. Alternatively they may choose to be followers and gain information on a range of areas that interest them with no obligation to contribute. Currently there is limited information on how people with a disability use Twitter, but this is an area of growing interest, particularly as people without a disability have noted that Twitter is a major medium for keeping in touch and sharing information. For a group of people who are information-poor, (see Balandin & Morgan 2001) the full potential of Twitter for people with a disability has yet to be realised.

Potential and real dangers of being part of a virtual community

In this section we discuss the often-cited potential dangers of being part of a virtual community through SM and point to studies that give evidence of the real dangers.

Feeling left out

Feeling left out of a community may not be deemed as serious as other dangers described later, but it can be significant for an individual's self-image. It may also be the factor that prevents access to the virtual community and to all the benefits of belonging to that community. Feeling left out may occur for a broad variety of reasons such as the individual not being able to overcome access issues regarding literacy, technology interface and caregiver restrictions, or not being allowed to access available media.

Cyber bullying

Didden et al. (2009), and Holmes and O'Loughlin (2014) described cyber bullying in online communities as a concern for people with an intellectual disability. In some online communities, such as virtual worlds in Second Life, there may be less evidence of cyber bullying. That may be due to the factor of anonymity. However, anonymity can in fact either discourage or encourage cyber bullying. To discourage cyber-bullying, the person with an intellectual disability must retain control over information that is visible on their public profile. They must know how to leave an unpleasant situation ('teleport' or turn off the computer) and understand that the anonymity of a virtual world ensures that they cannot be traced by an offender. On the other hand, anonymity can encourage cyber-bullying. Behind the mask of anonymity, some individuals may feel they are less accountable for their own behaviour. Or, bullying may occur unintentionally because the victim's identity is also anonymous and the offender may not know when their own behaviour is perceived as bullying.

Fraud and privacy

Personal information being shared unintentionally can happen anywhere and there are various sources of risk. For example, spam can arrive through email, leading a user to use invalid links and encouraging them to accept false offers. Phishing – when someone tries to compromise a password in order to gain access to personal email or other accounts – also occurs, as well as identity spoofing, which is when someone impersonates another user. People with an intellectual disability, in common with the general community, need to be aware of these dangers and know what to avoid. Security measures for basic computer hardware such as disabling scripts, using certificates, and installing most recent versions of software, are a digital necessity for any user. However, people with an intellectual disability may require additional support to understand basic safe use of technology and make sure that systems have the latest updates.

Managing the risks of using social media may be addressed with other measures in addition to controlling the hardware. For example, accounts for social usage may be set up that are separate from and different from accounts that contain payment information. This would allow the user to have freedom to use a virtual community without the worry of making a financial mistake, such as in-app purchases. Preventive measures will not always stop a person with an intellectual disability from falling victim to fraud or other identity crimes. This is a complex problem that presents risks to every sector of society. In response, some government bodies are working on legislation to protect people with a disability. For example, in North Carolina a new law has created a legal classification of the 'protected consumer' that is intended to protect the credit report of children and people with a disability from identity theft (Meyer 2015, NCGA 2015). Other states have implemented consumer protection laws against scammers who target older people and people with an intellectual disability (Fox 2013). We would emphasise the point that issues of fraud are societal challenges that we all face, and that need to be addressed so that all people, regardless of ability, have the right to use ICT services and not be excluded from such use because of their abilities or needs.

Character abuse

Other abuse such as sexual, verbal or emotional abuse can occur in virtual communities. Furthermore, poor understanding of both virtual communities and people with a disability can lead to an acceptance of myths or false ideas. For example, a caregiver in one of our studies refused to allow a person with a mild intellectual disability to join an ethically approved study in Second Life because they said the individual wouldn't know the difference between reality and the virtual world (Balandin & Molka-Danielsen 2015).

Concluding remarks

This chapter has highlighted the affordances and challenges of virtual communities in the lives of people with a disability. We have suggested that there is a need for ongoing research regarding the barriers to use of virtual communities. The barriers that present the greatest challenges are societal attitudes and the recognition that a diverse range of new technologies require training programmes and special support for people with intellectual disabilities. Longitudinal studies are needed to learn more about the potential benefits of inclusion and involvement of people with a disability in the virtual communities of their choice.

References

Balandin, S. & Molka-Danielsen, J. (2015) 'Teachers' perceptions of virtual worlds as a medium for social inclusion for adults with intellectual disability', *Disability and Rehabilitation*, 37(17): 1543–1550.

Balandin, S. & Morgan, J. (2001) 'Preparing for the future: Aging and AAC', *Augmentative and Alternative Communication*, 17: 99–108.

Burke, M., Kraut, R. & Williams, D. (2010) 'Social Use of Computer-Mediated Communication by Adults on the Autism Spectrum'. In: *Proceedings of the 2010 ACM Conference on Computer Supported Cooperative Work*. Baltimore, MD, USA, 15–19 February 2010, pp. 425–434.

Chadwick, D. Wesson, C. & Fullwood C. (2013) 'Internet access by people with intellectual disabilities: Inequalities and opportunities', *Future Internet*, 5: 376–397.

Cooper, L., Balandin, S. & Trembath, D. (2009) 'The loneliness experiences of young adults with cerebral palsy who use alternative and augmentative communication', *Augmentative and Alternative Communication*, 25(3): 154–164.

Didden, R., Scholte, R. & Korzilius, H. (2009) 'Cyberbullying among students with intellectual and developmental disability in special education settings', *Developmental Neurorehabilitation*, 12: 146–151.

Fox, S. (2011) 'Americans living with a disability and their technology profile', *PewInternet*. Washington, DC, USA http://pewinternet.org/~/media//Files/Reports/2011/PIP_Disability.pdf. Accessed 21 Dec. 2015.

Fox, T. (2013) 'New law establishes tougher penalties for scammers targeting Montana's most vulnerable consumers', *Montana Department of Justice*. https://dojmt.gov/new-law-establishes-tougher-penalties-for-scammers-targeting-montanas-most-vulnerable-consumers/. Accessed 21 Dec. 2015.

Guo, B., Bricout, J. & Huang, J. (2005) 'A common open space or a digital divide? A social model perspective on the online disability community in China', *Disability and Society*, 20: 49–66.

Hemsley, B., Dann, S., Palmer, S., Allan, M. & Balandin, S. (2015) '"We definitely need an audience": Experiences of Twitter, Twitter networks and tweet content in adults with severe communication disabilities who use augmentative and alternative communication (AAC)', *Disability & Rehabilitation*, 37(17): 1531–1542.

Hemsley, B., Palmer, S. & Balandin, S. (2014) 'Tweet reach: A research protocol for using Twitter to increase information exchange in people with communication disabilities', *Developmental Neurorehabilitation*, 17(2): 84–89.

Holmes, K. & O'Loughlin, N. (2014) 'The experiences of people with learning disabilities on social networking sites', *British Journal of Learning Disabilities*, 42: 1–5.

Kowalski, R. & Fedina, C. (2011) 'Cyber bullying in ADHD and Asperger Syndrome populations', *Research in Autism Spectrum Disorders*, 5(3): 1201–1208.

Kydland, F., Molka-Danielsen, J. & Balandin, S. (2012) 'Examining the use of the social media tool 'Flickr' for impact on loneliness for people with intellectual disability', *NOKOBIT 2012: Proceedings of the 2012 Norsk konferanse for organisasjoners bruk av informasjonsteknologi.* Trondheim, Norway: Akademika Forlag. http://dro.deakin.edu.au/view/DU:30062177. Accessed 5 Nov. 2015.

Löfgren-Mårtenson, L. (2008) 'Love in cyberspace: Swedish young people with intellectual disabilities and the internet', *Scandinavian Journal of Disability Research*, 10: 125–138.

Marzano, G., Lubkina, V. & Rezekne, I. (2013) 'Cyber bullying and real reality', *Society, Integration, Education*, l(1): 412–422.

Meyer, G. (2015) 'New Law Protects People with Disabilities and Children From Identity Fraud', *The Arc.* http://www.arcnc.org/news/2015-08-19/new-law-protects-people-disabilities-children-identity-fraud. Accessed 21 Dec. 2015.

Molka-Danielsen, J. & Balandin, S. (2009) 'Recognition and eDemocracy for members of the community with lifelong disability'. In: E. Tambouris & A. Macintosh A. (eds.), 'Electronic Participation: Proceedings of ongoing research, general development issues and projects of ePart', *First International Conference, ePart 2009.* Linz: Trauner Verlag, 59–66.

Molka-Danielsen, J. & Brask, O. (2011) 'Design of a social communicative framework for collaborative writing using blended ICT', *I: Proceeding from Norsk Konferanse for Organisasjoners Bruk av Informasjonsteknologi.* Trondheim, Norway: Tapir Akademisk Forlag, pp. 91–104.

— (2014) 'Designing virtual collaboration environment for distance learners: Exploring socialization as a basis for collaboration'. In: T. H. Commisso, J. Norbjerg & J. Pries-Heje (eds.), *Nordic Contributions in IS Research: 5th Scandinavian Conference on Information Systems*, SCIS, Springer, pp. 74–89

NCGA (2015). 'Allow Protected Consumer Security Freezes'. House Bill 607/ S.L.193. North Carolina General Assembly. http://www.ncleg.net/gascripts/ BillLookUp/BillLookUp.pl?Session=2015&BillID=h607&submitButton=Go. Accessed 21 Dec. 2015.

Sawyerr, W. & Pinkwart, N. (2011) 'Extending the Private and Domestic Spaces of the Elderly'. *The 2011 ACM Conference on Computer Supported Cooperative Work*, March 19–23, Hangzhou, China.

Schultze, U. (2010) 'Embodiment and presence in virtual worlds: A review', *Journal of Information Technology*, 25: 434–449.

Schultze, U. & Leahy, M. (2009) 'The Avatar-Self Relationship: Enacting presence in Second Life'. *International Conference on Information Systems Proceedings*. Paper 12.

Stendal, K. & Balandin, S. (2015) 'Virtual worlds for people with autism spectrum disorder: A case study in second life', *Disability and Rehabilitation*, early online 1–8.

Stendal, K., Molka-Danielsen, J., Munkvold, B. & Balandin, S. (2011) 'Initial experience with virtual worlds for people with lifelong disability: Preliminary findings'. *I: Proceeding from Norsk konferanse for organisasjoners bruk av informasjonsteknologi*. Trondheim: Tapir Akademisk Forlag, pp.105–118.

Social Exclusion of People with an Intellectual Disability: A Psychotherapist's Perspective

ALAN CORBETT

'Disability Therapy' is a relatively new term to describe a range of approaches used in the individual and group therapeutic treatment of people with disabilities. This chapter considers the ways in which the social exclusion of people with intellectual disabilities is determined by two layers of psychological functioning – the individual unconscious and the social unconscious. Here I will examine the role of the psychosocial perspective* in Disability Therapy using evidence from the psychoanalytic treatment of a woman with intellectual disabilities. Through this I examine how Disability Therapy needs to differ from therapy for people without disabilities in order to address the psychosocial needs of this particular client group. I also discuss the curious mirroring of experiences of exclusion between the disabled subject and the non-disabled professional, and the ways in which Disability Therapy has had to struggle to position itself within the confines of mainstream psychotherapy, just as people with disabilities struggle to move in from the margins of society.

'Othering' is the process by which one group is seen as 'us' and another as 'them', and has tended in the discourse of disability to ascribe power to 'us' and powerlessness to 'them'. In Kleinian terms it can be understood as a form of 'projective identification' (Klein 1946), whereby those aspects of the self that cause us pain and discomfort are located in others. When we then feel hate towards the 'other', that feeling is partly fuelled by hatred of aspects of our ownselves.

People with intellectual disabilities have been 'othered' in different ways across the course of history, and continue to

* An individual's psychological development in, and interaction with, a social environment.

perform an important societal role. By placing them on the margins of society, we unconsciously hope that we are safely distanced from our own cognitive deficits and failures in thinking. Our need to disavow our own pockets of disability is rooted in unconscious processes that tend to impede our capacity to both understand our own internal failings and acknowledge that the structures of the disabled and non-disabled self are ways of relieving us from the burden of non-thinking. When it comes to intelligence, the means by which we calculate our value to society and to each other, we are all on a spectrum between brilliance and stupidity. My use of the word 'stupidity' here draws attention to Sinason's (1992) research into the aetiology of the term 'learning disability', and how she traced its origins back to stupidity – meaning 'numb with grief', thus revealing a condition that all are vulnerable to, regardless of levels of intelligence.

Dagnan (2007) divides psychosocial interventions into four ecological levels.

1. Interventions with the individual, such as psychotherapy.
2. Interventions in the immediate social context of the person, such as the person's family or paid carers.
3. Interventions aimed at the wider social context of the person, including a focus on housing, leisure or employment.
4. Broader national interventions, such as, in the UK, the National Service Framework for mental health.

Dagnan and Waring (2004) highlight the impact of negative construction and reduced opportunity on the psychological structures used within individual therapies. They also consider the clinical implications of such models, and argue for:

the therapist stepping out of the therapeutic environment into the broader psychosocial world of the client, using the psychosocial formulation to collaboratively guide the broader intervention and bringing the psychosocial world of the client into the therapeutic setting through the careful and collaborative involvement of carers and family in the therapeutic process. (Dagnan 2007)

Individual psychotherapy cannot be conducted in a vacuum that sets the individual apart from their life outside. It needs to be interwoven within the immediate and wider social context of the person, and it places upon the therapist a responsibility to attune to the intrapsychic world[†] of their patient and the social environment in which the patient exists.

Powerful social forces drive the extent to which we exclude people with intellectual disabilities, both specifically within therapeutic services and generally within society. More value was accorded to this population in the pre-enlightenment age (Gilbert 2006), and high levels of support and care were provided throughout Europe, often by religious institutions. But the Industrial Revolution shifted the means by which society allocated value, with worth being ascribed to the ability to make money. People with disabilities, with their reduced ability to produce and contribute financially, began to be viewed as a burden on an increasingly individualistic and utilitarian society (Gilbert 2006).

Socio-economic disadvantage accounts for high rates of mortality and morbidity (Emerson and Hatton 2008), and children with intellectual disabilities, whose development is already compromised, are at increased risk of exposure to social conditions that are themselves inimical to healthy development (Emerson 2008). This creates a paradigm in which social exclusion and diminished brain function become mutually sustaining phenomena. An intellectual disability evokes a specific form of stigma, individually and societally, and engenders a dynamic that transcends race, beliefs and culture (Shah 1992). Thus intellectual disability is both a professionally ascribed diagnostic category and a social identity (Rapley 2004).

The British social model of disability tends to focus on the obstacles that prevent people with disabilities accessing and using the tools of modern life. Shakespeare and Watson (2001) highlight the inadequacy of this view, tending as it does to

†Internal psychological processes of the individual.

diminish or disregard the reality and impact of a disability in a person's life. We cannot ascribe all the problems of disability to society. If we do, we are in danger of disregarding the psychological and physiological impact of the disability itself. I have argued (Corbett 2011) that an exclusively social model of disability relieves us of the pain of acknowledging that disability is a wide spectrum in which we are all represented. We are all disabled in some way, the question is one of degree. The social exclusion of people with intellectual disabilities stems from a deeply unconscious urge to rid ourselves of anything that disturbs our view of our own selves as perfect, non-disabled beings. One of the reasons people with disabilities are so deeply troubling to us is that they remind us of our own vulnerability to and fear of disablement.

In exploring what takes place within the consulting room between non-disabled therapist and disabled patient, and, in turn, how this relates to the social structures that contain them both, I wish to illuminate the need for such therapeutic work to take place within a psychosocial context. Psychotherapy with people with intellectual disabilities is, in many respects, identical to psychotherapy with people without disabilities. It is a relational enterprise, a dyadic process[‡] in which issues such as identity formation, anxiety, depression, or cumulative trauma, are addressed through psychological processing. There are, however, significant differences from 'mainstream' psychotherapy in this process. The pace of work is slower, particularly when expressive or receptive communication skills are impaired. The psychotherapist has to pay particular attention to the patient's use of language, mindful that their tendency to comply can lead to the expression of understanding when little exists. Work with people with intellectual disabilities is largely dependent on the connection between the patient's internal and external worlds, and the extent to which the therapist is able to protect the boundary of their dyadic work with their patient, while at the same time maintaining a mutually informative relationship with the patient's support network.

‡ Dyadic describes the interaction between a pair of individuals.

Here, it is pertinent to introduce an anonymous vignette of a patient I have treated in psychotherapy. 'Olive' lives in a group home in London. She is thirty-eight years old, has no siblings, and was referred to the clinic in which I work because she had been raped the previous year. She has not received any form of justice for the crime committed against her, and because of her disability, she was judged to be unsuitable for interview by the police. The rape tended to be described using the less grave terms of 'sexual abuse', partly because the perpetrator also had an intellectual disability. Olive herself has a mild to moderate intellectual disability, fairly good verbal communication skills, and was able to give informed consent to the therapy.

The fact that even the most serious of sexual crimes against people with disabilities may be referred to as 'sexual abuse' reveals a deeply embedded 'othering', which is part of a societal response to disability that serves to diminish the impact of trauma. There is an underlying assumption that people with disabilities matter less than us, and the abuses perpetrated against them cannot be considered as crimes. This diminishing of the importance of crimes against people with disabilities increases their vulnerability – abusers target the disabled partly because they know their actions are less likely to be investigated and prosecuted than crimes against the non-disabled. People with disabilities are four times more likely to experience sexual crime than people without disabilities (Sobsey 1994), and yet these crimes are less likely to be taken seriously by the criminal justice system than crimes committed against victims without disabilities (Niehaus et al. 2013).

The session with Olive I will describe followed a lengthy process of her acclimatising to the therapeutic space. Much of the preceding six months she had been preoccupied with an ever-present anxiety about safety. Olive seemed, on the surface, to want to take part in the sessions, and stated that she did not have a problem with my being a man (in fact, she had stated her preference for a male rather than a female therapist). Olive was someone who exhibited many traits of 'outer directedness' (Bybee & Zigler 1999), which is a phrase to describe people with intellectual disabilities being overly compliant towards those they perceive as having more power than them, namely, people without disabilities. This is a vivid enactment of the power imbalance inherent in the lives of people with disabilities where they themselves personify powerlessness and their therapist personifies power. It is tremendously easy, then, for a psychotherapist to be convinced that their patient wants to be in the consulting room, understands all that is being said and has the capacity to comprehend the minutiae of what unfolds in the therapeutic process.

In the presence of Olive, I was painfully aware of how fragile she appeared and how paper thin her psychic skin (Bick 1968) was. She required much coaxing to stay in the sessions, often appearing to be overwhelmed by a transferential fear that something dangerous and hurtful would happen if she remained in the room with me. I interpreted this fear fairly early on both as a free-floating anxiety and as a symptom of her traumatic history.

To begin the session, Olive entered the consulting room, accompanied by her support worker. The worker stayed for a minute or so, and settled Olive into her chair, before leaving the room. It was a warm day, but Olive was dressed, as ever, in a thick winter coat, tightly buttoned up as if she needed to insulate herself against the harshness of the world. There was a lengthy silence before she started to speak, and I found myself thinking back to the previous week's appointment. Olive had used much of this session to describe the nightmares she'd been having. These dreams had troubled her for many years preceding the rape, and tended to feature mysterious male figures attempting to kidnap her. I tried to help her to think about the symbolic meaning of the men in her dreams – wondering what sense she made of them, and the feelings of panic and anxiety they evoked. Olive rejected these attempts to think about her dreams in anything other than concrete, black and white terms. 'It's something I must have seen on telly,' she stated, a rare note of certainty colouring her voice. 'Happens when I eat cheese as well. That's why I dream. Don't like the dreams.'

When she broke the opening silence of this next session, Olive told me what a terrible week she'd had. The bus to her day centre broke down at least three times. Her best friend at the centre was off sick and she had no-one to talk to. She lost her purse when out shopping with her key worker. Her voice was heavy with sadness, and I noticed how difficult it was for her to differentiate between misfortunes. Everything was an equally weighted trauma. I reflected back to her how sad all these events had been, and wondered what feelings they had left her with. 'Bad feelings,' she replied, not allowing for any thought or reflection, the words coming out of her mouth before I'd finished my question. We spent some time trying to decode these 'bad feelings', but Olive lost interest, wanting to tell me instead about how angry the bus driver had become each time his vehicle broke down. I realised we were in extremely concrete territory that day, with my attempts to think symbolically (What part of Olive feels broken down? What part of her anger might the driver be articulating?) stunted by her need to skate along the surface of her narratives. She eventually acknowledged that it was not just the bus driver who felt anger – she did too; so much so that she broke a number of plates in her kitchen and, as a result, had not been allowed to attend her regular Thursday night disco. I reflected that it sounded as if the plate smashing happened on the day we last saw each other – perhaps, I wondered aloud, her rage was connected to the nightmares we had been exploring in our last session, and the feelings of fear and anxiety they evoked. Olive started to cry, and said she was afraid of going home after that day's session. 'What if they tell me off when I get angry?' she cried. 'My head's full of bad feelings – keep remembering the bad men, and the bad man.'

This was Olive's first allusion to 'the bad man' rather than just 'the bad men', and I recognised that we were entering a new phase of her work in which the reality of her rape would be more explicitly explored. This is a necessary and ultimately positive part of the therapeutic process, yet I felt concern about the punitive response from Olive's support team to her rage. What, I found myself wondering, would it be like when she began to share the narrative of her abuse with me, connecting on an unconscious, and eventually a conscious, level with her feelings of violation, hurt and injury? Previously she had managed to fend off such overwhelming feelings through the use of concretised, impenetrable defences. What would happen to her and to her team when these defences began to be dismantled? In thinking about the broken plates, I wondered whether there was a risk that her team were struggling to manage emotions that would require careful holding and containment, rather than the enactment of something more punitive.

Psychotherapy with patients with intellectual disabilities is, I suggest, dependent on an understanding of their external world, as much as of their internal world. As such, I had to make some adaptations to the frame of the therapy at this stage, changing it from a primarily dyadic intervention to one that could accommodate the participation and involvement of others, such as those people involved in Olive's home care. I arranged a review meeting with her support team in order to:

1. review her level of consent for treatment;
2. ensure her team were responding sensitively and effectively to any post-session behavioural and/or psychological changes;
3. equip the team with an understanding of the role and function of her psychotherapy.

The second aim of the meeting is a vital component of psychosocially-informed treatment. A patient without an intellectual disability seeing a psychotherapist would not expect their therapist to brief their parent, partner, sibling or friend about how to deal with them before and after their sessions. The need for an equivalent process for the briefing of a support team to occur within Disability Therapy reflects:

• the extreme levels of dependence many people with intellectual disabilities have on their carers;
• the risk of behavioural and psychological changes being misinterpreted.

Many patients of Disability Therapists rely on a third party to pay for their therapy, to ensure that transport to and from sessions is provided and to assist in communicating with the therapist about holidays and cancellations. This places immense power in the hands of the third party and, by implication, threatens to disempower the patient. Psychotherapy is a relational and dynamic process that seeks to promote change in both psychological and behavioural levels. There are times when insight into past trauma, sharpened awareness of narcissistic wounds endured and clarity about one's emotional history can result in patients 'acting out' their internal distress. In Olive's case there was a risk that the anger emerging within her sessions was spilling out into the rest of her life, and being met with misunderstanding and a corresponding rage.

This highlights the need for those supporting the patient with intellectual disabilities to be equipped with an understanding of the psychotherapeutic process. Without this, one of two things may happen: the patient's behaviour will be met with a punitive response, or the therapy may be curtailed prematurely as it begins to be viewed as making the patient worse. In this case, both responses could be prevented by an ongoing process of psychoeducation for those responsible for Olive's care. If she did not have an intellectual disability, there would be no need for any form of contact between the therapy provider and her support team. An awareness of the impact of her disability on her sense of agency and autonomy underpins a systemic model of intervention that raises questions about the impact of the external system upon the deeply internal work being conducted within the therapy. None of the above steps can be taken without Olive's informed consent, a process that changes the patient's concept of the therapy as a purely dyadic, confidential process. This is one of the key factors that demarcates mainstream therapy from Disability Therapy.

Freud's creation of psychoanalysis did not allow for disability. His dictum that 'a certain measure of natural intelligence' was required of patients entering psychoanalysis led to an aversion to working with the intellectually disabled that still prevails in much contemporary psychotherapeutic practice (Freud 1901–1905). Bender (1993) put it beautifully when he referred to the 'unoffered chair' to describe the ways in which people with disabilities were prevented from accessing psychotherapy and counselling. Most psychotherapy trainings do not provide teaching on working with patients with disabilities, meaning that few psychotherapists feel equipped to meet the treatment needs of this patient population. Symington (1992) described the myriad ways in which his colleagues enacted contempt and disdain for their disabled patients in what was then called the Mental Handicap Workshop at the Tavistock Clinic. He became interested in how easy it seemed to be for therapists to be late for their disabled patients' sessions and to dress down on days when they were exclusively seeing patients with disabilities – things these highly trained and otherwise respectful professionals would not have dreamt of doing to their non-disabled patients.

The extent to which people with intellectual disabilities are excluded from society depends largely on the type of society in which they live. How we treat people psychologically does not then depend solely on engaging with the individual unconscious, it has to engage equally with the wider social unconscious, a phenomenon that is constrained and restrained by the history and structure of its society. Dalal (1998, p.210) defines the social unconscious as being 'a representation of the institutionalisation of social power relations in the structure of the psyche itself. In this sense it is a bridge between the social and the psychological'. In considering Olive's therapeutic needs, I had to think carefully about the context of the society in which she had been born and brought up.

My training as a psychoanalytic psychotherapist equipped me to work mainly within a dyadic context, and my interest in Kleinian analysis and the world of British Object Relations theory allowed little space to consider the broader social context in which patients lived. As a result I found my therapeutic work was in danger of missing the social context that had informed my previous work with people with disabilities in social care settings.

A challenge to the psychotherapist working with patients with disabilities is how to work within a psychosocial context without neglecting the internal world of the patient. Frosh and Baraitser (2008, p.354) critiqued a Kleinian way of working that privileges the 'inner reality' over the 'outer reality', and there are signs that this split between the internal and the external is being examined more creatively in contemporary clinical practice. As disability therapists, is our interest in the psychosocial a form of defence against engaging more exclusively with the internal world of our patients? Too premature or abrupt a departure into the psychosocial may prevent a more psychoanalytic dyadic exchange from taking place. Was my desire to look outside of the dyad a symptom of my own discomfort? In working out the answer to this question, it is important to examine the impact of transference and counter-transference in psychological work with patients with disabilities.

Freud first understood transference[§] as an unhelpful form of resistance to being analysed, but later amended his views to encompass the notion of transference as a necessary and useful element of psychoanalytic work. It is this latter understanding that resonates in a more contemporary view of the usefulness of transference and counter-transference. The therapist serves as a container for the experiences that the patient is unable to withstand, and by containing these unbearable experiences frees the patient to be able to commence the therapeutic mechanism of translating their experiences into words. A pathological counter-transference is the failure of the therapist to comprehend when the patient begins to reflect an aspect of the therapist that the therapist still has not learned to understand.

In working with people with intellectual disabilities, counter-transference is affected not just by un-analysed parts of the therapist's neurosis, but also by the therapist's relationship to their own disabilities. Freeman observed a preponderance of guilt, anger, over-sheltering, over-identification, overestimation of abilities and co-dependency with patients in this context (Freeman 1994). Being in the presence of a patient with a disability forces us into an encounter with those parts of our psyche that resonate with notions of lack and loss. Under the pressure of counter-transference feelings arising from both patient and therapist, the therapy itself is at risk of becoming disabled. In her study of cognitive analytic approaches to working with patients with intellectual disabilities, King (2005) notes the temptation on the part of the therapist to deny the presence of disability in their patient, leading to a lack of connection with

§ Transference can be loosely defined as the redirection of feelings or desires towards a new object. In this context this can mean the redirection of a past emotion, such as fear, anxiety or affection, from the patient on to a therapist.

what is, and has to be, real in the consulting room. Segal (1996) noted the propensity of some therapists to unrealistically limit their expectations of what therapy may achieve when working with patients with disabilities, a restriction based largely on a prejudicial view of the patient's ability to tolerate painful emotions.

In literature on the subject of transference, Aragão Oliveira and Milliner et al. (2004) focussed on the impact of a patient's physical disability upon the therapist, linking distortions in judging the patient's prognosis with the therapist's own castration anxiety. Levitas and Hurley (2007) discuss counter-transference as a factor in the over-medication of patients with intellectual disabilities, with the patients they studied being medicated in direct proportion to their caregivers' fear of them, rather than as a result of any quantifiable diagnosis. Drawing on psychoanalytically-oriented group psychotherapy with severely physically disabled patients, Watermayer (2012) has examined counter-transference responses to both the impaired mind and the impaired body. This study linked the universal unconscious conflicts evoked by impairment to a need to place those people with disabilities out of society's sight. The lens through which we seek to observe and assess our patients with objective neutrality is thus sharpened, focussed or unfocussed by the emotional experience of sitting in the presence of their disability. The result, then, is an impasse caused by unconscious counter-transference attitudes in the therapist that remain unaddressed. As Segal says, 'counter-transference is the best of servants but the worst of masters' (1986).

The Disability Transference (Corbett 2009, 2014) is a counter-transferential response to working with patients whose experiences of cognitive deficit impact significantly upon our own sense of internal lack. It can manifest itself in the therapist experiencing problems in thinking clearly inside and outside the therapeutic session, difficulties in holding on to clear memories of sessions and, in more extreme cases, problems in communicating. Something of the patient's disability gets projected into the therapist, resulting in an intersubjectively shared disablement being held in the consciousness of both parties. The decision to remain in the purely dyadic mode rather than adopting a more psychosocial approach depends largely on the capacity to analyse the effect of the Disability Transference upon one's attitudes towards the patient.

Disability Therapy is a clinical approach that has, over the short course of its history, evolved as a psychosocial endeavour. This is due in part to its place on the margins of mainstream clinical practice. Because of this position, Disability Therapists have felt able to diverge from some of the old mantras of classic analytic thinking. In many ways Disability Therapists mirror the marginalised status of their patients, as Hopper writes: 'our colleagues do not always get much gratification from their limited clinical "achievement"' (2012, p.230). Although it is marvellous when a learning-disabled patient has a breakthrough in, for example, his capacity to reflect upon his actions and gain some sense of having a mind of his own, this is often a consolation prize. In comparison to the presentations of certain kinds of psychoanalysts, which often begin with a few lines about their clients being highly intelligent, we cannot present our cases by saying 'Of course, he is highly stupid, in fact as thick as two planks'. In other words, we cannot identify with the brilliant. We must find other sources of gratification in our work.

The exclusion of people with intellectual disabilities from mainstream psychotherapy services can be viewed as part of a fractal process, stemming from a deeply embedded unconscious aversion to 'the other' within ourselves. This intrapsychic process is active not just in the dyadic context of psychotherapy, but is also alive in the organisational and the societal contexts, with the societal being coloured and shaped by the social unconscious.

Olive's case demonstrates the need for an integrated approach to be taken to psychotherapy with people with intellectual disabilities. This presents a challenge to all, as it involves the promotion of clear lines of communication between clinician and support network alongside the building of a safe and confidential dyadic space between clinician and patient. Such an endeavour can only succeed with the engagement of all players in a collaborative process that creates an elastic, but not breakable boundary. It is clear that, despite a slowly flowering interest in Disability Therapy, we are still at the early stages of its integration into mainstream practice. The failure of the mainstream world of psychotherapy to accommodate the patient with disabilities is evidence of the myriad ways in which 'othering' can filter into every section of society and service provision. It may also indicate a tension between what has traditionally been an individualised and internal view of psychology adopted by the psychotherapeutic profession (with exceptions), and a more integrated psychosocial connectedness that can help move people with intellectual disabilities from the outside to the inside.

To end on a note of hope, it is possible that the mainstream world of psychotherapy may have much to learn from the younger discipline of Disability Therapy, particularly through its interest in the psychosocial, and its struggle to erase the artificial split between 'us' and 'the others'. We are all the others.

References

Aragão Oliveira, R., Milliner, E. & Page, R. (2004) 'Psychotherapy with physically disabled patients', *Psychoanalytic Psychotherapy*, 58: 430–441.

Bender, M. (1993) 'The unoffered chair: The history of therapeutic disdain towards people with a learning difficulty', *Clinical Psychology Forum*, pp. 7–12.

Bick, E. (1968) 'The experience of the skin in early object-relations', *The International Journal of Psychoanalysis*, 49: 484–486.

Bybee, J. & Zigler, E. (1999) 'Outerdirectedness in individuals with and without mental retardation: A review'. In: E. Zigler & D. Bennett-Gates (eds.), *Personality Development in Individuals with Mental Retardation*. Cambridge: Cambridge University Press.

Corbett, A. (2009) 'Words as a second language: The psychotherapeutic challenge of severe disability'. In: T. Cottis (ed.), *Intellectual Disability, Trauma and Psychotherapy*. London: Routledge.

— (2011) 'Silk purses and sows' ears: The social and clinical exclusion of people with intellectual disabilities', *Psychodynamic Practice*, 17: 273–289.

— (2014) *Disabling Perversions: Forensic psychotherapy with people with intellectual Disabilities*. London: Karnac Books.

Dagnan, D. (2007) 'Psychosocial interventions for people with intellectual disabilities and mental ill-health', *Current Opinion in Psychiatry*, 20: 456–460.

Dagnan, D. & Waring, M. (2004) 'Linking stigma to psychological distress: Testing a social-cognitive model of the experience of people with intellectual disabilities', *Clinical Psychology & Psychotherapy*, 11: 247–254.

Dalal, F. (1998) *Taking the Group Seriously: Towards a post-Foulkesian group analytic theory*. London: Karnac Books.

Emerson, E. (2012) 'Deprivation, ethnicity and the prevalence of intellectual and developmental disabilities', *Journal of Epidemiology and Community Health*, 66: 218–224.

Emerson, E. & Hatton, C. (2008) 'Socioeconomic disadvantage, social participation and networks and the self-rated health of English men and women with mild and moderate intellectual disabilities: Cross sectional survey', *European Journal of Public Health*, 18(1): 31–37.

Freeman, A. (1994) 'Looking through the mirror of disability', *Women & Therapy*, 14: 79–90.

Freud, S. (1901–1905) *A Case of Hysteria, Three Essays on Sexuality and Other Works, I–VI*. London: The Hogarth Press and the Institute of Psychoanalysis.

Frosh, S. & Baraitser, L. (2008) 'Psychoanalysis and psychosocial studies', *Psychoanalysis, Culture & Society*, 13: 346–365.

Gilbert, P. (2006) 'Social care services and the social perspective', *Psychiatry*, 5(10): 341–345.

Hopper, E. (2012) 'Some challenges to the capacity to think, link and hope in the provision of psychotherapy for the learning disabled'. In: J. Adlam, A. Aiyegbusi, P. Kleinot, A. Motz & C. Scanlon (eds.), *The Therapeutic Milieu under Fire: Security and insecurity in forensic mental health*. London: Jessica Kingsley Publishers.

King, R. (2005) 'CAT, the therapeutic relationship and working with people with learning disability', *Reformulation*, 24: 10–14.

Klein, M. (1946) 'Notes on some schizoid mechanisms', *International Journal of Psycho-Analysis*, 27: 99–110.

Levitas, A. & Hurley, A. (2007) 'Overmedication as a manifestation of counter-transference', *Mental Health Aspects of Developmental Disabilities*, 10: 1–5.

Niehaus, S., Krüger, P. & Schmitz, S. (2013) 'Intellectually disabled victims of sexual abuse in the criminal justice system', *Psychology*, 4: 374.

Rapley, M. (2004) *The Social Construction of Intellectual Disability*. Cambridge: University Press.

Segal, H. (1986) 'Countertransference'. In: H. Segal (ed.), *The Work of Hanna Segal: A Kleinian approach to clinical practice*. London: Free Association Books.

Segal, J. (1996) 'Whose disability? Counter-transference in work with people with disabilities', *Psychodynamic Counselling*, 2: 155–166.

Shah, R. (1992) *The Silent Minority: Children with disabilities in Asian families*. London: National Children's Bureau.

Shakespeare, T. & Watson, N. (2001) 'The social model of disability: An outdated ideology?'. In: N. Sharron, B. Barnartt & M. Altman (eds.), *Exploring Theories and Expanding Methodologies: Where we are and where we need to go. Research in Social Science and Disability*. Bingley: Emerald Publishing Limited, 2: 9–28

Sinason, V. (1992) *Mental Handicap and the Human Condition: New approaches from the Tavistock*. London: Free Association Books.

— (1997) 'Gender-linked issues in psychotherapy with abused and learning disabled female patients'. In: J. Raphael-Leff & R. Perelberg (eds.), *Female Experience: Three generations of British women psychoanalysts on work with women*. London: Routledge.

Sobsey, D. (1994) *Violence and Abuse in the Lives of People with Disabilities: The end of silent acceptance?* Baltimore, MD: Paul H. Brookes Pub. Co.

Symington, N. (1992) 'Countertransference with mentally handicapped clients'. In: A. Waitman & S. Conboy-Hill (eds.), *Psychotherapy and Mental Handicap*. London: Sage Publications.

Watermeyer, B. (2012) 'Disability and countertransference in group psychotherapy: Connecting social oppression with the clinical frame', *International Journal of Group Psychotherapy*, 62: 392–417.

Wolfensberger, W. (1987) *The New Genocide of Handicapped and Afflicted People*. New York: Syracuse.

Community Health Care for People with an Intellectual Disability: A Pharmacist's Perspective

BERNADETTE FLOOD

Introduction

Health care outcomes for each person with an intellectual disability result directly from their interaction with the health care system in their communities. Members of this population group experience significant disparities in life expectancy, access to and use of health care services, morbidity, and mortality. Their health needs are complex, and intersect with the social and economic conditions these individuals experience in their community.

Health is essential for daily cognitive and physical function, and is a prerequisite for full participation and inclusion in the community. Over the last 20 years there has been an increase in the life expectancy of people with an intellectual disability. This may be due in part to improved health and wellbeing, the control of infectious diseases, the move to community living, better nutrition, and an improvement in the quality of health care services. This enhanced life expectancy places increased demands on health services and poses new challenges to pharmacists and other health care professionals caring for people with intellectual disabilities, wherever they live.

This vulnerable population of people with an intellectual disability is a heterogeneous one. The health care outcomes vary considerably according to the severity of their impairment, the cause of the intellectual disability, the risks involved in health problems, and environmental factors including their access to health care. Once an illness is diagnosed, patient care relies on pharmacological interventions (medication) as the major form of therapy, and the optimisation of medications is necessary to ensure their safe and effective use, result in the best possible outcomes. Data suggests that medicines are currently the cornerstone of chronic disease therapy in all population groups. However, the pharmacist, as a member of the health care team, is often 'invisible' in the care process for people with an intellectual disability and people with an intellectual disability may also be invisible to pharmacists as a group of people that are societally 'hard to hear' and 'hard to see'.

Rights, respect and responsibility interact at all stages in the lives and health care experience of people with intellectual disabilities. But if pharmacists and others concentrate on rights alone, without regard to respect and responsibility, this can place people with an intellectual disability in the position of making potentially unwise and unhealthy decisions in relation to use, or non-use, of medication. Often the person's 'right' to autonomy is recognised, such as their right to make unwise health care decisions, but this can lead to concerns about the 'respect' shown to them as a person deserving of the highest quality of health care, and the 'responsibility' of clinicians (including pharmacists) to protect that individual's 'right to health'. This 'right to health' was first articulated in the 1946 Constitution of the World Health Organisation, and was mentioned in the 1948 Universal Declaration of Human Rights as part of the right to an adequate standard of living. However, the apparent disconnect between universal human rights and the heterogeneous limitations of people with an intellectual disability have caused concern (Fyson & Cromby 2013).

Making efforts to understand more fully the real life situation of the person with an intellectual disability is one of the key aspects to managing this vulnerable population, and intervening when needed to address health inequality and poor care management. Clinicians, such as pharmacists, must try to understand the person's broader social and economic situation as this will significantly impact on how any patient fares in the health care system. It will also affect how they manage their own health outside the system in their living environment. Is the person able to manage aspects of their own health care, including medicine use, or does a carer take charge?

As the nature of the community and home for each person is unique, the care provided will also need to be tailored to each situation. People with an intellectual disability who live 'at home' often have a greater role in determining how, and even if, certain interventions in health care will be implemented. For example, in a residential care setting, nurses, physicians and pharmacists may all play a role in ensuring that the patient with an intellectual disability receives medication at therapeutically appropriate intervals. At home, however, the patient may choose, for a variety of reasons, to take their medication at irregular times, despite advice about the importance of a regular schedule. Interventions by pharmacists and others to promote patient safety and quality care in managing medication should take into account the fact that patients and their carers will sometimes choose to act in ways that are inconsistent with the advice given to make the programme of medication successful, with the result that the pharmacist's best efforts may not have the desired outcome.

Many patients with an intellectual disability receive assistance or support from family members or other informal caregivers. As professional clinicians, such as pharmacists, have no authority over these caregivers, a level of risk is introduced into the process of medication use. For example, non-adherence rates for anti-epileptic drugs have been found to vary according to living arrangements. Individuals with an intellectual disability living in family homes or in semi-independent settings have been found to be significantly less adherent to anti-epileptic drugs than those in group homes (Hom et al. 2015).

Good patient experience of health care is positively associated with improvements in clinical effectiveness and patient safety. There is evidence that a better patient experience leads to:

- higher levels of adherence to recommended prevention and treatment processes;
- better clinical outcomes;
- better patient safety within hospitals;
- less health care utilisation.

Health systems and professionals in all communities must pay serious attention to the personal experience of people with an intellectual disability and their carers, as this is an essential component of any episode of health care. Those professionals involved should work to acquire an insight into the challenges faced by people with an intellectual disability during the medication programme, in order to encourage more effective cooperation and support to ensure the best outcome of the recommended treatment.

Optimisation of the use of medication

There is a recognised need to improve clinical outcomes for people with an intellectual disability. Effective communication is central in the many stages of optimising the use of medication. Pharmacists, prescribers and others do not always understand the complexity of the tasks they ask patients with an intellectual disability, or their carers, to undertake during the recommended programme of medication. These tasks can include:

- usage of Monitored Dosage Systems (MDS);
- monitoring blood glucose;
- administering insulin;
- manipulating dosage, for example, decreasing a dose of steroids;
- administering medicines in different forms, such as tablets, liquids, suppositories, patches, creams etc.;
- administering epilepsy rescue medication in emergency situations.

'Always events' can be used to highlight the most important services and experiences in health care encounters for people with an intellectual disability and their carers. Health care providers and professionals should 'always' get these events right. Pharmacy-related 'always events' include:

- always being aware of common side effects of the patient's current medication;

- always receiving enough information about the patient's medication from a pharmacist;
- always being told about any change in their medication, such as if a dose is changed, stopped or started;
- always being given appropriate, accessible information.

To protect people with an intellectual disability in the use of medication, it is important that a risk assessment is undertaken to ensure that medication will be of high quality and is, among other things, safe, appropriate and cost effective. Pharmacists must discharge their professional responsibility to confirm that patients with an intellectual disability are 'competent' enough to self-administer medications, for example MDS, and/or insulin injections, and that patients are aware of storage conditions for certain products such as insulin and glucagon. In a case study of this process, reported by Irish pharmacists, one person with an intellectual disability and diabetes had stored all his insulin in a drawer in his bedroom, having first of all removed it from its original packaging (Flood & Henman 2015). There was evidence that he had used a MDS erratically and there was no indication of when the most recent dose had been taken.

Including patients in decisions concerning their treatment should be encouraged, and pharmacists should pay close attention to those individuals deemed 'at-risk'. Groups at increased risk of medication safety incidents within this population will include those:

- who self-manage their own health;
- prescribed multiple medications;
- with high-risk illnesses such as diabetes;
- taking high-risk medications such as insulin;
- for whom 'reasonable accommodations' were not provided by clinicians, including prescribers and pharmacists.

It is important to keep accurate documentation to review medications during each encounter with patients with intellectual disabilities. Frequent medication reviews and collaboration with members of the health care team, including pharmacists, should improve care and help to prevent adverse events associated with poor medication management. In England it is recognised that the sharing of relevant information can, on occasion, be as important as the duty to respecting patient confidentiality (HSCIC 2013).

Ambulatory care sensitive conditions (ACSC) are conditions that, given 'effective management' at the primary care level in the form of efficient community care and case management, should not normally result in an admission to hospital. People with an intellectual disability are more likely to be hospitalised for ACSC than people without. The crude rate of admissions for ACSC is 76 admissions per 1,000 per year for adults with intellectual disability associated conditions (Glover & Evison 2013). This is roughly five times the rate for other people, 15 admissions per 1000 per year. For example, people with both an intellectual disability and diabetes are more likely to be admitted to hospital as an emergency for diabetes-related complications; and this may indicate a potential weakness in primary care services for people with an intellectual disability (Turner & Emerson 2013). Strategies to avoid these hospitalisations in all population groups may include:

- after hours care;
- optimising use of ambulatory services;
- intensified monitoring of high-risk patients;
- initiatives to improve patients' willingness and ability to seek timely help;
- patients adhering to recommended medication. (Freud et al. 2013).

People with an intellectual disability rely on their carer for assistance and support across many aspects of their life, and it has been reported that for over 50 per cent of such individuals, it is others who make health care decisions and choices for them. Therefore, in all communities, family and paid carers can have a major impact on the health of people with an intellectual disability.

Medication use is the main therapeutic intervention in this population, and the frequency of experiencing side effects to medications may be greatly underestimated by doctors and pharmacists. Adverse effects are a problem for at least half of those taking psychotropic medication, and may offer a rational justification for a patient choosing to discontinue medication (Lambert et al. 2004). Evidence shows that clinicians prescribing antidepressants only ask roughly one in five patients how well the drugs are working, and only one in ten whether they are experiencing any side effects. These questions may be asked even more rarely of patients in vulnerable population groups. Individuals with both an intellectual disability and autism spectrum disorder, across multiple classes, who are prescribed psychotropic medications have been found to experience the most side effects (Hess et al. 2010). An examination of the practice of prescribing antipsychotics by a UK Intellectual Disability Psychiatry Department which operated in accordance with the standards adopted from nationally recognised guidelines, found that there was a lack of documentation regarding patients' physical health and the monitoring of side effects (Griffiths 2012).

Many people with an intellectual disability are 'invisible' to pharmacists. This may be due to a number of factors:

- lack of exposure to the population of those with intellectual disabilities on the part of the pharmacist, as many carers communicate/interact with the pharmacist on the patient's behalf;
- carers might be reluctant to encourage a person with an intellectual disability to visit the pharmacy;
- pharmacists education may not have included information on the population of those with an intellectual disability;
- pharmacists may not personally know anyone with an intellectual disability;
- lack of time for the pharmacist to interact with people in busy pharmacies;
- prescriptions may not indicate that the person has an intellectual disability.

This will hinder efforts to quickly determine the cause of any medication safety incident that occurs. If a person with an intellectual disability presents at a pharmacy with bruises that they cannot explain, it will not be known whether the cause is the result of a fall arising from low blood pressure, from an antipsychotic or anticoagulant prescription, from physical abuse, or from a blood abnormality. There may also be situational variables that present medication safety risks to patients with an intellectual disability, and these may be difficult or impossible for the clinician to eliminate. These can include the patient spitting out medication when the carer is not looking, the patient choosing not to self-administer medication due to side effects that they are unable to describe or choosing not to administer insulin due to 'insulin dread'*.

Risk assessment

Self-care in the community, or primary care, may not ensure quality medication use or the best outcomes for people with an intellectual disability who have high-risk illnesses and take high-risk medications. 'High-risk' medicines are those that are most likely to cause significant harm to the patient, even when used as intended. To protect people with an intellectual disability in the use of medication, it is important to undertake a risk assessment to ensure that the medication programme will be of high quality. Pharmacists must discharge their professional responsibility to confirm that patients with an intellectual disability are 'competent' enough to self-administer medications from a MDS, and that they are aware of the appropriate storage conditions for certain products such as insulin and glucagon. Elements of risk in the process may be reduced by educating and assisting caregivers such as families and providers.

Understanding the role human factors play in the use of medication is crucial to understanding how the entire process can be optimised. The Royal Pharmaceutical Society has undertaken

---

* In a survey that explored the impact of insulin injections and communication between patients and health care providers, one third (33 per cent) of patients identified that they have some level of dread associated with taking their daily injections, eight per cent strongly agreed that they dread injections and and 25 per cent somewhat agreed that they dread injections (Peyrot, Rubin, Kruger & Travis 2010).

extensive work in England in relation to the safety of home-care treatments (RPS 2014). An adaptation for use of these treatments in the intellectually disabled population is set out below.

Self-management of medication – Person with intellectual disabilities: Risk assessment

Patient needs include:

1. the patient's clinical condition;
2. the patient's willingness and ability to consent to self-administer medication at home;
3. availability of suitable contact details, such as a mobile phone, in case of any issues or medicine recall;
4. the patient's competence to self-administer the medicine, for example insulin or medication from a MDS, in accordance with the prescriber's instructions;
5. in the case of vulnerable adults or children, whether an appropriate additional care/support package is robust and in place;
6. the patient's (or carer's) ability to understand their responsibilities with regard to the treatment, for example:
    i)   attending appointments such as at diabetic or anticoagulant clinic;
    ii) taking required tests, for example, blood glucose testing;
    iii) adhering to the treatment, such as self-administering insulin;
    iv) reporting any adverse reactions or side effects like diarrhoea or falls;
    v)   storing the medicines appropriately as per manufacturer's directions;
    vi) being available to collect medications from the pharmacy, including having available transportation;
    vii) ensuring contact details are kept up to date and are shared between the patient's clinical team and support organisation.

It is necessary to monitor the quality of current medication-related processes in this vulnerable population. To improve these processes, people with an intellectual disability and/or their paid or family carers, should be encouraged to report medication safety incidents through national reporting systems. Incident reporting and effective management gives health care service providers the opportunity to learn from past events affecting the safe use of medication. Many people with an intellectual disability live in a 'home' environment in the community. The potential for medication safety incidents among those living in such an environment is thought to be greater than in other care settings because of the unstructured nature of their surroundings and the unique communication challenges present in the 'home' health care system. In England, the National Patient Safety Agency noted that more information is needed about medication incidents occurring in mental health and intellectual disability services. It found that a number of incidents in this population related to a confusion over what medicines patients had self-administered. This may have resulted from inadequate supervision or a lack of continued assessment of the patient's suitability for self-administration (NPSA 2009).

In the future, with the move towards community and primary care-based services, there will be a greater reliance of people with an intellectual disability on care providers and families supporting them with their health care and medication management. This may not be easy for the person with an intellectual disability and their carer, and may cause conflicts in the home setting. Caregivers, such as family members, may be concerned by the dilemma between providing good care, such as discouraging a person with an intellectual disability and diabetes from unhealthy eating and at the same time offering person-centred care and respecting the individual's autonomy. The current level of provision of information to people with an intellectual disability and carers is poor, with carers reporting that although they know how to administer medication, they know little about why the person is taking it and what the implications might be. This should be a wake-up call for all those involved in prescribing, dispensing and administering medication to this vulnerable population. Efforts should be made to improve disease-specific knowledge in order to enhance self-efficacy and promote the performance of self-care behaviours, including adherence to medication programmes needed to achieve desirable health outcomes.

Pharmacy

Pharmacists have a unique insight into the use of medication that differs from that of a physician, psychiatrist, nurse, and so on. Patients in the general population may ask questions and express concerns about their medication, which provides the pharmacist with an opportunity to tailor information to the patient's needs and level of understanding. When the patient has an intellectual disability they may be 'invisible' in the pharmacy, as it may be that their carer may be responsible for sourcing the medication supply. People with an intellectual disability are unlikely to seek information about their medication themselves, and as such it is the responsibility of health professionals to make that information readily available. Even if they do possess adequate information, people with an intellectual disability may experience difficulty in communicating the side-effects of their medication, for example reporting adverse effects such as 'blurred vision' or feeling 'dizzy'. Therefore, pharmacists and others must be receptive to the possible side-effects that people may experience.

Effective patient care services relating to medication management by pharmacists and others can lower total health care costs. Pharmacists can improve public health, and contribute to the care of people with long-term conditions, by encouraging the effective use of medicines promoting healthy lifestyles, supporting self-care, carrying out medication reviews, managing disease systematically within multi-professional teams, and working in partnership with case managers.

Many people with an intellectual disability are supplied with medications in a MDS, which may introduce a level of unidentified risk to the medication use process. The Royal Pharmaceutical Society recognises that, '... the use of multi-compartment compliance aids has become regarded as a panacea for medicines use and is often integrated into practice and service policy without giving due consideration to the alternatives available'(RPS 2013).

Repeat prescribing and dispensing systems have evolved, rather than been designed, and are therefore subject to variations in different communities. These systems normally rely on a patient with an intellectual disability, and/or the carer, prompting the continuity of supply; but this practice has serious drawbacks if the patient is non-compliant. Normally, these systems do not include any provision for regular checks on the patient's concordance with their medication or instructions.

Integrating pharmacists into direct patient care results in favourable outcomes across health care settings and levels of disease. Maximising the expertise and scope of pharmacists and minimising barriers to what is an already successful health care delivery model has been shown to improve the health system (Giberson et al. 2011). The limited evidence available in literature on the subject suggests that pharmacists, in collaboration with other health care professionals, carers and patients with an intellectual disability, can make positive interventions in relation to the quality of the medication programmes for such individuals (O'Dwyer et al. 2015).

Health literacy

Communication difficulties and reduced health literacy are determinants of health in people with an intellectual disability. Health literacy should be seen as a systems issue reflecting the complexity of both the presentation of health information accessible to people with an intellectual disability and navigation of the health and social care system in all communities. To improve these outcomes the emphasis must be shifted from the literacy skills of people with an intellectual disability, to the activities of health systems and health care professionals, such as pharmacists.

For the person with an intellectual disability health literacy skills may be the first step in a chain of factors impacting on their health status and medication use. Knowledge and understanding of health must always be examined in the context of the specific tasks that need to be accomplished, for example, MDS management, blood glucose measurement, administration of insulin and adequate nutritional intake. Four key strategies to support people with an intellectual disability in obtaining information about medication have been identified as:

1. spending more time providing and reiterating key information;
2. providing accurate, up-to-date, accessible information about medications;
3. providing training for carers in wider aspects of medication usage;
4. tailoring information to each person's individual needs (Heslop et al. 2005).

The health care of people with poor health literacy has been found to result in higher medical costs due to more medication and treatment errors, more frequent hospitalisations, longer hospital stays, and increased visits to their health care provider.

Conclusion

People with an intellectual disability in all forms of community have 'complex needs'. They may have more than one disability, may show behaviour that challenges, may have multiple morbidities, consume multiple medications, and may not use words to communicate. Medicines can be helpful when used appropriately, kept under review and monitored. The lack of review or challenge in relation to psychotropic medication use has been identified as a particular concern.

Unfortunately, the education of health care staff, from all professional backgrounds, does not prepare them well for the challenges of multi-morbidities, chronic illnesses, multiple medication use and the communication difficulties in this population. However, specific guidelines relating to people with an intellectual disability have been published that will benefit all health care staff (Hoghton et al. 2011) and carers (Bowers et al. 2013). The best use of medication will require access to quality medication programmes and competent, skilled pharmacists. Pharmacists in all communities, should ensure the uninterrupted supply of quality medicines to those in the local population with an intellectual disability. The management and responsible use of these treatments are vital components in improving the health of this vulnerable population leading to a narrowing of the gaps in health inequality and health inequity. Pharmacists need to be integrated into the care process for people with an intellectual disability, and be recognised for the skills and knowledge they possess and valued for their medication expertise.

Interventions to address risk in medication use may have an impact on health inequalities for people with an intellectual disability. To ensure good health outcomes from the use of medication, there is a need for a standard and uniform approach by prescribers, pharmacists and others to deliver adequate health and medication information. 'Joined up thinking' across all communities will ensure that health care professionals, such as pharmacists, coordinate their efforts to ensure people with an intellectual disability and carers have multiple access points, to ensure they receive care of appropriate quality.

Equal outcomes in health care are important factors for people with intellectual disabilities in all communities, but the evidence is sparse as to what form of intervention works. It is likely that any successful intervention to optimise medication and improve medication health related outcomes will:

- be context- and person-specific;
- be highly individualised;
- entail education and information transfer;
- involve the person with an intellectual disability and their direct caregiver;
- require skilled communicators;
- necessitate an awareness of the person's sensory profile, manual dexterity ability and mobility status; and
- be time-consuming.

A social responsibility exists to target services to this vulnerable population who are at high risk of medication safety incidents. The model of care used in each community should be determined locally, and based on the available professional resources, as well as the health and social care needs of the population who have intellectual disabilities.

References

Bowers, B., Nolet, K., Webber, R., Stumm, E. & Bigby, C. (2013) *Supporting Older People with Intellectual Disability to Age at Home: A manual for support staff and carers*. Queensland, Australia.

Flood, B. & Henman, M. (2015) 'Case study: Hidden complexity of medicines use: Information provided by a person with intellectual disability and diabetes to a pharmacist', *British Journal of Learning Disabilities*, 43(2): 234–242.

Freund, T., Campbell, S., Geissler, S., Kunz, C., Mahler, C., Peters-Klimm, F. & Szecsevi, J. (2013) 'Strategies for reducing potentially avoidable hospitalisations for ambulatory care-sensitive conditions', *Annals of Family Medicine*, 11(4): 363–370.

Fyson, R. & Cromby, J. (2013) 'Human rights and intellectual disabilities in an era of "choice"', *Journal of Intellectual Disability Research*, 57(12): 1164–1172.

Giberson, S., Yoder, S. & Lee, M. (2011) *Improving Patient and Health System Outcomes through Ambulatory Advanced Pharmacy Practice: A report to the US Surgeon General*. Rockville, Maryland: Office of the Chief Pharmacist, US.

Glover, G. & Evison, F. (2013) *Hospital Admissions That Should Not Happen: Admissions for ambulatory care sensitive conditions for people with learning disabilities in England*. Improving Health and Lives: Learning Disabilities Observatory.

Griffiths, H., Halder, N. & Chaudry, N. (2012) 'Antipsychotic prescribing in people with intellectual disabilities: A clinical audit', *Advances in Mental Health and Intellectual Disabilities*, 6(4): 215–222.

Heslop, P., Folkes, L. & Rodgers, J. (2005) 'The knowledge people with learning disabilities and their carers have about psychotropic medication', *Tizard Learning Disability Review*, 10(10): 10–18.

Hess, J., Matson, J., Neal, D., Mahan, S., Fodstad, J., Bamburg, J. & Holloway, J. (2010) 'A comparison of psychotropic drug side effect profiles in adults diagnosed with intellectual disabilities and autism spectrum disorders', *Journal of Mental Health Research in Intellectual Disabilities*, 3: 85–96.

Hoghton, M., Turner, S. & Murphy, K. (2011) *Improving the Health and Wellbeing of People with Learning Disabilities: An evidence based commissioning guide for emerging clinical commissioning groups (draft)*. Improving Health and Lives: Learning Disabilities Observatory.

Hom, C., Touchette, P., Nguyen, V., Fernandez, G., Tournay, A., Plon, L., Himber, P. & Lott, I. (2015) 'The relationship between living arrangement and adherence to antiepileptic medications among individuals with developmental disabilities', *Journal of Intellectual Disability Research*, 59(1): 48–54.

Health and Social Care Information Centre (2013) *A Guide to Confidentiality in Health and Social Care: Treating confidential information with respect.* London: Health and Social Care Information Centre.

Lambert, M., Conus, P., Eide, P., Mass, R., Karow, A., Moritz, S., Golks, D. & Naber, D. (2004) 'Impact of present and past antipsychotic side effects on attitude toward typical antipsychotic treatment and adherence', *European Psychiatry*, 19(7): 415–422.

National Patient Safety Institute (2009) *Safety in Doses: Improving the use of medicines in the NHS. Learning from national reporting 2007.* Dublin: National Patient Safety Institute.

O'Dwyer, M., Meŝtrović, A. & Henman, M. (2015) 'Pharmacists' medicines-related interventions for people with intellectual disabilities: A narrative review', *International Journal of Clinical Pharmacy*, 37(4): 566–578.

Peyrot M., Rubin R.R., Kruger, D.F. & Travis, L.B. (2010) 'Correlates of Insulin injection ommission', *Diabetes Care*, 33(2): 240–5.

Royal Pharmaceutical Society (2013) *Improving Patient Outcomes: The better use of multi-compartment compliance aids.* London: Royal Pharmaceutical Society.

Royal Pharmaceutical Society (2014) *Handbook for Homecare Services in England.* London: Royal Pharmaceutical Society.

Turner, S. & Emerson, E. (2013) *Making Reasonable Adjustments to Diabetes Services for People with Learning Disabilities*, Improving Health and Lives: Learning Disabilities Observatory.

Citizenship and Community: The Challenge of Camphill

DAN MCKANAN

When Helen Zipperlen first arrived at Botton Village in the mid-1950s she was intrigued and attracted by what she saw. The people she met were unusual in their speech, gestures and actions; but because Helen was young, and because society had not yet articulated a vocabulary of labels for disability, she could not readily explain what made them unusual. What most impressed her was that, for all their diversity, the people of Botton Village were hard at work. They were erecting houses, painting rooms, growing vegetables and caring for livestock. These people were building a new community, and all of them exuded a sense of pride and ownership in that community. Helen wanted to feel that same sense of pride and ownership, and so she cast her lot with Botton Village and the Camphill movement of which it is a part. Decades later, she remains a proud citizen of the Camphill movement, living in retirement at the community she helped to found: Camphill Village Kimberton Hills in Pennsylvania. With thousands of others, she has discovered Camphill to be a lively experiment in democracy. It is a place where people of all abilities work together to shape the social organisms that, in turn, shape their lives.

For the past fifteen years I have been visiting Camphill communities – sometimes alone, sometimes with my family, sometimes with groups of university students – and in almost every one I have felt the same sense of pride and ownership that impressed Helen sixty years ago. When I brought a class of graduate students to Camphill Village USA, in Copake, New York, for an overnight field trip one fall, we were greeted by a young villager with a mild disability. She assigned us bedrooms and gave us directions to the various houses where we would be eating our supper. She then led us on a comprehensive community tour that included a bookbinding workshop recently entrusted to her and her best friend. When my family spent a week at Newton Dee in Scotland, our days were anchored by the community's milkman, a middle-aged gentleman with an operatic voice who sang enthusiastically as he carried jugs of milk from the community dairy to each household. In most Camphill places, the residents with the longest tenure in the community are people with disabilities. As a result, both visitors and shorter-term residents turn to them for guidance in the ways of community.

I, too, have turned to Camphill for guidance in the work of building democratic communities in which we can all freely shape the circumstances of our shared lives. I am not a scholar of disability policy, and I have limited experience of the range of places other than Camphill that persons with developmental disabilities call home. As a historian of religion and social transformation, I first came to Camphill because I was interested in the ways that intentional communities shape broader processes of social transformation. Many kinds of intentional communities – ecovillages, cohousing communities, student cooperatives, Catholic Worker houses – are currently contributing to the renewal of democracy in the United States and beyond. But Camphill, with its deep commitment to individuals with intellectual disabilities, has a special contribution to make. By inviting people of all abilities to be true citizens, the Camphill community helps all of us to understand democracy more fully.

Democracy today faces multiple challenges. Since the revolutions in the eighteenth and nineteenth century established democratic control of government in many parts of the world, private corporations have steadily expanded the scope of their control over the lives of ordinary people. Even in ostensibly democratic societies, as a consequence, most people have limited capacity to shape those institutions with the greatest impact on their lives. Most people, most of the time, experience themselves as paid labour or passive consumers rather than as citizens. Another challenge is the paradox of equality and diversity. Democracy stipulates that each person has equal dignity and an equal right to practise citizenship, yet people are irreducibly diverse in their abilities, preferences and past experiences. Indeed, we have a right to have our diversity respected in a manner that does not compromise our equality as citizens. A final challenge stems from the fact that human citizens share this earth with non-human entities, including biological organisms and ecosystems, as well as human-made structures and technologies. The diversity among these entities is so vast as to preclude any talk of equality: for example, in what sense would a hummingbird have equal rights with the Internet? Yet the symbiosis between humanity and our environment is so deep that we cannot meaningfully practise democracy without taking non-human realities into account. The current environmental crisis is evidence of western societies' failure to learn this lesson.

Intentional communities in which people with and without developmental disabilities live and work together have a vital role to play in addressing these challenges to democracy. Neither Camphill nor any other community movement has fully resolved these challenges. To some extent, the anecdotes that began this essay convey an idealised vision of Camphill life. In practice, Camphillers do not fully 'own' their communities or exercise democratic control over all aspects of their lives. Legally, most Camphill communities are not governed by either their disabled or their non-disabled residents, but by self-perpetuating non-profit boards. In practice, most of these boards delegate many decisions to the interlocking network of committees that constitute Camphill's internal governance structure, and these groups are numerically dominated by the non-disabled residents in the community. Some Camphill boards include one or two persons with disabilities, but many do not. The same can be said for the decision-making committees within each community. Even where persons with disabilities do participate in formal community governance, their diversity – in linguistic ability, ease with social interaction and anxiety about responsibility – means that some individuals are more likely to have their perspectives honoured than others. Likewise, Camphill communities are far from perfect in the way they honour non-human beings in their governance. Many are justifiably proud of their biodynamic gardens and of the gentleness with which they allow baby calves to continue nursing even as their mothers are milked for human consumption. Many seek to preserve a healthy environment for more distant creatures by building biomass or solar energy systems that do not contribute to global warming. Yet, Camphillers still burn natural gas in their homes and gasoline in their automobiles. Many say that they aren't much ahead of their neighbours in recycling and other environmental practices; residents of one Camphill with exemplary environmental practices nevertheless bemoaned the fact that the initial construction of their buildings had constituted an act of violence to the hillside on which they were situated.

Therefore it is not my intent to lift up Camphill as it is now as a model to be emulated, for the movement hasn't yet attained the goal of being a fully democratic community. Instead, I offer Camphill as a beacon pointing toward that goal. The organisation is on a path toward the empowerment of people with intellectual disabilities as full citizens of the communities in which they reside, not merely as recipients of services or bearers of individual rights, but as shapers of a common future. This path, in turn, promises to enrich the possibilities for citizenship for all people, regardless of ability.

Camphill communities address the first challenge to democracy – the expansion of corporate power and consequent narrowing of the sphere of democratic decision making – in several ways. One way is by decentralising decision making. Most decisions are made in face-to-face conversation among the individuals directly affected by the outcome, with occasional community-wide gatherings in which individuals can identify problems and propose solutions.

Additionally, by guaranteeing a basic economic sustenance to every member of the community, Camphill places ensure that residents do not think of themselves as merely employees, valued only for labour. By limiting exposure to advertising and providing many goods from within the community, Camphillers also ward against the danger of seeing themselves primarily as consumers deriving their identity from passive choices among pre-packaged alternatives.

Many Camphillers would be quick to point out that these distinctive practices are less universal in the movement now than they were a generation ago. Though the classic Camphill model calls for each person to work on behalf of the others and to receive sustenance from the work of those others, with no one receiving a salary, virtually every Camphill place today has some salaried employees. Old rules limiting exposure to television and other media have faded in the name of individual freedom. Yet these changes hardly constitute a complete acquiescence to corporate consumerism. Camphill homes are still full of objects, such as wall art and rugs, that residents have made themselves rather than purchasing at stores. Camphill employees may receive salaries, but many were drawn to the community because of its egalitarian ethos. Changes that have softened the boundaries between Camphill and the larger world have likewise enhanced Camphill's capacity to share its distinctive communal wisdom with its neighbours. Perhaps most significantly, the challenges that currently face Camphill traditions have emboldened many Camphillers to articulate the reasons for those traditions more publicly.

Camphill communities address the second challenge, that of equality and diversity, by deliberately crafting communities in which persons with and without developmental disabilities live and work together in roughly equal numbers. In the stereotypical 'institution', the residential community consists exclusively of persons with special needs. Non-disabled 'staff' reside offsite or live in sequestered apartments that insulate them from the daily experience of the residents. This is not so for most Camphill co-workers, who eat the same food, use the same bathrooms, and celebrate the same seasonal festivals as the villagers or students.

It is true that, to varying degrees, Camphills have moved away from the traditional model of having residential co-workers provide all support services to their residents with disabilities. It is also true that many Camphill communities today include persons with disabilities who are present for only part of the day, perhaps to attend school, participate in a sheltered workshop, or join in an artistic activity. These changes have complex implications for the practice of democratic citizenship in Camphill, and are the subject of intense, ongoing reflection within the movement. At the time of writing this, however, it is universally true that in the Camphill movement all residents with disabilities are expected to build community together with persons without disabilities, and vice versa.

This is important, because all people have a right to forge relationships with those who are like themselves *and* with those who are different. Long-repeated experience has shown that both ghettoisation and tokenisation undermine democratic participation for members of minority groups. When people are ghettoised or restricted to communities where everyone is like themselves, they lose access to resources that are held primarily by people who are unlike themselves. People separated by ghetto walls lose the capacity to see one another as individuals because they cannot build one-to-one relationships, and instead they assign to others the stereotypical qualities associated with the group to which they belong. In some cases, they may cease to regard members of the other group as fully human. This is why European Jews struggled to leave their ghettoes, why African Americans fought against Jim Crow segregation and the 'separate but equal' doctrine that restricted their access to education, and why people with physical disabilities have demanded full access to public spaces and activities. It is why western societies have abandoned the old 'institutions' that once housed the majority of persons with developmental disabilities.

Though the dangers of ghettoisation are widely recognised, tokenisation can be equally damaging, both to the individual and to society. When individuals are placed in situations where they are the only representative of their particular group, they may face intense pressure to conform to the habits of the majority group or, alternatively, to 'perform' the uniqueness of their own group in a stereotypical manner. Tokenised persons risk losing their individuality, since neither they, nor the people around them, can readily discern which of their traits are uniquely individual and which ones reflect their group identity. As these individuals lack the opportunity to process their own experiences with others who have had similar experiences, they cannot readily judge which of their negative experiences are the result of prejudice and mistreatment, and which ones might stem from other causes. These factors make it difficult for tokenised persons to be advocates for themselves, which is an essential aspect of full democratic participation. For this reason, universities, businesses, and other organisations that seek to integrate members of previously excluded groups have generally found that it is more helpful to include cohorts of people than individuals one at a time.

In modern western societies, persons with developmental disabilities are often able to avoid the pitfalls of ghettoisation and tokenisation only because different demographic patterns occur in their households, their neighbourhoods, and their workplaces. A person might live in a group home populated entirely by those with special needs, situated within a neighbourhood in which there are no other persons with developmental disabilities. Or they might live with their family of origin, as the only person with a disability in the household, but work in a sheltered workshop with others very much like themselves. Such mixed circumstances, which seem to be favoured by policy makers, have the potential to inculcate the mixed experience of sameness and diversity that is key to democratic participation. But this is so only if there is some fluidity between the various settings, for example, if the participants in a sheltered workshop know enough about one another's home settings that they can collectively process (in whatever manner is appropriate for them) the experiences they have with individuals unlike them. If this fluidity does not exist, for example if residents feel safe in their homogeneous group home but unsafe in the diverse neighbourhood surrounding it, people in these situations might suffer the negative effects of both ghettoisation and tokenisation.

Camphill places, especially traditional Camphill villages in rural areas, take a different approach. Household, neighbourhood, and workplace, along with religious and cultural spaces, are fully integrated, so that the community one experiences in any of these areas is identical to, or overlapping with, the community in the others. For this reason, some social care policymakers have seen Camphill communities as less than ideal settings for persons with disabilities, seemingly on the grounds that residents do not experience a sufficiently diverse array of social interactions to equip them for full democratic participation. Such concerns certainly deserve to be taken seriously, but often fail to take

145

into account the offsetting factor; because of the balanced composition of Camphill communities, residents have abundant opportunities for relationships of both sameness and difference at home, at play or in work. It should be noted that here I am referring only to differences related to disability. In far too many Camphills, persons from racial or ethnic minorities are in fact tokenised, though this is gradually changing.

I make no claim to know whether, on balance, democratic participation for persons with developmental disabilities is better served in tightly integrated, demographically balanced communities like Camphill, or in the mixed situations that are more typical today. A systematic researcher might find that the answer would vary widely from individual to individual. For this reason, I would not advocate for social care authorities to regard Camphill as the ideal setting in every case, merely that they should create placement structures that make it easier for persons with special needs to discern for themselves whether Camphill is right for them.

One might plausibly argue that Camphills are problematically 'artificial' in that they are home to a much higher percentage of individuals with disabilities than would be found in the wider population. The logic of 'mainstreaming' assumes that people fare better in social settings that are as similar as possible to the social environments occupied by other kinds of people. But this logic is falsified by the observable behaviour of virtually every minority group that has enjoyed the freedom to determine its own residential and workplace patterns. Traditionally, for instance, gays and lesbians have migrated to urban neighbourhoods in order to build the critical mass necessary to exercise political power. Refugees who are initially resettled in widely scattered locations, likewise, typically relocate to cities that have developed significant ethnic neighbourhoods. These people are not ghettoising themselves, since they rarely constitute the majority of residents in the cities or neighbourhoods they choose. They are simply choosing a demographic balance that allows them to experience both sameness and diversity. Camphill makes it possible for persons with developmental disabilities to make similar choices.

I should add that the democratic benefits of Camphill's 50/50 demographic mix do not accrue only to those Camphillers who have developmental disabilities: non-disabled co-workers also benefit. As previously noted, my initial interest in Camphill had very little to do with disability, and focused more on my interest in radically democratic community-building. My observation is that Camphill communities have some distinct advantages over many others that have been founded primarily to promote democratic practice. Those communities can be intensely homogeneous, populated only by well-educated, politically leftist people with boundless energy for participating in formal democratic processes. This has a paradoxical consequence, for a degree of taste for politics is itself a diversity that should be present in a healthy democratic community. People who spend all their time with other political junkies lose the capacity to honour the preferences of, and learn from the experiences of, neighbours who do not translate every challenge into a political idiom.

Camphill's antidote to this is to put people whose primary motivation is to build radical democracy alongside those motivated by a desire to care for other humans, as well as individuals motivated by a deep connection to the land. By including people whose disabilities prevent them from participating in politics in the usual sense (for example, nonverbal individuals, or individuals with social phobias), Camphill challenges their politically-minded companions to imagine more diverse and subtle strategies for achieving political inclusion.

The multi-faceted challenges involved in helping people of diverse abilities participate in political decision-making are closely related to the challenge of giving the natural world a democratic voice. Most Camphills are ideally situated to help residents incorporate plants and animals into decision-making processes. As many residents live and work in the same space, they have the opportunity to pay close attention to natural rhythms and the way these rhythms can be disrupted by human behaviour at local and global levels. Most communities include gardens, livestock, and wild spaces, so Camphillers get to know wild and domesticated plants and animals, gaining insight into their diversities and commonalities.

The diverse abilities of Camphillers similarly widen the overall community's awareness of plants and animals. For example, some people who have trouble reading the emotions of other human beings are deeply sensitive to the emotions and needs of animals, and can communicate these insights to their less sensitive human companions. Individuals who may be 'slow' at achieving physical or mental tasks may be correspondingly deep in their capacity for close attention to the here and now. People who are unusually sensitive to changes in seasonal or daily rhythms, and thus prone to extreme reactions when those rhythms are disrupted, can help others of us understand the ways we may be harmed by rhythmic disruptions that we would not otherwise notice.

I mentioned above that technology and the built environment must also be taken into account in democratic practice. It might appear that Camphill places, with their relatively low-tech lifestyles, might not have much to contribute to this challenge. I argue, however, that Camphill has much to teach us about how to live in a future in which technological advances change nearly everyone's relationship to productive work. Five thousand years ago, a rough equality prevailed among individuals because most of the goods available to any one person had to be produced by that person's own labour. Today, by contrast, the vast majority of the goods that I enjoy are the product, not of my own labour or that of my neighbours, but of the accumulated technological capital of past generations – and that technological capital is growing at an unprecedented rate. In the United States especially, there are no good mechanisms for ensuring that the wealth of past generations is equitably distributed; hence, income inequality is rapidly increasing with the expansion of technology.

My preferred antidote to this problem, one shared by many Camphillers, would be the distribution of a universal basic income. Under such a system, similar to what is already in place in many Camphills, every person would be guaranteed sufficient income to provide for their food, shelter, clothing, education and other basic needs. Many would still choose to work for additional income, but they would have greater freedom to choose activities that are socially and individually beneficial. No-one would be forced to work under unjust circumstances, or in an enterprise contributing to social harm, merely in order to survive. The environment would also benefit, as people would spend less time producing unnecessary consumer goods and more time engaged in intrinsically rewarding activities.

A universal basic income would create a new set of challenges for the many people who have come to experience identity and self-worth primarily in terms of their capacity to generate income. However, these challenges will beset us even without a universal basic income, as robotics and artificial intelligence increasingly replace human labour. Some experts predict, for example, that self-driving cars will become widespread within a decade, displacing thousands of people currently employed as truckers, taxi drivers, and transit workers. As robots replace factory workers and then middle managers, more and more of us will need to find meaning and purpose in 'non-productive' activities, and will need to resist the concentration of political power among the technocratic elite.

Camphills are home to many people who have already been judged incapable of being economically 'productive' on the terms of the mainstream economy. These people have already been developing alternative paths to identity and purpose, paths that might include practising a traditional craft, maintaining a loving household, forging lifelong friendships, meditating, and spending time in nature. As Helen Zipperlen's experience illustrates, these are the qualities that draw so-called non-disabled persons to Camphill.

In short, the Camphill movement is a laboratory for a new democracy that touches all aspects of human experience, that honours the equal rights of people who are very diverse in ability, and that is adapted to both the environmental crisis and the technological revolution that face humanity today. It is not the only such laboratory: similar work is being done in the 'New Economy' and 'Transition Town' movements, among social entrepreneurs, creating organisations that are neither traditional charities nor profit-obsessed businesses, and in some cases within activist groups created by persons with disabilities. As each of these impulses expands and learns from the others, society as a whole may soon achieve a new commitment to democratic community.

The Widening Impact of
an Intentional Supportive Community

DIEDRA HEITZMAN

Introduction

Just like family life, healthy community life can be challenging. As our perceptions become global, relatedness to neighbours and our locality can become less personal and important. We are stretched between what we long for on a macro level, such as peace, justice and sustainability, and relationships on a micro level, and between what we have to do and what we want to do. What really matters? How can our communities and societies shape themselves to address macro and micro levels, global and personal? How can we nurture personal dignity and health and at the same time contribute to, rather than detract from, global and planetary health? Can we attend to our own personal needs without compromising someone or something else? Can each person's inviolable spirit be honoured along with the wellbeing of our planet?

In intentional supportive communities such as Camphill villages, these questions can be asked, along with others that are related: can we live responsibly and authentically with people who have different mental and emotional challenges? Can we learn with them – often, but not only, lessons of the heart – and apply these lessons more widely to our lives and communities? Can we in this way discover how to make life better?

Camphill was founded by refugees with tragic past experiences from the Second World War, who embodied high ideals nourished from studying Rudolf Steiner's works, and by children with so-called 'intellectual and developmental challenges'. The study of ideas from Steiner's work, including social, economic, educational, artistic, therapeutic, agricultural, medical and developmental indications, led to an intensely creative community life, and opened up ways to address the questions posed above. Camphillers came to see that people with disabilities are not to be left out of the earth's positive evolutionary equation. The qualities and needs of people with disabilities call forth others' gifts, and thus these qualities and needs make true contributions to the micro and macro community. From a socially conscious life-sharing model comes precious and personal, life-changing growth for everyone open to serious community involvement. Personal growth, regardless of ability or challenges, can coalesce with community strength to expand culturally, socially and productively into the wider society.

Personal growth and community

Some progressive child-rearing experts advise telling a child, 'share because you want to, not because you have to', in order to teach that sharing is a free deed. To do the very best work from our own fount of capacities, we need to be clear and truthful about our own ability to share – to give, or not give, to others in healthy ways. Therefore, having something to share means, at its best, having the inner strength and resourcefulness to know when, how and what to share. Unlimited sharing can enable dependency, while a lack of charity can cause abuses and unnecessary suffering. One of the ideals of Camphill is finding how to be of help in truly healthy ways, which therefore calls for contemplative practice, self-knowledge and self-development. It is a call to witness and inspire self-knowledge in others, so that developing, encouraging and challenging each other becomes uplifting community practice.

In turn, an interactive community culture can potentially maximise personal growth. It is relevant here to note Rudolf Steiner's maxim that the healthy social life is found when the whole community finds its reflection in each individual's soul, and when the virtue of each one is living in the community. We coexist and depend on others for countless services and other things, whether that be shoes or other products that we use daily. In recognising our interdependence, we can shape our daily lives, not just according to our own personal wishes and benefit, but also to the advantage of others who in turn may help meet needs in our lives. From this, a culture develops that can then support larger goals which serve beyond ourselves and the community. Support is given by agreed schedules, shared use of resources, following through on commitments, and a willingness to change what needs to be changed. In Camphill communities, shared culture is a support, and can be especially helpful to those who might founder in unstructured or self-structured environments. In such a culture, there is space to make choices for more significant issues as the less significant issues are 'givens'.

The Camphill experience weaves together ideals and capacities, putting ideas to work 'on the ground'. Ways are found to work effectively together, and to offer and demonstrate that work to the wider world, even if only in local and humble ways. Elements of social renewal are brought, so strongly hoped for by those refugees from Central Europe's devastation in the 1940s, into today's society and future endeavours. One such enduring community was established in 1972 by a number of experienced Camphillers, with land and buildings donated by the Myrin family in Pennsylvania, USA.

Camphill Village Kimberton Hills

There are a number of reasons why you might visit Camphill Village Kimberton Hills. You might simply think of it as a place to get your vegetables each summer. Or you might know it as a biodynamic training centre, or as an example of intentional community living, or perhaps as a friendly neighbour and community partner. Perhaps you might see it as a place where people with intellectual and/or developmental disabilities live alongside their non-labelled counterparts, a model for home–integrated elder care, a local source for wholesome food, or maybe as a place to attend or participate in performances, workshops or conferences. You might view it as a place to help students of varying ages learn about all manner of skills, including sustainability, agriculture, health care and therapies, as well as innovative management, building design or entrepreneurial partnerships. You might see it as a valuable place to volunteer for a day, a year or a lifetime.

The mission of Kimberton Hills is:

> to create and maintain a land-based community including adults with special needs. Inspired by Anthroposophy, members of the community support one another to contribute to the wider society through biodynamic agriculture, craft, and other ecological, social, cultural and educational endeavours.

Residents of Kimberton Hills live in diverse households, work together in enterprises throughout the village, and interact with the surrounding community in a variety of ways. There is an emphasis on engendering resilience, including use of sustainable practices, biodynamic farming and ecological building. The community has the dual aspects of a nonprofit corporation and an intentional community, and encourages participation in decision-making and governance. It includes people of all ages, with children and seniors seen as valuable contributors. As a community it values intelligent communitarian use of resources in partnership with local businesses, dedicated donors and social enterprises. Members work to create congruence between community ideals and all areas of involvement.

Locality presence and community life

Kimberton Hills is home to about 120 people but its activities engage a population of well over three thousand people comprising neighbours, volunteers, employees, partners, donors, and customers, among others, who are involved in its community life in any one year. It includes a public café, the organic/biodynamic Sankanac Community Supported Agriculture Garden (CSA) with 300 or more shareholding families, a certified organic grass-fed raw milk dairy with local sales, the privately owned Sweetwater Bakery and Birchrun Hill Farm artisan cheesemakers. Fibre arts, herbs, clay, and orchard workshops make products sold on-site and at local stores, farmers' markets and craft fairs.

Residents of Kimberton Hills experience a variety of social interactions and vocational opportunities, as well as a range of healthy life options. The community's organisational structure is participatory and process oriented to help everyone express their capacities. All adult residents are acknowledged partners in the community's wellbeing, and are given opportunities to participate in decision making groups and on the board. The community encourages volunteers by hosting one-, two-, and three-year residencies for individuals from across America and around the world. Some interns are accepted for shorter amounts of time, and some people with and without disability labels settle to become long-term village residents.

Vulnerable people

While a wide range of people can be considered vulnerable in these times, individuals with intellectual and developmental disabilities often need significant support due to experiencing unemployment, poverty, and poor health. Trends in care for adults with disabilities show a shift away from locating individuals in large institutions towards including them in small-scale dispersed housing. Though the aim of this goal is to improve the quality of life for adults with disabilities, inclusion in dedicated housing does not in itself lead to increased social connectedness or better health. The experience of real community participation (Bigby 2004, Lutz 2015), access to stable, permanent and valued work (Fresher-Samways et al. 2003) and good physical health (Robertson et al. 2000) can be lacking. Even in the best economic circumstances, people with developmental disabilities continue to experience higher rates of unemployment, discrimination, poor health, and low social status compared with the general population (Cummins 2001, Havercamp et al. 2004, Jackson 2015).

Results from a recent evaluation conducted by the Camphill Association of North America, in partnership with researchers from the University of Toronto and Immaculata University, confirmed that Camphill communities in North America, including Kimberton Hills, provide a high quality of life for adults with disabilities. This particular form of intentional community living scored higher than the four other options considered by the researchers, namely: large congregate settings ('institutions'), small congregate settings (group homes), independent living, and family inclusion. Camphill was also shown to be a particularly successful and viable alternative to those other forms, providing a lifestyle of engagement for adults with disabilities and enabling them to exercise meaningful control over life choices (Goeschel & Heitzman 2010).

However, by way of contrast, in many situations, adults with intellectual and/or developmental disabilities are either recipients or consumers of a service in which there is a differentiation between those who serve and those who receive that service; or between those who contract services and those who provide them. These situations can fail to give credit to the abilities that people possess, or, by design, create a hierarchy that diminishes the dignity of the person with disabilities or the caregiver, or both. Significantly, with care models that are run as businesses, where people are seen as consumers or clients, the reverse of independence often results, with human dignity undermined (Jackson 2015).

While past cases of negligence and abuse have prompted current foundations and charitable organisations, such as the ARC for People with Intellectual and Development Disabilities and the Mental Health Foundation, to encourage independent decision-making by the consumers of service, Camphill intentional communities seek to address the need for independence by acknowledging that, as human beings, we all need the help of others, and to learn from, and care for, each other.

An important question here is, what makes for a good life? While individual choice is significant, there is good reason to believe that, beyond food, housing and basic needs, most people need genuine social engagement and authentic relationships to fulfill their lives – something to live for, feel secure in, and through which to develop and be recognised. As Atul Gawande suggests in his book, *Being Mortal*, people need to feel they are 'of use' (Gawande 2014).

The human longing for a home is strong, and notably refugees suffer that deep longing. We feel that a sense of belonging is important, and we all need a place where we can move at ease and where we can be supported by those who know us and who help us to know ourselves. A secure and loving home life can allow us to go confidently into the world, while a thoughtful and responsive community can give each person a genuine sense of belonging and usefulness. This happens in and around Kimberton Hills, where the fabric of interconnectedness generates increased creative interconnections.

Toward healthy cooperation

Intentional community living emphasises both independence and interdependence, providing work and living situations in which to make active contributions. Kimberton Hills' emphasis on practical living and environmental sustainability creates a variety of responsibilities; everyone is needed to help out and by so doing can develop personal competencies. Residents here have real, meaningful lives with opportunities for individual growth, social connectedness and authentic community participation.

In Kimberton Hills, each adult works mornings and afternoons during the week, returning home for shared meals. Some may visit other houses, the café or other local restaurants for meals. Some work alongside others in households, as homemaking is considered a significant vocation. Others help at the organic/biodynamic garden, at the café and craft shop, or deliver bread to the local store. After work there are opportunities to attend events in the village, or at the local school, bookstore, or theatre. Adults may volunteer at the nearby animal shelter, or as firefighters. Others take goods to local farmers' markets or fairs, and attend area social and/or self-advocacy groups. Some are involved in local government initiatives. Abilities and interests change as we age, and these often can be accommodated in village life. In elder years, each person can be valued, and those who become infirm can live in a house specially designed to bring life, culture, and care into balance.

A strong educational emphasis at Kimberton Hills includes cultural events open to the public, and internal and open courses. Specific adult educational opportunities take place, including participation in the college-level integrative Camphill Academy courses. Spiritual life as well as self-development, study, and celebration are also nurtured. There is an active culture of review meetings for all elements of the community, and encouragement for each individual adult to help each other meet challenges and flourish.

There is a choice of spiritual opportunities available for community members, such as attending a non-denominational Christian worship service held weekly in the village, a Christian denomination's monthly services, and/or visiting other local churches or temples. Holidays are celebrated, with the four seasonal Christian festivals (Easter, Midsummer or St John's, Michaelmas, and Christmas): all times of profound celebration.

Creativity is encouraged, and paintings from professional and/or amateur artists hang in every house, with changing gallery exhibits in shared spaces. Many residents are artistically engaged in activities that vary from individual initiatives and workshops to the village orchestra, music lessons, plays, study or therapeutic work. Learning to do things well through craft, can help establish a sense of competency and strengthen the will to follow through on initiatives.

Village residents eat mainly biodynamically and/or organically grown food, and get regular exercise and plenty of fresh air. Positive outcomes of this have been well-documented; for example, there are currently no issues of obesity, diabetes or pre-diabetic conditions present in the community, and the average level of prescribed medication among those with disabilities is even lower than the population of non-disabled people in the same age group (Stagnitti 2006). The community's lifestyle appears to contribute to health and wellbeing in many ways, and in some situations may make behavioural medications, as well as other pharmaceutical interventions, unnecessary. Of course, life is not risk-free, and accidents and illnesses occur, so a health centre is available for support and walk-in visits. This houses two part-time nurses with anthroposophical training, as well as other practitioners who provide therapies and health education.

A genuine choice is crucial for those who may consider joining the village. During a trial visit, applicants live in a household and join different workshops or job activities, meeting many of the community members. If the visit proves a mutually good fit, then arrangements are made to integrate new members into the community when openings occur.

Those who make the community their lifelong home and those who come for shorter periods of time have opportunities to develop genuine and long-term friendships, as well as new relationships. These friendships contribute to a deep sense of belonging. They develop regardless of labels, and are facilitated by an environment in which it is possible to walk to a friend's house, share meals, work together with others and enjoy spontaneous and planned activities and celebrations. Over time they can deepen the ability to genuinely accept and appreciate differences in both oneself and others. Learning to be oneself, making allowances, acknowledging and encouraging others, finding avenues for growth, and developing a deep awareness of one another are all challenges which are difficult to quantify. Jean Vanier refers to this when he states, 'People are crying out for authentic community where they can share their lives with others with a common vision, where they can find support' (2001, p.2). This kind of involvement gives rise to what Helen Zipperlen calls developing the 'thinking heart' by allowing each person to be cherished and to develop further.

> The guiding image, the culture of the thinking heart
> discloses that we can only be responsible when we accept
> the personal and communal discipline of actively integrating
> commitment, action and thinking. This discipline is what we
> need from one another; without it no system of safeguards
> and no approach to service can realise the opportunities in
> our crisis... (Zipperlen & O'Brien 1994, p.73).

The 'crisis' Zipperlen refers to is that of funding, of alternatives and of safety which affect the disabilities movement and individuals.

Economic stability

People who live in the Camphill community choose this life. The benefits are not to be found in financial rewards, as neither those with or without disabilities are salaried. Each person's work is valuable to the whole, regardless of how society might see its value. Budgeting is done collectively, allocating funds to household and workplaces based on varying need. People with and without disabilities contribute government entitlement funds, those with less economic viability contribute funding, and all contribute by abjuring salaries and equity.

While frugal and careful, the community still relies on income from some families or trusts. For much of its history, people with significant challenges have joined regardless of an 'ability to pay'. In these circumstances, therefore, the community has relied on charitable contributions and sales of its own products. Currently, with some exceptions, those newly admitted with special needs bring cost-covering payments until there can be a sufficient reserve to invite others without such funding. Here the cost for adults with disabilities is substantially less than that of traditional models, currently estimated to be between one half and one sixth the cost of state-funded, or other private, options (Larson et al. 2010).

Kimberton Hills is able to achieve this cost management through intelligent communitarian use of resources, partnerships with local businesses, rentals, dedicated donors, and enterprises that provide income and vocational opportunities. The village enterprises regularly fund one quarter or more of the cost of the community's operating budget. Another quarter comes from charitable support that friends, neighbours, foundations and corporations contribute. Entitlement funds that go to individuals and family pledges make up the other half. Because the village contains well over one hundred people, cooperative purchasing is possible. There is a moderate degree of self-sufficiency, as households get a large amount of fruit, vegetables, dairy products and bread from enterprises within the village. Community members donate time to pick up, distribute, and compost food from local health food and specialty stores, thus cutting food waste. They also recycle the packaging that would otherwise be sent to landfills.

It is estimated that current resident volunteer contributions (those who would otherwise be employable and drawing salaries) offset *at least* $1.5 million of the potential operating cost of Kimberton Hills. This community employs eight people (five of whom are part-time) who live outside the village and relies on independent contractors for some infrastructure projects and auditing. The village maintains a strong eco-sensitive ethos by recycling, upcycling, sharing and making do by using what is available.

Kimberton Hills maintains several rental properties on the premises which provide both income and flexibility. A few facilities, such as woodworking and cheese-making, fall in and out of village use based on the interests and skills of individuals. Here, the community approach shows itself to be different from an institutional or business model. By renting available space to local enterprises or individuals, the community is more involved in the local economy. For instance, several years ago a local dairy farming family was struggling financially. As it happened Kimberton Hills had unused cheese-making facilities that were doubling as storage space. This space was subsequently rented to the family, who now pay a low rent, and a percentage of their gross profits goes to the village for the use of space and equipment. The family's artisan cheese sales have allowed the farm to thrive. The village maintains a similar relationship with a family-owned bakery that operates in the heart of the village, and a local retired university pottery teacher uses workshop space in exchange for mentoring village potters.

Environmental sustainability

Developing sound ecological practices is a fundamental tenet of Kimberton Hills. The village has won, among other awards, the 2008 Pennsylvania Environment Council's Sustainability Award, and the 2012 Gene Wilson Climate Protection Award, with citations from the Pennsylvania Senate and House, and the Chester County Commissioners for its commitment to environmental sustainability. Several buildings were constructed or substantially renovated in 2003–8, and now feature sustainable recycled and/or recyclable materials, rooftop water catchment systems, sunlight tubes and an attic fan system to replace or augment air conditioning. There is a constructed wetland garden that filters wastewater and has native wetlands plants. Solar panels mounted on a nearby garage, built by village residents with windfall lumber, partially meet the community's electricity needs, and additional electricity that is purchased by the village comes from renewable sources. The café and bakery are heated and cooled using a geothermal system. Residents use many ecologically sound daily practices, and usually opt to walk or bike to and from work; cars and errands are shared. Yet with aging buildings (some built as early as the late 1700s), there is still much to improve.

Kimberton Hills received a perfect rating from the Cornucopia Institute (2016) for its dairy which provides milk to village households, to the locally-owned Kimberton Whole Foods, and the local organic company, Seven Stars Yogurt, as well as manure for compost to add to nutrition in the fields. The Institute assessed approximately 110 farms and distributors for best practices in organic dairy farming. The Sankanac CSA garden is run on biodynamic principles by village garden managers and crew, including apprentices in biodynamics, and provides food for 300 families or more. Along with the dairy, orchard, and herb garden, the community produces a seasonal mix of vegetables, meat, eggs, herbs, fruit and flowers for village households, the café, and the surrounding community. Mixed CSA livestock includes bees, cows, draft horses, goats, sheep, pigs, and donkeys. The emphasis is on creating a balanced ecosystem by utilising biodynamic preparations and practices, and forgoing chemical pesticides, herbicides or factory produced fertilisers. A corollary is an appreciation of insect and other wildlife: for instance, bat houses, beehives, bluebird and swallow houses have been built and used on site and are also sold. The community has hosted public lectures and workshops on effective composting and ecological beekeeping, while Sherry Wildfeuer, a village resident, creates the Kimberton Hills Agricultural Calendar called *Stella Natura*, and has done so for nearly forty years. It is commercially available to home and professional gardeners worldwide: www.stellanatura.com

Some of the community's 100 acres of woodlands border French Creek, a river with an 'Exceptional Value' designation. A study commissioned by the French and Pickering Creeks

Conservation Trust found that the healthiest part of the creek was found to border Kimberton Hills' property. This is likely to be attributable to biodynamic practices as well as riparian buffer zones enhanced by community members and other volunteers.

Financial ideals into practice

The Kimberton Hills community philosophy includes aligning money management with its philosophical and spiritual intentions. Although the village does not have an endowment *per se*, its cash reserves are placed with organisations that are dedicated to operate in ways that:

- are socially responsible and renewable;
- are environmentally sound and corrective;
- benefit their communities and employees;
- work out of, or are supportive of, anthroposophy (as introduced by Rudolf Steiner).

The reserves are invested in local banks and otherwise pooled for investment by professional, socially-responsible managers. Kimberton Hills has loaned money to the locally-owned Kimberton Whole Foods to help develop additional stores. Thus, the village utilises an investment strategy to reflect its values outside its premises, as well as within its own community (Heitzman & Yen 2011).

Sharing with others

Kimberton Hills maintains an intimate connection to the land, with strong and enduring connections to the wider surrounding community, particularly in its work in the arts, education and culture. All these aspects are supported by the community's commitment to both study and integrate ideas developed from the work of Rudolf Steiner (1861–1925), and pediatrician and social innovator Karl König (1902–1966), the originator of the Camphill village concept.

Interacting with customers, volunteers, and visitors is part of Kimberton Village life. A varied landscape makes it welcoming for educational groups, from middle schoolers studying sustainability to university students undertaking service learning projects. The village has attracted classes studying architecture and land use, those learning about sustainable lifestyles and people interested in alternatives to conventional care situations. There are courses in biodynamic gardening and farming, social therapy, anthroposophy, movement, and the art of caring for elders, as well as nursing, nutrition and therapy workshops. The community provides a venue for other local initiatives to hold workshops and meetings. The community's Myrin Library, open to village residents and the general public, houses a large collection of Rudolf Steiner's works and related books.

At the centre of the community is Rose Hall, which hosts workshops, conferences, lectures, plays, dances, parties and concerts. Designed by Camphill Architect Joan Allen, it was designated the 'Best Live Music Venue' in Chester County by the *Philadelphia Inquirer* in 2008. It serves as a centre for local anthroposophical activities, as well as for other public events. This community venue is similar to other halls and centres found in Camphill communities throughout the world, allowing initiatives that foster community cohesion and varied interaction, as well as creative ventures.

Conclusion

Community members do not consider Camphill Village Kimberton Hills a community for people with disabilities because they see themselves living alongside each other and working together to create an unpretentiously valid and useful life. While it is possible to describe many aspects of this community, as has been done above, it is in fact the totality of the intentions, work, creativity, processes, ideals, products, support and experiences that together make it possible to create something that makes good sense. Something larger than each of these aspects is born when they are working together. That synergy can be radiant for those who discover it.

Many aspects of life are integrated in ways that not only affirm, but also evolve and adapt the original intentions of the Camphill founders. There is ongoing work to refresh the original impulses and develop these naturally in response to arising needs. This involves study, personal development work, community practices, openness to initiatives, critical analysis and review, substantial planning, and the will to evolve. It involves being open and inviting to those in the surrounding area, to local and world needs. A cosmopolitan approach to world issues can be experienced in the promotion of sound ecological practices and social inventiveness. The Camphill community, in uniting people from diverse backgrounds, ages and abilities in reciprocal and authentic relationships, makes it possible to create together what would otherwise be difficult to achieve. Those in the community aim and, to an extent, are able, to serve not only their own needs but also those of the wider world.

References

Bigby, C. (2004) 'But why are these questions being asked? A commentary on Emerson', *Intellectual and Developmental Disability*, 29: 202–205.

Cornucopia Institute (2016). *Organic Dairy Scorecard.* http://www.cornucopia.org/dairysurvey/index.html.

Cummins, R. (2001) 'Living with supports in the community: Predictors of satisfaction with life', *Mental Retardation and Developmental Disabilities Research Reviews*, 7: 99–104.

Fresher-Samways, K., Raush, S., Choi, K., Desrosiers, Y. & Steel, G. (2003) 'Perceived quality of life of adults with developmental and other significant disabilities', *Disabilities and Rehabilitation*, 25: 1097–1105.

Gawande, A. (2014) *Being Mortal: Medicine and what matters in the end.* New York: Metropolitan Books/Henry Holt & Company.

Goeschel, J. & Heitzman, D. (2010) *Providing Quality of Life through Intentional Community Living: Outcomes evaluation for the Camphill AmeriCorps Education Award Program of the Camphill Association of North America (Inc. University of Toronto).* The Camphill Association of North America.

Havercamp, S., Scanlin, D. & Roth, M. (2004) 'Health disparities among adults with developmental disabilities, adults with other disabilities, and adults not reporting disability in North Carolina', *Public Health Rep*, Jul–Aug, 119(4): 418–426. http://www.ncbi.nlm.nih.gov/pmc/articles/PMC1497651/.

Heitzman, D. & Yen, J. (2011) 'Camphill Village Kimberton Hills: Innovations in intentional supportive community living', *The Philadelphia Social Innovations Journal.* http://philasocialinnovations.org/journal/articles/disruptive-innovations/359-camphill-village-kimberton-hills-innovations-in-intentional-supportive-community-living.

Jackson, R. (2015) *Who Cares? The impact of ideology, regulation and marketisation on the quality of life of people with an intellectual disability*. Sheffield: The Centre for Welfare Reform. http://www.centreforwelfarereform.org/library/by-az/who-cares1.html.

Larson, S., Ryan, A., Salmi, P., Smith, D., & Wuorio, A. (2010) *Residential Services for Persons with Developmental Disabilities: Status and trends through 2010*. Minneapolis: University of Minnesota, Research and Training Center on Community Living, Institute on Community Integration.

Lutz, A. (2015) 'Who decides where autistic adults live?' *The Atlantic*. http://www.theatlantic.com/health/archive/2015/05/who-decides-where-autistic-adults-live/393455/.

Robertson, J., Emerson, E., Gregory, N., Hatton, C. Turner, S., Kessissoglou, S. & Hallam, A. (2000) 'Lifestyle related risk factors for poor health in residential settings for people with intellectual disabilities', *Research in Developmental Disabilities*, 21: 469–486.

Stagnitti, M. (2006) 'Average number of total (including refills) and unique prescriptions by selected person characteristics', *Medical Expenditure Panel Survey: Statistical Brief #245*, 1–8. http://meps.ahrq.gov/mepsweb/data_files/publications/st245/stat245.pdf.

Vanier, J. (2001) *Community and Growth*, Paulist Press, Mahwah, NJ.

Zipperlen, H. & O'Brien, J. (1994) *Cultivating Thinking Hearts: Letters from the Lifesharing Safeguards Project*. Camphill Village Kimberton Hills.

Re-thinking Work in Relation to Community Inclusion

MARIA LYONS

Introduction

Access to employment has become a key component of strategies to improve levels of community participation and inclusion for people with intellectual disabilities. This chapter begins by describing the thinking behind this objective and some of the ongoing obstacles facing people with intellectual disabilities in their efforts to secure employment. It goes on to suggest that these obstacles cannot be surmounted without a fundamental re-examination of the framework within which we are operating, specifically regarding the differences, both real and potential, between the concepts of 'employment' and 'work'.

This chapter argues that the cultural and economic trends which have seen work become defined increasingly narrowly as an activity performed to earn pay, have a particularly negative impact on people with intellectual disabilities, both in terms of ensuring that their rights are respected, and that their gifts and contributions to society are fully honoured. Here Camphill is seen as illustrating a framework which has developed an alternative approach to disability and work, resting on an interpretation of 'work' which de-emphasises the pecuniary aspect at the same time as celebrating the qualities of service and personal fulfilment. Some practices resulting from this conceptualisation of work, and evidence of outcomes for people with intellectual disabilities, will also be discussed.

Employment as a route to inclusion

There are many reasons why, in recent years, access to employment has come to be such a prominent feature in policies affecting people with an intellectual disability. From a human rights perspective, the case is quite simple: most people work, so why should people with intellectual disabilities not have equal prospects in this sphere of life? Work is often a crucial factor in identity formation, something that is acknowledged in the UK Government's 2009 strategic report on learning disability:

> Work defines us: what will you be when you grow up?
> What do you do for a living? These are questions we all face from others when people want to get to know us.
> But they are questions seldom directed towards people with learning disabilities. (Department of Health 2009, p.86)

Beyond the basic argument of an individual's rights, work represents many other potential benefits for people with intellectual disabilities. Greater financial freedom can increase autonomy and lead to a sense of empowerment as individuals experience previously unknown levels of control over their own lives and the world around them. This in turn can lead to greater confidence, independent decision-making and heightened self-awareness. Having a job has the potential to improve social integration and a sense of community, as it creates opportunities for forming relationships and social interaction both within and outside the workplace. A job also tends to confer social status. It is well established that both the social and self-determination dimensions of work have an impact on the subjective quality of life indicators, particularly psychological wellbeing and mental health (Jahoda 2008, Trembath 2010). Objective quality of life can also be positively affected, since going to work constitutes a regular daytime activity or excursion, counteracting sedentary lifestyles and the associated health problems that are known to disproportionately afflict people with intellectual disabilities.

A further reason for the emphasis on work is that the increasingly common practice of consulting service users themselves has revealed a significant proportion expressing the desire to work. A survey of close to three thousand adults with an intellectual disability in England, commissioned by the Department of Health in 2003/4, reported that 65per cent of those who were unemployed would like a job (Emerson 2005). This figure is frequently repeated by influential disability advocacy groups and in policy documents. A survey of six hundred people with an intellectual disability, carried out in Scotland in 2006, reported that 'at least as many again as are working want to work' (Curtice 2006, p.34). Positive responses to the question 'do you want to work' have generally been interpreted as a desire for paid employment. Where responses are ambiguous or negative, there is speculation that the cause is a lack of familiarity with the option, rather than a lack of motivation for, or interest in, work. Indeed, the White Paper *Valuing People Now* identified low expectations as the strategy's 'biggest challenge' (Department of Health 2009, p.87).

Improving employment figures for people with intellectual disabilities thus requires a two-fold approach: on the one hand, a campaign to transform entrenched attitudes relating to work and disability, and on the other, the development of practical schemes and support programmes to enable greater participation in the world of work. Since 2001, it has been a key target of successive UK governments to move people with intellectual disabilities, wherever possible, into paid work, with the ultimate goal of achieving parity with other disabled people in the workforce (Department of Health 2001, p.85). Numerous policies, tax and benefit reforms, and cross-departmental strategies have been introduced to facilitate this, all sitting within the broader framework of the 'welfare to work' agenda that has been a core ideological commitment of all main political parties since the 1990s.

The clearest expression of a shift away from welfare to what has become known as 'workfare', is represented by the introduction of the Employment and Support Allowance which replaced incapacity benefits in 2008. The terminology itself reveals the intention to link eligibility for state support more closely to the labour market, with receipt of benefits for the majority of claimants becoming conditional on seeking, or engaging in, paid employment. In 2011, what was previously a collection of specialised support schemes was incorporated into one universal marketised welfare–to–work programme. This plan has overseen the task of achieving sustained employment outcomes for those at risk of long-term unemployment (with or without the label of disability) outsourced to a variety of mainly private sector organisations. The Work Programme is designed to incentivise work providers by rewarding them on the basis of results, where results are defined in terms of the length of time a participant is employed: 'The longer a customer stays in work, the more delivery partners will be paid' (Department for Work and Pensions 2012, p.3).

In spite of this agenda, there has been only limited success over the last decade in moving people with intellectual disabilities off benefits and into paid work. Research between 2011 and 2013 suggests that in England approximately seven per cent are in some form of paid employment, and these positions are predominantly part-time and low-paid (Beyer 2014). People with intellectual disabilities are shown to be considerably more disadvantaged even than other so-called 'impairment groups' in terms of rates of employment, types of work and levels of unemployment (Coleman et al. 2013). The barriers to work facing people specifically with learning or mental health-related problems are multiple and complex. Personal barriers include low expectations and low motivation, possibly linked to a lack of confidence, anxiety and/or unfair treatment and prejudice, whether actually experienced or merely anticipated. People with intellectual disabilities are more likely to lack formal qualifications, to have low levels of numeracy and literacy, and to lack work experience, than those with physical disabilities or those without disabilities. Individuals with intellectual disabilities are also more likely to present challenging behaviour and have difficulty in understanding tacit codes of conduct and communication in work settings (Coleman et al. 2013, Trembath 2010, Milner 2005).

Externally, a major obstacle has been the inadequacy, and in some cases even counter-productivity, of the very mechanisms set up to help people find work. In particular, this occurs where a one-size-fits-all approach requires especially vulnerable people to take part in mainstream schemes which do not observe these vulnerabilities. As indicated above, the fundamental reasoning of the workfare agenda is that it is the interaction between social security benefit rules and employment which constitutes the principal 'disincentive' to work (Department of Health 2001, p.85). In a study analysing the failure of the Coalition Government (of 2010–2014) to come even close to targets set for people with disabilities in employment, Hale found that it is this 'mistaken assumption' at the heart of Government policy that has created 'a regime of conditionality and sanctions'. This system has left participants 'demoralised, and further away from achieving their work-related goals or participating in society than when they started' (Hale 2014, p.5). Instead of receiving personalised support, people with diverse types of disability are compelled to perform mandatory activities which take no account of the large gap that may exist between a capacity for work-related activity and the capacity to find and keep a job in a competitive labour market.

> This gap is not caused by a culture of dependency
> and won't be narrowed by compulsion to engage with
> the labour market. The generic work preparation activities
> imposed on respondents, such as CV writing, appears
> of little benefit while their limited capability for work,
> resulting from their disability or illness, remains unaddressed
> (Hale 2014, p.6).

While the deficiencies of welfare-to-work programmes are well recognised, the greatest impediment to increasing levels of employment for people with intellectual disabilities is one which raises fundamental and unanswered questions both about the viability and the value of this objective in itself. The reality is that there are not enough jobs that match the skills and limitations of people with intellectual disabilities. Employers must be highly committed to the task, and adequate support networks must be in place to help employees overcome the multifaceted challenges and vulnerabilities referred to already. Few mainstream businesses are able or willing to accommodate this need. Moreover, employment as a route to inclusion seems all the more untenable in an economic environment where technological advances are fast reducing demand for unskilled and low-skilled labour, and competition for such work grows increasingly fierce.

Beyond the practical barriers to participation caused by contradictory trends in the market and official policy, government focus on measuring the 'success' of work programmes purely in terms of employment duration, means insufficient attention is being given to exploring the social and emotional impact of employment on people with intellectual disabilities where it has been provided. There is evidence to suggest that, while employment often enhances opportunities for social engagement, for some people with intellectual disabilities the contact that they have with work peers does not necessarily translate into a sense of belonging, or the development of reciprocal and supportive relationships (Jahoda 2008). The rush to present employment as the answer has, to a certain extent, overshadowed the original question, which was how to foster meaningful inclusion. The Scottish survey quoted above revealed that respondents with an intellectual disability had varied, and often quite loose, understandings of the concepts 'work' and 'job'. A genuinely personalised approach would need to probe more deeply into the meaning behind the language in individual cases.

When work becomes labour

For the disability rights movement, the effort to enable people with intellectual disabilities to access employment is based on the recognition that interacting with others in work is often fundamentally related to a person's sense of self-worth, identity, purpose and belonging within a social context. In his famous hierarchy of needs, Maslow identified 'commitment to an important job' as a key factor in 'the business of self-actualisation'. Morin captures all these elements in defining work as:

> primarily an activity whereby a person inserts himself into
> the world, exercises his talents, defines himself, actualises
> his potential and creates value, which in return gives him
> a sense of accomplishment and personal effectiveness, and
> possibly even a meaning to life (Morin 2008, p.2).

Significantly, Maslow's conception of 'work' incorporated caring, volunteering, artistic creation and scholarly endeavour as much as paid employment (Dean 2007). Although volunteerism and the self-organisation of civil society are increasingly promoted in political rhetoric as a public good, political practice firmly prioritises economic activity as the highway to social improvement, and construes the meaning of work in terms of waged or salaried labour.

> This restriction of the meaning of work to its economic
> aspect engenders or reinforces the contractual relationships
> between the individual and the employer organisation,
> conferring importance on remuneration to the detriment
> of the spirit of service and community (Morin 2008, p.1).

The devaluation of community service corresponds to an ideological presumption that individuals will only contribute something of value to their community or society as a whole if they are incentivised by mechanisms of financial reward and sanction. As such, unpaid activities, most notably caring for others, caring for house and home and caring for the land and our natural environment, go unrecognised and unrewarded, despite the undeniable reality that without freely given contributions in precisely these areas, the formal productive economy could not function.

Where welfare is concerned, the prevailing ideology promotes citizens' responsibility to unburden the system by maximising their 'human capital'. 'Policy therefore focuses on the opportunities that are made available to individuals to enhance their productive potential and their labour market readiness' (Dean 2007, p.18). While in the UK the Department for Work and Pensions (2006) labels this 'empowering', certain aspects of government policy are at best paternalistic and at worst morally authoritarian, where welfare dependents are hassled or coerced into taking on jobs, 'never mind how low paid, uncongenial or inappropriate' (Dean 2007, p.19). This sits uneasily with the notion of a human rights agenda honouring personal choice and autonomy. Moreover, treating an individual's productive potential exclusively in terms of economic capital 'has crucial ideological significance since it privileges a particular construction of what is to be valued about a person and her abilities' (Dean 2007, p.21).

As Amartya Sen pointed out:

> 'empowerment' is derived not merely from the ability to
> do something, but the freedom to do it. By insisting the
> individual must embrace for themselves a 'responsible'
> or correct form of functioning (i.e. labour market
> participation), advanced liberalism is, arguably, as much a
> corruption of the liberal ideal as the utilitarianism of the
> Poor Law era had been. (Dean 2007, p.22)

This confusion of agendas and ideologies forming the background to welfare-to-work has significant consequences for people with intellectual disabilities. Environments dominated by a competitive, individualist ethos, where 'negotiators pay more attention to salaries than to the treatment of human relations' (Morin 2008, p.1) will be an additional obstacle for those who are emotionally vulnerable, who have difficulty forming relationships, or who communicate and express themselves in unusual or unique ways. Likewise, for those whose capacities may not extend beyond simple household activities, like making a cup of tea or raking leaves, this framework amounts to automatic exclusion not because they cannot work, but because what they can do is not considered worthy of the term.

A final factor that is often overlooked in the job-placement strategy is that it is not any old job, but an important job, that has the potential to offer self-actualisation. How a worker perceives the relative importance of his or her work is vital, and this perception will be connected to an experience of how tasks relate to a wider purpose. This is not, therefore, a question of how menial or complex the task is, but a question of context. In the case of the intellectually disabled as much as for those without disabilities, policy and practice:

> should proceed not from the premise that 'work' is
> an enforceable individual obligation, but that it must
> necessarily have some socially constituted value and
> meaning if it is to be a means to social inclusion
> (Dean 2007, p.23).

Work as service: Camphill's approach to work and disability

As publicly contracted providers of support for people with intellectual disabilities, Camphill villages do not market themselves primarily as work placement programmes, even though what were once known as 'sheltered' workshops form a core part of daily routines in adult communities. Traditionally Camphill represents a 'whole package', where care is transformed into a lifestyle rather than a selection of individual services. Here, the jobs taken on by the less able are situated within a complex network of community activities, rituals and relationships. This integration or contextualisation is a key element in the Camphill approach to work.

A further feature that sets Camphill apart from the mainstream is the decoupling of work and money. Neither the disabled, nor their live-in staff are paid a salary. Money is distributed according to specific needs, for food, board, training, travel, dependents and leisure, but is not linked to specific tasks or roles. The communities operate on the basis that work is a voluntary social contribution. Introducing a wage incentive into the mix turns 'work' into 'labour', a process which is believed to distort not only the relationship between activities and their value, but also the quality of the relationships between the people carrying them out (Christie 1989).

This attitude to work has its roots in the economic and social theories of Rudolf Steiner, whose teachings heavily influenced the founders of Camphill. Lecturing in the early twentieth century, Steiner challenged the conventional notion that the defining principle in modern economic life is competitive individualism. He argued that competition, the free expression of individuality and the cultivation of difference, are characteristic features of the 'spiritual-cultural' sphere of social life, but that the logic of economic development points entirely in the opposite direction. Economic exchange is driven by material need, and in every transaction freely entered into, there would be no agreement without a mutual satisfaction of needs. This principle of mutuality can be seen on a larger scale in the tendency towards the division of labour and the growing interdependency of all economic agents. In practice, the more interconnected an economic system becomes through the division of labour, the less any individual participant can be said to work for himself or herself. All the products of individual labour are passed on to other people, and what the individual requires in turn is provided by wider society (Steiner 1972).

According to Steiner, then, altruism in economic relations is not simply an ethical consideration but an observable reality. This reality is obscured by the institutionalised norm of tying labour to wages. To work for wages is to provide predominantly for oneself, that is, in contradiction to the inherent logic of the division of labour. One sees oneself as working only to earn a living and not to meet a social need through the production of certain goods or services for the general community. The distinction has more than theoretical implications. To sell one's labour (rather than the products of it) means that the remuneration one receives has nothing to do with what one creates, or with the enterprise as a whole; the activity is performed for money rather than because it is considered intrinsically worthwhile by the person performing it, or indeed because it is desirable from a social perspective (Steiner 1972).

It was the notion that paid work has lost not only its social context but its social value that Camphill founder Karl König perceived to be of fundamental significance in any attempt to build inclusive communities. König led the group of women and men who started the first Camphill residential homes for 'handicapped' children and adults. He understood humans as essentially social beings, unable to thrive without genuine communication with and recognition by others. It is this self-defining or self-valorising contact with others which creates a sense of community, and it is the 'social womb' of community that people with intellectual disabilities are most frequently deprived of or isolated from (König 1959).

Today, this deprivation and isolation is well known; counteracting it is the main aim behind the ongoing de-institutionalisation of care facilities. It is also increasingly acknowledged, however, that relocation to mainstream settings alone seldom leads to social integration. To make up for the lack of naturally occurring support networks for people with intellectual disabilities an 'army of professional help has been mobilised' (Christie 1989, p.102). Writing in the 1950s, König fully appreciated the difficulties arising from the professionalisation of care. In particular, that contracted help is necessarily both rule-bound and nonreciprocal.

> Wages (not money!) create a barrier between the one who receives and the one who pays. To give and to take is a matter of mutual human relationships; the true relationship goes as soon as wages intervene. Paid service is no service; paid love is no love; paid help has nothing to do with help (König 1959, p.35).

Whereas practical assistance might be the obvious need on a physical level, at a psychological – some might say spiritual – level it is *friendship* which engenders the most powerful experience of being included. This is why the structures and practices of Camphill community life are designed to dissolve the association between tasks and monetary reward, in an effort to preserve the quality of service between friends and as such the equality of relationships between individuals with vastly dissimilar cognitive and practical abilities (Christie 1989, König 1959).

Attempting to transform what have become the normalised dynamics between able and disabled people is one aspect of Camphill's approach to work. Another relates to how the provision of work and skills development opportunities is socially contextualised. As we have seen, Steiner suggested that the commodification of labour undermines the relationships not only between merit and rewards, but between work, value and identity. For the waged or salaried employee, compelled by material need and the structure of the system to sell her labour, the amount of money it pays is inevitably associated with judgements about the value of the work, and thus with the level of self-esteem derived from it. This is in contrast to the volunteer, the parent, the lover or the friend, where the aims or purpose of the task will be more immediate than its financial returns and will also be the real source of its importance. Any sense of pride or status arising from it will be determined by the overall success of the endeavour, whether this is measured in terms of its usefulness to self, to others or to the planet. Furthermore, a key feature of the modern labour market is the tendency for ever higher degrees of removal between the specific tasks carried out by an individual and their end result, or between individuals' tasks and the objectives of the firm or organisation as a whole. In this scenario employees are left with little option but to identify with the wage rather than the work. Again, this working culture has particular implications for people with intellectual disabilities. Within it, the greater the severity of someone's cognitive, psychological or behavioural challenges, the less likely she will be able to perform the kind of job which confers social status or leads to the types of self-affirming experiences employment schemes are intended to offer.

Camphill thus aims to create situations where work is embedded into communal life in such a way that participants can experience directly how their contribution fits into a larger process. This means it is an advantage to have relatively enclosed or 'bounded' spaces, which is why many communities are modelled on the traditional rural village, with a small collection of households, a farm, a village store, a cafeteria, a bakery, and a variety of craft or trade workshops. Ideally in this setting, if a person's work is to prepare vegetables in one of the neighbouring households in the village, she will see by sitting down with them at lunch time that her actions benefit the members of that household; if she works in the bakery, she is partly responsible for producing food for the village; if she works the till in the village shop or makes tea in the cafeteria, she is literally serving visitors from the wider locality; if she makes furniture in the joinery, the small-scale dimension of the enterprise means the end result can be experienced as a personal as well as collective achievement.

A workshop is a mini community. A community where we can all feel equal. It is easy to see that all activities are important for the final product. If one link disappears,

177

consequences follow for the whole process … For each participant it is important to know that she or he is of importance to the totality (Leinslie, cited in Christie 1989, p.39).

In developing an alternative cultural framework around work, therefore, the Camphill approach assumes that there will be qualitative differences between having a job as one of the village cooks and taking on the duties of a kitchen porter in a large hotel, even if the skills employed are the same. The appropriateness of one or the other setting will depend completely on the personalities involved.

It is in the question of the appropriateness of setting that Camphill's methods appear on the surface to diverge from current views on what constitutes best practice for people with intellectual disabilities. To heighten levels of interconnectedness the 'totality' must of necessity be shrunk and contained to some extent. Camphill working environments are artificial in so far as they are unlike what the average person is accustomed to. In contrast, national policies reflect a broad consensus across the disabilities sector that specialised workshops are outdated, even unacceptable, and that integrated employment is preferable given the potential for exploitation, discrimination and other negative outcomes within segregated facilities.

However, what is rather emotively termed 'segregation' is only harmful where it in fact produces these undesirable experiences, just as integration can only be regarded a success where it mitigates or eliminates them. As a case study, Camphill illustrates the risks to diversity of rejecting or favouring either contained or integrated settings purely on principle. Research shows that not only are Camphill communities consistently rated as high-quality care providers according to generalised standards, but that it is specifically the two features discussed here – reciprocity and the social re-contextualisation of work – which are most consistently linked to reported experiences of meaningful participation, a sense of being valued, a sense of purpose and a sense of belonging (Lyons 2015).

In a climate where cost effectiveness is top of the agenda for public services, it remains unclear how Camphill's practices of shared living, volunteering and collective financing affect the public purse. This is something worth investigating in the light of the political focus on workfare and its twin policy of austerity. As Christie noted, however, it is not financial input that is the most interesting aspect of Camphill economies, but 'how they use their resources' (Christie 1989, p.42) to set up individually tailored responses to what are arguably universal human needs. This is by no means to suggest that the choice to enter the competitive labour market should be denied to people with intellectual disabilities, but rather to suggest that where normal life is not conducive to wellbeing, the fault may lie with the norms and not with the people attempting to live them.

Conclusion

Initiatives offering access to work are vital to enhancing community inclusion for people with intellectual disabilities, but they will have only limited success until what is regarded as 'work' allows for a far broader range of activities and pursuits than is currently represented by the formal labour market. The Camphill example demonstrates that even in the context of a national political preoccupation with contractual employment and the perceived imperatives of the financial economy, there is still considerable scope for local community projects and service providers to offer varied and meaningful daytime activities which take as their starting point participants' specific needs and abilities. Most importantly, while arrangements for funding support services undergo major changes, a crucial question will be whether the reforms help or hinder the capacity of providers to be innovative with available resources and offer people with intellectual disabilities the diversity of work-related opportunities they deserve.

References

Beyer, S., Meek, A. & Davies, A. (2014) *Supported work experience and its impact on young people with intellectual disabilities, their families and employers.* Regional SEN Transition to Employment Initiative (Real Opportunities).

Christie, N. (1989) *Beyond Loneliness and Institutions: Communes for extraordinary people*. London: Norwegian University Press.

Coleman, N., Sykes, W. & Groom, C. (2013) *Research Report 88: Barriers to employment and unfair treatment at work, a quantitative analysis of disabled people's experiences*. Equality and Human Rights Commission.

Curtice, L. (2006) *How Is It Going?: A survey of what matters most to people with learning disabilities in Scotland today*. Scottish Consortium for Learning Disability and ENABLE Scotland.

Dean, H. (2007) 'The ethics of welfare to work', *Policy and Politics*, 35(4): 573–590.

Department of Health (2001) *Valuing People*. London: HMSO.

— (2009) *Valuing People Now: A new three year strategy for people with learning disabilities*. London: HMSO.

Department for Work and Pensions (2006) *A New Deal for Welfare: Empowering people to work*. London: HMSO.

— (2012) *The Work Programme*. London: HMSO.

Emerson, E. (2005) *Adults with Learning Difficulties in England 2003/4*. London: HMSO.

Hale, C. (2014) *Fulfilling Potential? ESA and the fate of the Work-Related Activity Group*. Sheffield: The Centre for Welfare Reform.

Jahoda, A., Kemp, J., Riddell, S. & Banks, P. (2008) 'Feelings about work: A review of the socio-emotional impact of supported employment on people with intellectual disabilities', *Journal of Applied Research in Intellectual Disabilities*, 21: 1–18.

König, K. (1959) 'Camphill Essential'. In: J. Bang (ed.), (2010) *A Portrait of Camphill: From founding seed to worldwide movement*. Edinburgh: Floris Books.

Lyons, M. (2015) *Rethinking Community Care*. Sheffield: The Centre for Welfare Reform.

Milner, C. (2005) *Employment Issues for Young People with Learning Disabilities in Tynedale*. Hexham: Disability North.

Morin, E. (2008) *The Meaning of Work, Mental Health and Organisational Commitment*. Quebec: Institut de recherche Robert-Sauvé en Santé et en Sécurité du Travail (IRSST).

Steiner, R. (1972) *World-Economy: The formation of a science of world-economics*. London: Rudolf Steiner Press.

Trembath, D., Balandin, S., Stancliffe, R. & Togher, L. (2010) 'Employment and volunteering for adults with intellectual disability', *Journal of Applied Research in Intellectual Disabilities*, 7 (4): 235–238.

Employment Services for People with an Intellectual Disability: Building Connections in Vermont

BRYAN DAGUE

Vermont culture

Vermont is a small rural state in the north-eastern United States that is home to the nation's second-smallest population. Based on the 2014 US Census, the residents of Vermont number 626,562 with the majority living in the Burlington area. According to the Vermont Council on Rural Development, Vermont residents highly value a sense of community, defined here as 'a shared feeling of belonging, acceptance and trust; a sense that the success of each neighbourhood, town, county, and the state depends on the contributions and engagement of every individual' (2009, p.9). In addition to community, residents value the environment, hard work, independence and privacy, as well as the small scale of the state and its unique identity defined by history and traditions. The Vermont state motto, 'Freedom and Unity', aptly describes the culture as seeking balance between the personal freedom and independence of the individual citizen with the common good of the larger community. It is known for setting trends in terms of progressive social politics and social responsibility. Vermont has been a leader in disability services as well as being one of the first to implement community-based employment services, close the state institutions, and end sheltered and segregated employment for individuals with intellectual and developmental disabilities (ID/DD).

State institution

Despite the current culture and inclusive nature of services for individuals with developmental disabilities, Vermont shares a similar dark history with the rest of the American nation. People with developmental disabilities, such as intellectual disability, cerebral palsy, and autism, have a long history of discrimination and exclusion from society. People with developmental disabilities in the United States have been institutionalised and segregated from society since the 1850s. Often referred to as 'feebleminded' or 'idiots', the isolation and segregation of such individuals was based on the prevailing attitudes of the time, namely that people with developmental disabilities were to be protected and sheltered from society, and/or society itself should be protected from them (Wolfensberger 1975).

From 1854 onwards, numerous institutions were built around the country to house, or warehouse, people considered different and inferior because of their disability. These institutions catered also for children, and were the standard of care for over one hundred years; although 'care' is not an appropriate descriptor. The conditions in these institutions were often deplorable, yet hidden from the public view and the collective conscience (Blatt & Kaplan 1974, Blatt, McNally, & Ozolins 1978, Shapiro 1993).

Institutions of this kind were both highly secretive and secure, and were able to keep the secrets of their internal workings for many years. In the 1960s, a number of exposés by journalists and university researchers, such as the hidden-camera photographic essay *Christmas in Purgatory* (Blatt & Kaplan 1974), revealed some of these secrets and made the public aware of the dreadful conditions in which people with developmental disabilities were forced to live (Blatt & Kaplan 1974, Blatt, McNally et al. 1978, Shapiro, 1993). The public was outraged and demanded reform. In 1972, a television exposé on Willowbrook State School in New York State made national headlines, further fuelling the deinstitutionalisation movement. Geraldo Rivera and his WABC Eyewitness News crew gained unauthorised access to

Willowbrook, having evaded armed guards and heavy security, to televise the shocking conditions that six thousand people with developmental disabilities were enduring (Rivera 1972). These and other public exposures strengthened the deinstitutionalisation movement across the nation, and prompted the gradual closure of many institutions (CHP 1979, Shapiro 1993, Shoultz et al. 1999, Stancliffe & Lakin 1999).

Brandon Training School was an institution that housed people with developmental disabilities in the state of Vermont between 1915 and 1993. During its 78 years of operation, a total of 2,324 people lived there. Former Governor Howard Dean, who oversaw the final closure, remarked, 'over the past centuries, people with disabilities have been not only feared and discriminated against; they have been relegated to the shadows of society. Well-intended and humane as it was intended to be, the Brandon Training School was emblematic of those shadows' (Twentieth anniversary of closure 2013).

The idea to close Brandon Training School began in the mid-1970s, when some key leaders in the disability field attended workshops conducted by Wolf Wolfensberger and his colleagues, leading them to adopt the concept of 'normalisation' as a philosophy that should be applied in Vermont. Closing the institution became a part of their overall mission, so that people with developmental disabilities, once free, could become part of their communities. Nearly 250 people moved into the community in the late 1970s and early 1980s, due in part to the state's successful application for, and use of, the federal Medicaid Home and Community Based Services Waiver (Shoultz et al. 1999).

Closing the institution was further prompted by a lawsuit filed on behalf of several residents who wanted to move into the community. The settlement in 1980 included a ten-year plan for developing community resources and moving most of the approximately three hundred residents out of Brandon Training School.

Community services

The closure of Brandon Training School in 1993 was a turning point in the care for individuals with developmental disabilities, as it marked the end of reliance on an institutional model of care provision. It also underscored the State's commitment to creating support and services necessary for people with intellectual disabilities to live with dignity, respect and independence within their communities. The Vermont State Legislature embedded into law the Developmental Disabilities Act of 1996 requiring the Department of Disabilities for Aging and Independent Living, through the Developmental Disabilities Services Division, to adopt the 'State System of Care Plan' that described the nature, extent, allocation and timing of services that would be provided to people with developmental disabilities and their families.

The System of Care Plan is intended to instruct how legislatively-appropriated funding will be allocated to serve individuals with significant developmental disabilities, to help these people achieve their personal goals, and to continuously improve the system of support within available resources for individuals with developmental disabilities. The adult service system is not an entitlement programme. Since resources are never sufficient to meet all needs, eligibility criteria were established, and are determined by the designated agency in each county. Although an individual may meet eligibility criteria as a person with a developmental disability, they do not automatically qualify for funding. The System of Care Plan is designed to serve those with the greatest need. The Developmental Disabilities Act states: 'The law does not guarantee support or services to all people who need or want them. Resources are limited to the funding approved each year by the Legislature. Each year, the System of Care Plan will describe what funding and services will get state support'. Funding and provision of services follows the guide of 'no more, no less'. Although not all may receive funding, many individuals with developmental disabilities in Vermont are actively involved in home and community life, working and living alongside the non-disabled population. If not eligible for developmental disability services, people may be entitled to receive support from the Division of Vocational Rehabilitation in order to become employed.

Employment services

Sheltered workshops grew in popularity throughout the country in the 1950s and 1960s, when parents had few choices other than institutional placement or home care (McLoughlin, Garner & Callahan 1987). Sheltered workshops are segregated facilities where workers with disabilities are paid a piece-rate, which is frequently far below the minimum wage, based on what they actually produce, not the hours they work. The national average wage in sheltered workshops is $2.46 an hour, with average weekly earnings of $64.00 (Butterworth, Gilmore & Kiernan 2000, Fried & Schmitt 2014). The sheltered workshop became popular with families as it freed them from child-rearing duties that extended well beyond those needed for most children, and provided a place where they knew their sons and daughters would be safe and occupied. The tasks were brought into the workshop by outside companies on a contractual basis, with the result that there was little contact with the general community or people without disabilities (McLoughlin et al. 1987, Murphy & Rogan 1995). People in sheltered workshops seldom made it out into the 'real world' of employment (Bellamy et al. 1986).

In his book *Crossing the Unknown Sea: Work as a pilgrimage of identity*, David Whyte defines work as, 'an opportunity for discovering and shaping; the place where the self meets the world' (2001). Our work often becomes our identity as we are generally defined in our society by the work we do. Too often people with significant disabilities have been denied an opportunity to 'meet the world' and establish themselves in society. Whyte suggests, 'the consummation of work lies not only in what we have done, but who we have become while accomplishing the task' (p.5). By excluding people with disabilities from the general workforce, they are removed from an important aspect of community life and identity. Rather, the affixed label of 'disability' often defines their lives (Goffman 1963, Shapiro 1993).

American society began to change markedly with the advent of legislation such as the Rehabilitation Act of 1973, the Education for All Handicapped Children Act in 1975, now known as the

Individuals with Disabilities Education Act (IDEA), and the impact of the deinstitutionalisation movement. At this time, people with developmental disabilities were finally becoming integrated into society. The concept of supported employment was developed in the late 1970s as a way of helping people with more severe disabilities to obtain and maintain community-based employment at a competitive wage. Supported employment programmes enabled individuals to participate in jobs in the community with the support of a designated helper, known as a 'job coach' or 'employment consultant'. The job coach provides advocacy and systematic training until the person learns the trade, then gradually withdraws their presence to the extent that is possible (Wehman 1986). Successful supported employment demonstration efforts for people with developmental disabilities were established in various universities across the country in the late 1970s and early 1980s, including Project Employability at Virginia Commonwealth University, the Specialised Training Programme at the University of Oregon, and the Employment Training Programme at the University of Washington.

In the late 1970s, Vermont State and university leaders noticed that improved educational programmes for students with disabilities were highlighting discrepancies in the adult services field. Graduating students were much better prepared than their predecessors, yet were ending up in segregated, sheltered facilities rather than in community-based employment and activities (Vogelsberg 1986). To counter this, a state-supported employment demonstration project called 'Project Transition' was funded in 1980 in Barre, Vermont. The project recruited new referrals and workers from sheltered workshops to participate in the model demonstration. The programme director, Bill Ashe recalled that, before the demonstration project:

> the staffing ratio was somewhere in the 1:10 range. There
> were lots of behavioural issues, usually daily, which of course
> were impossible to solve. Almost everyone was in a single
> large room spending most of the day there from 9:00–4:00.
> Project Transition took 3–4 years to successfully move about
> 70 people out of the facility into the community (Personal
> correspondence).

The initial demonstration project followed the phases of referral, job development and evaluation, placement and on-the-job training, and follow-up.

A local newspaper carried a story on the first woman in Vermont, previously labeled as 'unemployable', to move from a sheltered workshop to a community job through the new employment programme. The article reported, 'she has a lot more self-confidence and pride now that she has a legitimate job, she dresses better, her personal hygiene has improved and she speaks clearer'. The report further states that the move has created new dimensions in her life, 'she has new friends and she has gone to a bar where, though she only drank soda, she had a great time' (Glitman 1980). This marked the beginning of inclusive employment in Vermont.

The success of this initial demonstration project led to replication at other Vermont sites. Project Transition II was established in 1981, followed by several more. Before the project, approximately 1,400 individuals with intellectual or developmental disabilities were located in sheltered workshops throughout Vermont. The overall success of these various demonstration projects led the US Department of Education-Rehabilitation Services Administration to fund states with multi-year grants in order to implement a statewide change of system in support of employment efforts. The initial federal investment in systemic change in the 1980s and 1990s exceeded $100 million, with funding for more than fifty-five grants lasting three to five years (Mank 1994).

The state of Vermont was a recipient of one of these federal grants, through which it was able to further expand supported employment throughout the state. The change of system project was a collaborative effort among the state stakeholders of the Division of Vocational Rehabilitation, Developmental Disabilities Services, Mental Health Services and the University of Vermont Center on Disability and Community Inclusion. The University of Vermont provided training and technical assistance for the duration of the grant, and after that resource was exhausted the state continued to fund training and technical assistance. This continuous training and assistance was key to the long-term success of the project. The respective state divisions also committed to continue funding their supported employment staff after the grant, ensuring a strong commitment to community-based employment from all divisions.

The supported employment initiative was implemented throughout the state in all fourteen counties. As part of it, the State of Vermont contracts directly with the fourteen private, non-profit community developmental disability service providers to meet the support needs of eligible people in their regions. This network provides integrated employment services using Vermont's Medicaid home- and community-based services waiver.* Vocational Rehabilitation grants complement agency Medicaid by paying for infrastructure, such as job development and job training. The blended system provides the required employment support for individuals with intellectual or developmental disabilities; Vocational Rehabilitation provides up-front support for assessment, job development and training, and Medicaid waiver-funding provides the longer-term support. Currently, Vermont only funds individualised integrated community employment. It does not support group settings.

Vermont's supported employment programmes provide a full range of services which enable people with disabilities to access and succeed in competitive employment, including self-employment. Services have been developed from a philosophy that presumes competence and employability of everyone, given that the right supports are provided. Person-centred planning, creative job development, meaningful job matches, systematic instruction, adaptive technology and natural supports are utilised for full inclusion in the Vermont workforce. The close geography of the state allows the fourteen supported employment coordinators to meet in person on a regular basis. These meetings with state and university officials have been instrumental in providing cohesive services and keeping up with current best practices.

Vermont's current employment rate for individuals with intellectual or developmental disabilities is 44 per cent in employment compared to the national average of 19 per cent (Braddock et al. 2014), although some Vermont agencies have placement rates as high as 80 per

---

* States can apply for federal Medicaid waivers to provide long-term care solutions for individuals with developmental disabilities in home and community settings rather than institutional settings.

cent (CCS 2015). Vermont's supported employment services rank among the highest in the nation (Butterworth et al. 2014). In the fiscal year 2013, the Developmental Disabilities System served over 2,700 working-age adults (16–64), of which 1,142 were employed. Supported employment is a sound investment, garnering significant fiscal and social returns for all Vermonters. It is estimated that individuals with intellectual or developmental disabilities receiving supported employment services earned approximately $3,800,000 in wages, and as wage-earners they contribute back to the economy through purchases, taxes and a reduction in government benefits. A 2014 survey of Vermonters with developmental disabilities reveals that 97 per cent like where they work, 97 per cent think the work they do is important, 98 per cent felt the people they work with treat them with respect and 46 per cent wanted to work more hours. For those not employed, 62 per cent said they would like to have a job (DDSD Annual Report 2014).

Since the initial supported employment project in 1980, inclusive employment of individuals with developmental disabilities has steadily increased. All the sheltered workshops gradually closed as people found employment in the community or became involved in other community services. In 2002, Vermont closed its last sheltered workshop for people with intellectual and developmental disabilities, making Vermont the first state with no sheltered work. Former Vermont Senator Jim Jeffords noted, 'as we close this chapter on work centers in Vermont, I hope that we encourage others to follow Vermont's lead to a place where all of us work side by side'.

I was closely involved with the conversion of the last sheltered workshop and conducted a study of the process, including an examination of how stakeholders navigated the conversion effort. With a 35-year history, there were significant issues and barriers to this agency's conversion. Conflicting matters emerged with families' different histories, cultures, values, philosophies, and expectations of their children and their childrens' inclusion in community. There were initial fears by some regarding safety and consistency, exploitation in the community, and loss of friendships, while others welcomed and expected full inclusion in the community.

The families and participants who had a long history with the workshop had a difficult time with the conversion process. They had become entrenched in a model that remained essentially unchanged for thirty-five years. They simply could not envision life without the workshop. Embracing this drastic change was not easy for those people, whereas the younger generation of families had high expectations of full community inclusion. Despite the issues and obstacles, the agency successfully converted their services, and participants and their families were satisfied with the final conversion as long as they could maintain social contacts and find acceptable employment in the community (Dague 2012).

Shift in philosophy and resources

The shift in philosophy from facility-based to community-based employment services also shifts energy and resources. Since Vermont has no segregated employment, other opportunities are nurtured. One emerging trend is for university/college options for students with intellectual and developmental disabilities. In 2010, grants were awarded to twenty-seven colleges from US Department of Education federal funding for Transition and Postsecondary Programmes for Students with Intellectual Disabilities (TPSID). This was to enable the colleges to create or expand high quality, inclusive-model comprehensive transition and postsecondary programmes for students with intellectual disabilities. The University of Vermont was awarded one of these grants and developed the Think College Vermont programme on two campuses. Think College Vermont is an innovative, inclusive, academic, social, and vocational programme for students with developmental and intellectual disabilities who are seeking a college experience and career path. Participants earn a 12-credit 'Certificate of College Studies' designed to include academic enrichment, social and recreational activities, independent living and self-advocacy skills, and work experience and career skills. The programme incorporates student-centred planning, academic advising, and peer mentors for an inclusive, supportive college experience. Individuals with intellectual and developmental disabilities who in the past may have been consigned to sheltered workshops, are now attending college earning certificates of studies. Throughout their two-year college experience, students gain the soft-skills and employability skills that companies are seeking. Students follow a career path and attain better jobs, and programme graduates have a 90 per cent employment rate. The success of Think College Vermont has led to the programme being replicated at other Vermont colleges.

The concept of self-employment or micro-enterprises has also been beneficial to a number of individuals who may struggle with traditional employment. One such individual is Patrick who is blind with cerebral palsy, and with family support runs his own business, 'Purely Patrick' (2016). He creates mixes for soups, cookies, dog and bird treats, hot cocoa and chai tea using a switch-activated device specifically designed for pouring ingredients. He layers them into decorative bags and mason jars, and sells them at local inns, farmers' markets and online at http://www.purelypatrick.com. Another self-employment example is illustrated by 'Nickering Nuggets', a healthy and natural horse treat business, with honour-system buckets set up in local stables. Visitors can feed the horses homemade biscuits and leave money in the bucket. This business encourages a young woman's love of horses and supports the cyclical nature of her disability. She can schedule her work hours to meet her needs.

Conclusion

The Vermont Developmental Disabilities Council is a statewide board that works to increase public awareness about critical issues affecting people with developmental disabilities and their families. Their mission is, 'to help build connections and supports that bring people with developmental disabilities and their families into the heart of Vermont communities' (VTDDC 2015). Vermont's system of employment services for individuals with intellectual and developmental disabilities is certainly not flawless, and there is much work that needs to be done. But as services and resources have shifted to be more community-based, Vermonters with developmental disabilities seem to be getting closer to the heart of their local communities and making their own contributions.

References

Bellamy, G., Rhodes, L., Bourbeau, P. & Mank, D. (1986) 'Mental retardation services in sheltered workshops and day activity programmes: Consumer benefits and policy alternatives'. In: F. Rusch (ed.), *Competitive Employment Issues*. Baltimore: Paul H. Brookes Pub. Co.

Blatt, B. & Kaplan, F. (1974) *Christmas in Purgatory: A photographic essay on mental retardation*. Syracuse, New York: Human Policy Press.

Blatt, B., McNally, J. & Ozolins, A. (1978) *The Family Album: Views of residential settings for mentally retarded people*. (Slide show) Syracuse, New York: Human Policy Press.

Braddock, D., Hemp, R., Rizzolo, M., Tanis, E., Haffer, L. & Wu, J. (2014) *Annual Report on Developmental Disabilities Services for State Fiscal Year 2014*. Coleman Institute and Department of Psychiatry, University of Colorado.

Butterworth, J., Gilmore, D. & Kiernan, W. (2000) *Choose Work*. Paper presented at the Association for Persons in Supported Employment, Richmond, VA.

Butterworth, J., Winsor, J., Smith, F., Migliore, F., Domin, D., Timmons, J. & Hall, A. (2014) *State Data: The National Report on Employment Services and Outcomes. Institute for Community Inclusion*. UMass: Boston. http://www.statedata.info.

Center on Human Policy (1979). *A Time to Take Sides*. http://thechp.syr.edu/a-time-to-take-sides-1979/.

Dague, B. (2012) 'Sheltered employment, sheltered lives: Family perspectives of conversion to community-based employment', *Journal of Vocational Rehabilitation*, 37(1): 1–11.

Fried, C. & Schmitt, D. (2014) *It's Time to Address Sub-Minimum Wage*. Maryland ARC. http://www.thearcmd.org/app/document/1580767.

Glitman, R. (1980) 'Mentally handicapped adults finding way into workplace', *Burlington Free Press*, pp. 8D and 11D.

Goffman, E. (1963) *Stigma: Notes on the management of spoiled identity*. Englewood Cliffs, NJ: Prentice-Hall.

Mank, D. (1994) 'The underachievement of supported employment: A call for reinvestment', *Journal of Disability Policy Studies*, 5(2):1–24.

McLoughlin, C., Garner, J. & Callahan, M. (1987) *Getting Employed, Staying Employed: Job development and training for persons with severe handicaps*. Baltimore: P.H. Brookes Pub. Co.

Murphy, S. & Rogan, P. (1995) *Closing the Shop: Conversion from sheltered to integrated work*. Baltimore: Paul H. Brookes Pub. Co.

Purely Patrick (2016) Specialty items with a splash of country flare and a taste of Vermont. http://www.purelypatrick.com.

Rivera, G. (1972) *Willowbrook: The last great disgrace*. http://geraldo.com/page/willowbrook.

Shapiro, J. (1993) *No Pity: People with disabilities forging a new civil rights movement*. New York: Three Rivers Press.

Shoultz, B., Walker, P., Hulgin, K., Bogdan, B., Taylor, S. & Moseley, C. (1999) *Closing Brandon Training School: A Vermont story*. New York: Syracuse University.

Stancliffe, R. & Lakin, K. (1999) 'A longitudinal comparison of day programme services and outcomes of people who left institutions and those who stayed', *The Journal of the Association for Persons with Severe Handicaps*, 24: 44–57.

State System of Care Plan for Developmental Disabilities Services (2014) Developmental Disabilities Services Division, Department of Disabilities, Aging and Independent Living Agency of Human Services, State of Vermont.

Vermont Council on Rural Development (2009) *Imagining Vermont: Values and vision for the future*. 43 State St, Montpelier, VT 05602

Vermont Developmental Disabilities Council (VTDDC) (2015) *Annual Report: 2015*. 103 South Main Street One North, Suite 117 Waterbury, VT 05671-0206.

Vermont Disabilities Services Division (2014) *Vermont State Annual Report on Developmental Disabilities Services for State Fiscal Year 2014*. Developmental Disabilities Services Division, Department of Disabilities, Aging and Independent Living, Agency of Human Services, State of Vermont.

Vogelsberg, R. (1986) 'Competitive employment in Vermont'. In: F. Rusch (ed.), *Competitive Employment Issues and Strategies*. Baltimore: Paul H. Brookes.

Wehman, P. (1986) 'Competitive employment in Virginia'. In: F. Rusch (ed.), *Competitive Employment Issues and Strategies*. Baltimore: Paul H. Brookes.

Whyte, D. (2001) *Crossing the Unknown Sea: Work as a pilgrimage of identity*. New York: Riverhead Books.

Wolfensberger, W. (1975) *The Origin and Nature of our Institutional Models*. Syracuse, New York: Human Policy Press.

Community Living, Inclusion and Disability in China

CHRIS WALTER

In 2014 I was invited to contribute to the developing curative educational work on intellectual disability in China; partly as a lecturer, but also as a practitioner working on a residential programme with children with an intellectual disability and their families. Over a period of eighteen months I visited China on three occasions and saw at first hand both the challenges and opportunities of this exciting work. This chapter draws on those experiences by considering disabled identities in the context of Chinese culture. It also details the way in which an innovative educational programme in China, inspired by Camphill philosophy, aims to support families and young people as they develop a more strength-based – as distinct from incapacity-based – understanding of disability.

Instead of seeing identity as something located within the person, this chapter adopts the symbolic interactionist view that identities are socially produced and relational. Accordingly, societal values and beliefs shape behaviour and thus different social constructions of disability will have practical consequences for both families and their children who have these conditions (Lawler 2014). The concluding section of the chapter will outline some of the professional learning involved when working within a very different cultural context.

The work of Mead (1863–1931) has been highly influential within a sociological understanding of identity and is useful in addressing this issue. He distinguished what he termed the 'I' of a person as the ongoing experience of selfhood, from the 'Me' as the internalised attitudes of significant others within that individual, and saw these as constantly interacting elements. As Jenkins (2014) suggests, in Mead's view we cannot perceive our own selves at all without also seeing ourselves as others see us. As I have discussed elsewhere (Walter 2010), children's vulnerabilities are often initially interpreted through a disabling lens of 'normality/abnormality'. In consequence, some identities are seen as less valuable than others. Goffman (1963) in his work on stigma referred to the 'master status' of a particular identity which overwhelms all other aspects of the self. He provides an example of the way in which disabled people are constructed as fundamentally different to 'normal', non-disabled people, through the way in which a particular feature of their experience (such as autism) becomes the dominant category or 'master status' for external identification. The individual is then in danger of being labelled as different and treated as 'another type of person' or even non-person who can then, perhaps legitimately, be excluded, ignored or patronised (Wickenden 2010).

Wolfensberger's (1983) concept of 'social wounds' is relevant in this regard as it refers to the way vulnerable individuals may develop socially devalued roles. Such individuals can lose access to what he terms 'the good things in life' such as family, friends, leisure activities and meaningful work. His social role valorisation theory called for changes in society so that people are valued despite their differences.

The cultural context in any society is based on a shared symbolic world that is sustained by everyday practices and provides a sense of identity and belonging. Confucianism was and still is to a great extent the dominant belief system in China and has over the last century provided a foundation for social welfare ideology in Chinese culture (Hutchings & Taylor, 2007). It has been said that every Chinese person wears a Confucian thinking cap! The core values of Confucianism include reciprocity, filial piety, loyalty to one's family, and consensus and harmony in the wider community. Confucius stressed the importance of concern for one's fellow human being ('jen' in Chinese) which was based on the ideal of reciprocity: 'Do not do to others that you do not wish others to do to you' (Mah 2001).

In the context of China's leap into modernity many people yearn for such older forms of community and consolation (Chu 2014) which they hope will lead to more humanity and feeling of connection to others. Informal care and family obligations are valued in Chinese tradition and are still important principles of the contemporary welfare system. However, family size has decreased over the years due to China's 'one-child' policy, whilst the divorce rate has increased, meaning that there are fewer people in stable family relationships to share the responsibility of caregiving. Due to rapid urbanisation, many rural residents have left the land and migrated to cities to make money, whilst their elder parents and young children are left behind in the countryside. Those grandparents who have moved with their children to the city can feel isolated in a very different world, cut off from their social connections. All of these developments can add to the stress of raising a child with any form of intellectual disability.

The need to 'save face' means that it can be difficult for families to speak honestly and openly about their views. The danger of the Confucian emphasis on consensus and harmony is that it can lead to conformity and unwillingness to risk social disapproval. In consequence, it can feel like a big disgrace and failure to have a disabled child. This may be a particular problem in China due to cultural beliefs that disability is due to bad thoughts and a lack of willpower. Chinese parents may see their children as 'bad seed'. Mak and Cheung (2008) conducted a quantitative study of what they termed carers' 'affiliate stigma', the negative self-perception due to being related to someone with an intellectual disability. Caregivers with high levels of affiliate stigma tended to experience a lot of shame about their offspring. They often saw their child as a disgrace to the family and even attempted to conceal their difficulties from the wider family. This was particularly so if their child had autism. As they argue, given that kinship support is very important in China, these cultural issues are likely to increase their levels of stress. They recommend that support groups should be established to empower caregivers and reduce feelings of alienation. This is an interesting recommendation in the light of the Mignon programme that will be discussed later in this chapter as these are some of its principal aims.

The Constitution in China provides a general principle regarding the protection of people with disabilities, with Article 45 establishing that, '... all citizens ... have the right to material assistance from the state and society when they are old, ill or disabled.' The Law regarding the 'Protection of Disabled Persons' enacted in the year 1991 is of particular significance to the protection of the rights of children with disabilities in China (www.disabled-world 2010). There appears little doubt that attitudes to disability are changing and the government has instigated a number of projects to facilitate this. However they face a huge task due to the size of the population: according to the second National Sampling survey in 2006 the total population of people with disabilities reached 82.96 million, or 6.34 per cent of the total Chinese population (International Labour Organisation 2008), with 5.4 million having intellectual disabilities.

Special education for children with an intellectual disability began in the 1980s and (in common with Western approaches) has historically taken a medical and behaviourist approach emphasising the importance of diagnosis and individualised behavioural programmes. However it has been increasingly influenced by the Quality of Life model with its eight domains emphasising social inclusion and self-determination as well as physical and emotional wellbeing (Xu et al. 2005). Consequently the law in China places great emphasis on the importance of rehabilitation, with the government including rehabilitation in national and social development programmes. The Chinese government has both developed and supported rehabilitation programmes with the goal of mainstreaming and facilitating the participation of people with intellectual disabilities in society. Unfortunately these programmes are often run by staff with insufficient training and at a high cost to parents (Baldwin 2015).

Whilst there are doubtless many examples of good intentions and also good practice in Chinese schools, it is also true that many teachers struggle to include children with intellectual disabilities in the classroom. This is a particular issue in rural areas where the attitude still lives on that there is no need to educate such children. A report from Human Rights Watch '…. found little to no accommodation in mainstream schools for these students at all stages of education. One parent was explicitly told by the school that since her child is in "a normal environment" it is the child with the disability who must adapt, not the other way round' (Guardian

2013). In such a context there is the danger that schools will resort to behaviour management approaches that do not sufficiently take into account a child's needs and experiences.

Thomas (2007) has argued that the effects of discriminatory attitudes on the way disabled individuals see themselves have not been sufficiently acknowledged. She refers to 'psycho-emotional disablism' which '... involves the intended or unintended "hurtful" words and social actions of non-disabled people (parents, professionals, complete strangers, others) in inter-personal engagement...' (Thomas 2007, p.72). Consequently, not only are there societal barriers that place limits on what individuals can do, there are also barriers on what they can be as their sense of self is corroded in everyday life. Because children with an intellectual disability are so easily objectified, people may not even consider their inner experiences or attempt to understand them beyond their actual behaviour.

Families and young people with an intellectual disability in China experience high levels of stress in supporting their children and coping with pessimistic attitudes towards their children's abilities (Wang et al. 2011). In this context it is not surprising that parents feel under pressure and at a loss about how to meet their children's needs. Anxiety levels rise and in the middle of all of this, the young person can feel isolated, incapable, with low self-esteem and high levels of anxiety. As described earlier, families and young people can often struggle with a stigmatised identity, feeling excluded from their local community. However, if children and their families are to build a more positive, empowered view of their situation, this is most likely to happen within a supportive, empathic environment.

Work in China based on the spiritual, holistic world view of Rudolf Steiner (1861–1925) has developed rapidly over the last ten years, beginning with the founding of a Waldorf school in Chengdu. Since then there has been growing interest in this alternative approach to education and there are now over three hundred kindergartens and thirty-five schools, some of which are still very small. In 2011 Barbara Baldwin established a curative education foundation course to meet the need for parents and teachers to develop a deeper understanding of intellectual disability in China. Trained as a speech and language therapist, she has had a long experience of curative education, both in Camphill in the UK and in the curative movement in Australia where she subsequently moved. Curative education is a translation of the German term *Heilpaedagogik* which means 'healing education' (Monteux 2006). In developing educational approaches within this tradition, Steiner wanted to challenge the predominant medical narrative regarding disability which focused on children's lack of ability rather than their strengths (Walter 2010).

Mignon programmes for parents and their children with intellectual disability began originally in Japan and have been running in China since 2012 (Baldwin 2015). They offer a residential experience for five to ten days providing immersion in a therapeutic, rural environment for children and families. A 'breathing space' is provided where they can engage in crafts, artistic activities, relax together and make new connections. There are separate programmes for children and their parents, although they have time to be with each other in the evenings as they settle down for a night's sleep. Unique features of the programme in the Chinese context are the high child/adult ratio and intensive pedagogical support from curative education students who in turn receive daily mentoring from experienced practitioners. As Barbara Baldwin, the inspiration behind the Mignon programmes has stated:

> The purpose of this programme is to give parents the opportunity to review their current situation and to gain a new understanding of themselves as parents of a child with special needs. It is specifically designed so that parents can have some quality time for themselves, as well as spending time with other parents who share their concerns and all the time knowing that their child is in a safe environment in structured and supervised care (Baldwin 2012).

Meaningful relationships form the bedrock of working with children and young people, providing them with a sense of connection and trust, for without this, significant growth and change is not possible. Many of the children who come to the Mignon programme have experienced negative messages about their behaviour, even disrespectful and over controlling approaches in some cases where the focus has been on 'managing' their behaviour rather than building connections. All of the family can feel overwhelmed, in despair and at a loss how to help their children who are often socially isolated and even depressed. In Mead's terms they have internalised a negative identity, habitually reacting to stress in self-defeating ways such as aggression, anxiety and self-harm. Their greatest need is to re-build a sense of belonging and connectedness within a positive environment where they feel liked and valued.

The Mignon programme offers what Perry (2006) has termed a relationally enriched environment, a setting filled with moment-by-moment positive human interactions (in contrast to the rushed, hectic lifestyle many children are exposed to in the modern world). Whether it is in the joy and laughter of sharing a meal together, playing outside in nature, riding bikes along country lanes or peacefully playing a game, there are countless opportunities if we look for them. If those working with children do not insist on compliance but rather take an interest in what is important to them, take time to listen, show they trust them and welcome them back after a challenging moment, they begin to build a sense of belonging and community. This is also fostered through working together to achieve something where children can feel they have a contribution to make (Beck & Malley 2003). On a recent programme, for instance, the parents prepared a mime to perform for their children and we asked some of the young people if they could cut some bamboo sticks, which could be used as props in the play. They came into the rehearsal room with pride in their achievement obvious in their faces as they handed over the sticks to their parents.

Another important aspect of Mignon's therapeutic environment is the rhythmically structured day that gives the children a feeling of familiarity and security. Every morning the whole community meets for a morning gathering where we sing together, and greet each other in preparation for the day ahead. Every evening we gather again in a circle and this is also an opportunity for the children to show what they have made in the craft workshops. In this way they receive positive appreciation from the whole group for their achievements that in turn helps them to feel more confident and valued. As Mead argues, our social identity is built up in such moment-by-moment interactions with significant others (Jenkins 2014). However, in many school settings, children and young people with intellectual impairments are not given the time and space to develop a more strength-based identity. In settings which move away from behaviour management and recognise the holistic needs of the child, a space can open up for real growth and development.

Clearly children will not be able turn their lives around in five days, but Mignon's potential lies in its emphasis on working with parents to help them to reframe their child's situation in a more positive light. As Barbara Baldwin has written:

> ... parents can learn a lot and change their attitudes and their habits around their children and this is perhaps the greatest follow-up: that the parents have learned to think about their children in a new way and also to treat them differently, engage with them differently (Baldwin 2012).

Mignon is intended to be an intensive experience of mutual support. Whereas for children and young people it aims to be a social and active experience in a relationally enriched environment few have in daily life, for their parents it can be a time for reflection, connection, in-depth conversation and individual guidance about their children's needs. Through meeting other parents and sharing difficulties and challenges, parents can feel less isolated and stressed and consequently develop a sense of belonging. For many, this is the first experience of being listened to with respect and genuine interest. These connections are often maintained and strengthened afterwards through local support groups, social media and attendance at subsequent programmes. One of the results of this engagement is that parents can begin to feel a greater sense of self-efficacy. It is noteworthy that coping strategies such as reframing children's difficulties in a positive light have been identified in the literature as an important pointer to increased parental wellbeing (Woodman & Hauser-Cram 2013).

It has been said that Chinese people 'live in the eyes of

others', being predominantly concerned with social approval and reputation (Faure, no date). Confucius saw society as being like one large family and believed that social harmony was to be achieved by controlling emotions, acting morally and avoiding competition. This remains a powerful narrative by which many Chinese people live their lives. Westerners coming to work in China need to take this into account if they are not going to impose pre-conceived ideas on a different culture. Parents will not easily speak about their emotions and may conceal their judgments behind a polite smile in the interest of social cohesion. As mentioned earlier Mak and Cheung's (2008) research into 'affiliate stigma' found that Chinese parents felt the disgrace keenly of having a child with an intellectual disability, particularly if they have autism. It is almost as though they have failed in their duty to the community and wider society and in doing so are cut off from vital sources of support, thus feeling acutely their difference from others.

Lack of social approval has led many parents to feel demeaned and excluded and they are often longing for an experience of mutuality, trust and respect. If parents are supported to challenge the negative narratives about their children the traditional Chinese cultural resources of connectedness and concern for others ('jen') can be drawn upon to create a positive 'circle of influence' (Brendtro 2010). The Mignon programme is such a setting where parents can connect with others who share similar experiences and so develop a common 'sense of things' that is mutually validating. Identity is a reflexive process. In identifying similarities and differences with others we also form our own identity (Jenkins 2014). Hopefully, they will come away not only with a greater understanding of their children but also with a different and less stigmatised sense of themselves as parents.

The experience of working in China raised my own awareness of similarity and difference as I attempted to connect with parents and students across the language and culture barrier. Every sentence I spoke needed to be translated as the majority of participants did not understand English sufficiently well. I became much more aware of what I was communicating, both verbally and non-verbally and needed to negotiate a number of misunderstandings due to the different cultural context. For example, I became aware after my second session with parents during the Mignon programme that in my rush to be helpful I had not spent sufficient time listening to their experiences and trying to understand a very different cultural background. I had reacted to my own need for certainty in this new situation by offering answers in a more categorical and prescriptive manner than I normally would do. In doing so, I may have presented an identity of the 'Western expert' that in turn influenced how others responded to me.

Curative educational language, ideas and practices are of course strange and unfamiliar for new participants in China and there needs to be a lot of effort put into cultural translation. From my personal experience it was evident that a vast amount of careful thought had gone into the choice of traditional Chinese songs and verses (as well as sensitive translations of Steiner verses) for the morning and evening gathering on the Mignon programme. These rituals acted as a symbol of shared belonging as Cohen (1985) has pointed out, thereby providing participants with a sense of collective identity. In this sense, Steiner's understanding of the human being can provide hope and certainty, almost like a life raft in the stormy waters of Chinese society. At the same time, his ideas are complex and potentially confusing; I was always concerned when working in China to allow sufficient space for questions and clarification. If parents and professionals are indeed going to develop a greater sense of self-efficacy, they need the time and space to explore their understanding and develop their own meaning of these ideas. I was very happy when a parent in one session spoke honestly about her questions and doubts about what she had been hearing, although there was a slight sense of shock in the room that she had been so forthright. Once again, I had to ask myself whether I had allowed sufficient space for questions in my wish to transmit such complex ideas.

I am reminded of Confucius' injunction that was mentioned earlier: 'Do not do to others that you do not wish others to do to you' (Mah 2001). This could be a wise maxim to follow when connecting with others in a different cultural context. It is tempting when encouraging others to look at their beliefs and attitudes to transmit one's own cultural certainties and thus reinforce the very stereotypes one is trying to question. It is an ongoing challenge to see ourselves as others see us and to realise the ways in which our beliefs shape our perceptions and behaviour.

References

Baldwin, B. (2012) Short articles

—, (2015) Personal communication.

Beck, M. & Malley, J. (2003) *A Pedagogy of Belonging*. https://www.researchgate. net/publication/234733484_A_Pedagogy_of_Belonging. Accessed 22 Dec. 2015.

Brendtro, L. (2010) *The Vision of Urie Bronfenbrenner*. http://www.cyc-net.org/ cyc-online/cyconline-nov2010-brendtro.html. Accessed 8 Jan. 2016.

Chu, B. (2014) *Chinese Whispers: Why everything you've heard about China is wrong*. London: Phoenix.

Cohen, A. (1985) *The Symbolic Construction of Community*. London: Tavistock.

Disabled World (2010). 'Overview of Disability in China', http://www.disabled-world. com/news/asia/china/disability-china.php#bottom. Accessed 7 Dec. 2015.

Faure, O. (undated) *China: New values in a changing society*. China Europe International Business School. http://www.ceibs.edu/ase/Documents/ EuroChinaForum/faure.htm. Accessed 23 Dec. 2015.

Goffman, E. (1963) *Stigma: Notes on the management of spoiled identity*. New York: Simon and Shuster.

Hutchings, A. & Taylor, I. (2007) 'Defining the profession? Exploring an international definition of social work in the China context', *International Journal of Social Welfare*, 16: 382–390.

International Labour Organisation (2008) *Facts on People with Disabilities in China*. International Labour Organization. http://www.ilo.org/wcmsp5/groups/public/- --asia/---ro-bangkok/---ilo-beijing/documents/publication/wcms_142315.pdf. Accessed 7 Dec. 2015.

Jenkins, R. (2014) *Social Identity*. (Fourth edition) London: Routledge.

Kaiman, J. (2013) 'China's disabled pupils face exclusion amid pressure to adapt, warns HRW', *Guardian*. http://www.theguardian.com/global- development/2013/jul/16/china-disabled-pupils-human-rights-watch. Accessed 7 Dec. 2015.

Lawler, S. (2014) *Identity: Sociological perspectives*. (Second edition) London: Polity Press.

Mah, A. (2001) *Watching the Tree to Catch a Hare*. London: Harper Collins.

Mak, W. & Cheung, R. (2008) 'Affiliate stigma among caregivers of people with intellectual disability or mental illness', *Journal of Applied Research in Intellectual Disabilities*, 21: 532–545.

Monteux, A. (2006) 'History and philosophy'. In R. Jackson (ed.), *Holistic Special Education: Camphill principles and practice*. Edinburgh: Floris Books.

Perry. B. (2006) 'Applying principles of neurodevelopment to clinical work with maltreated and traumatised children'. In: N. Webb (ed.), *Working with Traumatised Youth in Child Welfare*. New York: Guilford Press.

Thomas, C. (2007) *Sociologies of Disability and Illness: Contested ideas in disability studies and medical sociology*. London: Palgrave Macmillan.

Walter, C. (2010) *Camphill: Understanding children and childhood*. MSc Dissertation. Glasgow: Strathclyde University.

Wang, P, Michaels, C. & Day, M. (2011) 'Stresses and coping strategies of Chinese families with children with autism and other developmental disabilities', *Journal of Autism and Developmental Disorders*, 41(6): 783 –95.

Wickenden, M. (2010) *Teenage Worlds, Different Voices: An ethnographic study of identity and the lifeworlds of disabled teenagers who use AAC*. University of Sheffield. http:// etheses.whiterose.ac.uk/860/2/wickenden_final_thesis.pdf. Accessed 7 Dec. 2015.

Wolfensberger, W. (1983) 'Social role valorisation: A proposed new term for the principle of normalisation', *Mental Retardation*, 21(6): 234–239.

Woodman, A. & Hauser-Cram, P. (2013) 'The role of coping strategies in predicting change in parenting efficacy and depressive symptoms among mothers of adolescents with developmental disabilities', *Journal of Intellectual Disability Research*, 57(6): 513–530.

Xu, J., Wang, M., Xiang, Y. & Hu, X. (2005) 'Quality of life for people with intellectual disabilities in China: A cross-culture perspectives study', *Journal of Intellectual Disability Research*, 49(10): 745–749.

Gross National Happiness as an Alternative Development Paradigm, and its Relevance for Community Living

HA VINH THO

In the course of history, there comes a time when humanity is called to shift to a new level of consciousness, to reach a higher moral ground. A time when we have to shed our fear and give hope to each other. That time is now.

The late Wangari Maathai, Nobel Peace Laureate

My path from Camphill to Vietnam and Bhutan over the warzones of our time

Together with my wife Lisi and our two children, I lived for many years in Perceval, a Camphill community in Switzerland. I consider those years of community practice, sharing our life and work with people living with intellectual disabilities, as some of the most formative experiences on which all my later work and social understanding are built. After Camphill, I worked for the International Committee of the Red Cross and spent time in most of the conflict areas of the beginning of the twenty-first century: from Afghanistan to Palestine and from Darfur to Pakistan. These experiences led me to the conclusion that the physical violence that I was witnessing was but the tip of the iceberg and that I had to uncover the underlying root causes that were not addressed in the humanitarian response to these tragic events. It became more and more obvious that systemic or structural violence was the deeper cause of the outer events and that we had to try and understand these systemic problems if solutions were to be found.

This led me to develop a critical view of the current economic and development paradigm and to search for alternatives. On a local community scale, my experience in the Camphill Movement seemed to offer a valid model of a different way to organise work, finances and a social organism. Nevertheless the question remained to find a model that would be applicable on a much larger scale, such as a country. This is how I encountered the Gross National Happiness framework in Bhutan. At the end of 2011, the Prime Minister of Bhutan decided to create a Gross National Happiness Centre as a learning institute and community to teach and experiment GNH in action. They were looking for a Program Director for the new centre and posted an international recruitment offer. I applied and was selected and this is how I moved to Bhutan at the beginning of 2012. At the same time, since the 1990's, my wife and I had set up an NGO[1] in Vietnam – *Eurasia Foundation*. Here we started our work in the field of special education. During the Vietnam war many children had been affected by the consequences of Agent Orange[2] and as a result there was an unusually high percentage of children with disabilities; at the same time, the government lacked the resources and the expertise to offer appropriate support and education to these children and young people. Gradually our work expanded from special education to general education, to embrace ecology, community building and social entrepreneurship. We built many schools and workshops, trained the first generation of teachers in the field of curative education and social therapy and, in 2009, we created the Peaceful Bamboo Family, an intentional working and learning community inspired by the Camphill Movement and the Gross National Happiness Framework in Vietnam.

The challenges of our time and the need to transform the current development paradigm

The crisis of our time isn't just a crisis of a single leader, organisation, country, or conflict. The crisis of our time reveals the dying of an old social structure and way of thinking, an old way of institutionalizing and enacting collective social forms.

Otto C. Scharmer

Otto Scharmer has identified three major challenges that we face as humankind. He calls it the three divides[3]:

1. The Ecological Divide
2. The Social Divide
3. The Spiritual-cultural Divide

It seems appropriate to add a fourth one that is a consequence of the three previous ones:

4. The Leadership Divide

1. The ecological divide: The alienation between self and nature

Since the beginning of human history until the late 1970s, mankind used far less of the abundant natural resources that Planet Earth so generously provides than was available. But this changed dramatically during the last three decades of the twentieth century. Modest UN scenarios suggest that if current population and consumption trends continue then by the 2030s we will need the equivalent of two Earths to support us. And of course, we only have one. Turning resources into waste faster than waste can be turned back into resources puts us in a global ecological overshoot, depleting the very resources on which human life and biodiversity depend[4]. As a consequence, one third of our agricultural land has disappeared over the past forty years. According to a World Bank report[5], dramatic climate changes and weather extremes are already affecting millions of people around the world, damaging crops and coastlines and putting water security at risk. There is growing evidence that warming close to 1.5°C above pre-industrial levels is locked into the Earth's atmospheric system due to past and predicted emissions of greenhouse gases, and climate change impacts such as extreme heat events may now be unavoidable. As the planet warms, climatic conditions, heat and other weather extremes which occur once in hundreds of years and considered highly unusual or unprecedented today would become the 'new climate normal' as we approach 4°C – a frightening world of increased risks and global instability.

These are only some examples to illustrate the unprecedented ecological challenges we are currently facing. The inner dimension of this challenge is the fundamental disconnect between humans and nature. This alienation is a side-effect of the current materialistic world view that has become predominant over the past centuries: the idea that our planet is but a heap of matter ruled by merely physical and chemical laws. Without reclaiming the spiritual dimension of Nature, mere political agreements will fail to address the fundamental crisis that underlines these issues.

2. The social divide: Alienation between self and others

Two and a half billion people on our planet subsist on less than $2 per day. Although there have been many attempts to lift people out of poverty, this number has not changed much over the past several decades. In addition we see an increasing polarisation in society in which the top one per cent has a greater collective worth than the entire bottom 90 per cent. According to Barack Obama, income inequality is the 'defining challenge of our times', while Pope Francis states that 'inequality is the root of social ills'. Human beings have deep-seated psychological responses to inequality and social hierarchy. The tendency to equate outward wealth with inner worth means that inequality colours our social perceptions. It invokes feelings of superiority and inferiority, dominance and subordination – which affect the way we relate to and treat each other. Research shows[6] that, as well as health and violence, almost all the problems that are more common at the bottom of the social ladder are also more common in more unequal societies – including mental illness, drug addiction, obesity, loss of community life, imprisonment, unequal opportunities and poorer wellbeing for children. The effects of inequality are not confined to the poor. A growing body of research shows that inequality damages the social fabric of the whole society. Health and social problems are between twice and ten times as common in more unequal societies.

Although mankind produces more goods and services than ever before, even when taking into account the current size of the world population, there has been hardly any progress in terms of fairness and equity in the distribution of wealth. Some

795 million people in the world do not have enough food to lead a healthy active life. That's about one in nine people on earth. Poor nutrition causes nearly half (45 per cent) of deaths in children under five (3.1 million children each year). Sixty-six million primary school-age children attend classes across the developing world, hungry.[7]

These figures are a sad expression of the level of alienation between oneself and others and a devastating outcome of our current economic system: our fellow humans being perceived as competitors, rather than sisters and brothers.

3. The spiritual-cultural divide: Alienation between self and self

Our current economic system is based on an assumption about human nature: the so-called *homo economicus* or economic man. This concept portrays humans as narrowly self-interested agents always trying to maximise their benefit as consumers and their profits as producers. In other words, we have a heartless egoistic being only pursuing material benefits without any consideration for values, ethics or simply human relations based on love and friendship. No wonder that this implicit assumption creates an economic system that manifests as a self-fulfilling prophecy, resulting in a massive institutional failure and collectively creating results that nobody wants. This is not to pretend that these tendencies do not exist but traditional wisdom saw them as the shadow aspect (C.G. Jung), as the 'double' (R. Steiner) or, according to Buddhist psychology, as the 'poisons of the mind'. Moreover, if we internalise and identify with this distorted view of what it means to be human, we disconnect from our highest potential and true nature. This is fuelled by the illusion that material consumption can fulfil our deeper aspiration for meaning, identity or self-actualisation. Some of the results of this alienation are obvious in today's world, from growing suicide rates, to epidemics of depression and stress-related illnesses becoming the major factor of morbidity in the developed countries.

4. The leadership divide: Alienation between self and the greater good

On a personal level, the leadership divide manifests as a lack of self-leadership leaving the individual to fall prey to all sorts of manipulations, from marketing to numbing media influence, and substance abuse, from compulsive consumerism to Internet and technology addiction[8]. On the collective level, it manifests as the helplessness of most world leaders who are unable to overcome narrow national interests to live up to the global challenges that we are facing as humankind; they restrict the horizon of their thinking to the next electoral deadline and not to mid or long term goals.

It appears that the current economic and development model has come to its limits. Change is bound to happen; the only question is whether we – as mankind – can lead the change consciously or if we passively undergo the changes because outer circumstances force us to do so. It also appears that the most vulnerable will be the first victims and this holds true globally: the poorest countries will be the first to bear the brunt of the negative impacts and this is also true within developed countries. Obviously, people living with intellectual disabilities belong to the most vulnerable segment of society. This is one of the reasons why I believe that rethinking about community living, inclusion and intellectual disability should be done within a larger context of rethinking the overall development paradigm.

As Einstein once famously observed: 'we cannot solve our problems with the same thinking we used when we created them'. Gross National Happiness is one of the global frameworks that can help us rethink the overall goals of societal development.

Gross National Happiness: A new development paradigm

In 1968 Robert Kennedy pointed out that: 'Even if we act to erase material poverty, there is another great task; it is to confront the poverty of satisfaction – purpose and dignity – that afflicts us all. Too much and for too long, we seemed to have surrendered personal excellence and community values to the mere accumulation of material things... Gross National Product counts air pollution and cigarette advertising... It counts special locks for our doors and the jails for the people who break them. It counts the destruction of the redwood and the loss of our natural wonder in chaotic sprawl. It counts napalm and nuclear warheads... It counts the television programs that glorify violence to sell toys to our children. Yet, the Gross National Product does not allow for the health of our children, the quality of their education or the joy of their play. It does not include the beauty of our poetry or the strength of our marriages... It measures neither our wit nor our courage, neither our wisdom nor our compassion... It measures everything in short, except that which makes life worthwhile.'

'Gross National Happiness is more important than Gross National product'. With this famous declaration made in the 1970s, Jigme Singye Wangchuck, the fourth King of Bhutan challenged conventional, narrow and materialistic notions of human progress. He realised and declared that the existing development paradigm – GNP (or GDP) – did not consider the ultimate goal of every human being: happiness.

Old wisdom for a modern age

Inspired by age-old Buddhist wisdom in the ancient Kingdom of Bhutan, the fourth King concluded that GDP was neither an equitable nor a meaningful measurement for human happiness, nor should it be the primary focus for governance, and thus the philosophy of Gross National Happiness was born.

Since that time this pioneering vision of GNH has guided Bhutan's development and policy formation. Unique among the community of nations, it is a balanced 'middle path' in which equitable socio-economic development is integrated with environmental conservation, cultural promotion and good governance.

The folly of the GDP obsession

The folly of an obsession with GDP, as a measure of economic activity which does not distinguish between those activities that increase a nation's wealth and those that deplete its natural resources or result in poor health or widening social inequalities, is so clearly evident. If the forests of Bhutan were logged for profit, GDP would increase; if Bhutanese citizens picked up modern living habits adversely affecting their health, investments in health care systems would be made and GDP would increase. All of these actions could negatively affect the lives of the Bhutanese people yet paradoxically would contribute to an increase in GDP.

Four pillars and nine domains

The intuitive guiding principle of Gross National Happiness led to a practical conceptualisation of the idea. The foundation is made of four pillars:

1. **Environmental conservation as an antidote to the ecological divide**
   Environmental conservation is considered a key contribution to GNH because in addition to providing critical services such as water and energy, the environment is believed to contribute to aesthetic and other stimuli that can be directly healing to people. Bhutan is absorbing three times more CO_2 than it produces and has pledged to remain a carbon sink and to become 100 per cent organic by 2020.[9]

2. **Fair and sustainable socio-economic development as an antidote to the social divide**
   GNH economics is a spiritual approach to economics. It examines the functioning of the human mind and aspires to transform ignorance, greed and violence that direct most of the current economic activity. It aims to clarify what is harmful and beneficial in the range of human activities involving production and consumption, and tries to support people in making ethical choices. It strives towards a middle way balancing economic development and human values.
   It holds that truly rational decisions can only

be made when we understand the nature and the functioning of the mind. When we understand what constitutes desire and craving as a cause of suffering, we realise that all the wealth in the world cannot satisfy it. We become aware of the importance of contentment and of leading a simple but dignified life.

GNH economics challenges the vision of homo economicus that underlies current economic models: from a GNH perspective, attributes such as altruism and compassion are innate qualities of the mind. Economic development is important but it must be fair in terms of distribution and sustainable in order not to deprive future generations of their right to a good life.

3. **Preservation and promotion of culture as an antidote to the spiritual–cultural divide**
   Culture, includes science, arts, and spirituality.
   All three elements are important and must be equally promoted and developed for a society to thrive.
   If culture is reduced to its economic dimension and when it is determined by financial indicators only, a society gradually loses its identity and values and individuals are reduced to economic actors: producers and consumers. Bhutan is a good example of a country that has been able to preserve and to further develop its unique Buddhist heritage and values.

4. **Good governance as an antidote to the leadership divide**
   Good governance is considered a pillar for happiness because it determines the conditions in which people thrive. While policies and programmes that are developed in Bhutan are generally in line with the values of GNH, there are also a number of tools and processes employed to ensure the values are indeed embedded in social policy. Bhutan is also a unique example of a peaceful transition from absolute monarchy to democracy initiated by the King himself.[10]

Nine domains

The four pillars are further elaborated into nine domains, which articulate the different elements of GNH in detail and form the basis of GNH measurement, indices and screening tools.

1. Living standards
2. Education
3. Health
4. Ecological diversity and resilience
5. Community vitality
6. Time balance
7. Psychological wellbeing
8. Good governance
9. Cultural diversity and resilience

These nine domains, clearly demonstrate that from the perspective of GNH, many inter-related factors are considered to be important in creating the conditions for happiness. Income and material security are obviously part of these conditions, but many other factors must also be taken into consideration. Similarly, the happiness of human beings is not seen as separate from the wellbeing of other life forms, and ecological diversity and resilience are included in the measure of GNH. The balance between material and non-material development, and the multi-dimensional and interdependent nature of GNH are key features that distinguish GNH from GDP as a measure of a country's progress.

The universal human goal to pursue happiness and the existence of planetary boundaries are the two fundamental premises of GNH. The current economic model, based on the doctrine of limitless growth has resulted in the destructive attempt to use the earth's finite resources to satisfy infinite wants. The envisaged new paradigm differs in essence from the existing one by making sustainability of life on earth the top concern and recalibrating development to ensure that life – of humans, other species and the earth itself – is valued and prioritised.

THE GNH Framework

PLANETARY BOUNDARIES

SOCIETAL HAPPINESS

A. Needs

All human beings, regardless of the environment in which they live, require adequate satisfaction of their need for food, water, shelter, security & respect. All of this, in turn, is dependent upon a sustainable environment

B. Holistic Development Agenda

A transformative agenda with interconnected solutions (the four pillars of Gross National Happiness):
- **Environmental conservation**
- **Sustainable & equitable socio-economic development**
- **Preservation & promotion of culture**
- **Good governance**

C. Responsible use of resources

Natural, social, human and economic resources to ensure present and future sustainability

D. Outcome: Equitable & Sustainable Society

Progress assessed through indicators including:
- Living standards
- Education
- Health
- Ecological diversity and resilience
- Community vitality
- Time balance
- Psychological wellbeing
- Good governance
- Cultural diversity and resilience

E. Happiness Skills

Drawn creatively from human historical experience, wisdom traditions and modern science

Happiness skills

The GNH framework seeks to find a balance between the outer and the inner conditions leading to happiness and wellbeing. Seeing happiness as a skill is a relatively new and unusual idea in current western culture, but most traditional wisdom, from ancient Greek Philosophy to Asian spirituality has shared this vision and developed methods to cultivate the inner qualities leading to happiness. However, there is now a strong convergence between traditional contemplative wisdom and the latest scientific findings – especially in the field of neuroscience[11] – that allows a better understanding of the way we can train the mind to enhance inner qualities such as mindfulness, compassion and altruism, and how these abilities have a strong correlation with happiness and wellbeing. In the field of education, there is a growing awareness of the need to complement intellectual and academic skills with Social and Emotional Learning[12] (SEL) and with the training of attention: Mindfulness practices.[13]

Likewise, there is also a strong momentum in cultivating Mindful-ness in many fields of social life, including in the British Parliament:

> The Mindfulness Initiative is an advocacy project, aimed at increasing awareness of how mindfulness can benefit society. The Initiative is working with parliamentarians, media and policy makers to develop recommendations on the role of mindfulness in public policy and the workplace. Scientific research is generating substantial evidence of the benefits of mindfulness to wellbeing.[14]

Similarly, there is an increasing interest in Mindfulness in the business community. Some years ago, it would have been unthinkable to expect the world political and business leaders to sit in meditation in a high level meeting, but this is exactly what is now regularly happening in the World Economic Forum (WEF) in Davos.[15]

These few examples illustrate the fact that the inner dimension of happiness and wellbeing has moved from a marginal interest to a mainstream concern in many fields of society, far beyond specialist concerns of psychologists or spiritual seekers.

From economic growth to happiness and wellbeing

Whilst the one sided neo-liberal economic ideology and the focus – and even obsession – with economic growth is still powerful, it is more and more challenged and not only marginally, but also in international arenas such as the UN. On April 2, 2012, the Royal Government of Bhutan convened a High-level Meeting on Wellbeing and Happiness: Defining a New Economic Paradigm. More than 800 participants including political and government leaders, representatives of governments, international organisations, civil society organisations, media, and business, as well as leading economists, scholars, academics, and spiritual leaders from the world's major faiths participated in the proceedings.[16] One of the outcomes of this meeting was that the March 20 was proclaimed by the United Nations as the International Day of Happiness.[17] Many countries, including the UK, Germany and France, have developed new sets of indicators to measure the wellbeing of their citizens as a complement to the conventional GDP measurement. Furthermore twenty US States have adopted Genuine Progress Indicators (GPI)[18] as an alternative measurement of their development. Major economists including Joseph Stiglitz (recipient of the 2001 Nobel Memorial Prize in Economic Sciences and the John Bates Clark Medal) have clearly shown that the current GDP based economic system does not meet the needs of our time.[19]

There is a growing tension between the old economic model based on narrow financial metrics and the emerging development paradigm based on happiness and wellbeing and this tension also manifests in the field of social care and especially in the field of intellectual disability.

The Gross National Happiness framework applied in a Camphill community in Vietnam

When we created the Peaceful Bamboo Family community in Hue, Central Vietnam, our fundamental intention was not focused on caring for young people with an intellectual disability, but rather on creating a conducive environment that would allow these young people to unfold their full potential in a way that would enable them to make a positive contribution to society. And these contributions have been manifold.

When we started our community, it was not yet possible for NGOs in Vietnam to buy land and to run a privately owned Centre. Due to the many years of work in the field of special education, the local government had confidence in our Foundation and granted us an exception so that we could create the first private and free centre entirely based on our values and principles inspired by the Camphill Movement and later by the GNH framework.

The Four pillars of GNH in the Peaceful Bamboo Family

1. Environmental conservation

In Vietnam, as in many developing countries the so-called modernisation of agriculture has created a lot of damage to the environment and even to the health of the population due to the misuse of pesticides and fertilisers. Especially among young parents, there is a growing concern of the negative effect of harmful food on the health of their children. Our community started the first biodynamic organic horticulture garden in Vietnam which became rapidly a pilot project where students of the local agricultural college could come to learn about a different way to take care of the earth and produce healthy food. As a result, we eat mainly our own organic, locally grown vegetables.

As a community, we are trying to reduce as much as possible our ecological footprint; we have solar panels for warm water and electricity, our own water source and the means to collect rainwater Our next project is to become a zero waste community and to recycle human waste into compost and biogas.

2. Fair and sustainable

Our aim is to become economically and financially sustainable and to generate enough income to gradually become autonomous. Our community is also a vocational training centre and the young people who have graduated and want to remain in the community are hired as co-workers. Our current focus is to develop social entrepreneurship in partnership with other like-minded companies. We process tropical fruits from our garden into delicious jam, juice and ice cream, we have a bakery and produce several types of cookies, and we sell these products through a partnership with an online health food store from Saigon.

Our lacquer-ware workshop combines traditional techniques with spontaneous creativity allowing the young people to express themselves freely while learning age-old Vietnamese handicrafts. We organise exhibitions and auctions to sell the paintings, and it is very moving to experience how proud the youngsters can be when they realise that people actually appreciate their creations and are willing to buy them. We also have an incense workshop producing high quality incense made of natural organic medicinal plants according to an ancient recipe.

We have opened a teahouse in our front-yard with a beautiful flower and rock garden; this gives us the opportunity to sell some of the products of the workshops and the garden, including our own organic green tea. Likewise, it is also an opportunity for the youngsters to learn the skills of service industry, and to practise useful abilities such as counting, reading and writing, speaking in an appropriate way with strangers.

All these projects have a dual purpose, creating situations where young people living with an intellectual disability can learn useful skills and train for a job, thus contributing to society, and also generating income for the centre. This year, the centre was able to generate over 50 per cent of its running costs through these activities. But of course such a centre will always need some financial support to be able to develop further and flourish.

3. Preservation and promotion of culture

When we started the Peaceful Bamboo Family, we were inspired by the ideals of the Camphill Movement, but we wanted to create a community that was completely embedded in the Vietnamese context. We did not want to import foreign values and cultural practices in a country that has suffered too much and for too long from destructive foreign influence, whether from French colonialism, American imperialism or Soviet communism.

At the same time, we knew from our experience in the Camphill community of Perceval the importance of spiritual and cultural practices to structure the life and cycles of time of a community. So our challenge was to find the essence of the practices that we had experienced in a Western, largely Christian context located in a temperate climate zone, and to recreate comparable forms and rituals born out of the Vietnamese, largely Buddhist and Confucian, tropical context. I explicitly mention the climate zone because most religious festivals are related to the season: Christmas near the Winter Solstice, Easter at the Spring Equinox, St John at the Summer Solstice and Michaelmas at the Autumn Equinox.

So we structured our yearly cycle around traditional Vietnamese and Buddhist festivals that are connected to the moon cycle rather than the sun cycle; including ancestor and Earth-spirit worshipping ceremonies which are held on New and Full Moon.

Likewise, we organised the weekly rhythm with a day of Mindfulness and an evening called 'Sharing from the Heart' where each member of the community has an opportunity to share how they feel, what makes them happy or worries them and heard in an atmosphere of respect and non-judgemental listening.

We also hold regular seminars and workshops for both co-workers and youngsters in a spirit of lifelong learning for all, and we have created the 'Eurasia Learning Institute for Happiness and Wellbeing' (ELI) to share our experience well beyond our limited field. As an example, we have started a training Programme for forty university professors from Saigon who want to implement a 'Mindfulness Based Compassion and Happiness

221

Programme' with their students. We are also working with the Education Department of Hue province and have implemented a mindfulness and compassion educational programme: 'A call to Care' in primary schools in Hue.

These are just some of the many examples of the way we have consciously included the spiritual and cultural dimensions in the community life and how it can spread beyond our community.

4. Good governance

Of course our community has a leadership structure that is responsible and accountable, but our effort is to create a participatory leadership-style that includes everyone, long-term co-workers, volunteers, and the residents alike and we regularly hold seminars to redefine and co-create a common vision and mission that is shared by all. When new projects emerge, the whole community is consulted so that they can voice their ideas or doubts. For instance, in the recent past, we have created an inclusive kindergarten, a sector for young teenagers with behavioural challenges and we are designing an ambitious zero waste programme. All these projects were discussed and designed with the entire community at many open meetings. Beyond the Four Pillars, we have also used the nine domains of GNH as an assessment tool to pilot and improve the functioning of our community.

The social experiment of Camphill in the light of the challenges of our time

In Vietnam, our centre is considered as being an innovative pilot project and has drawn a lot of attention from the media, civil society and government alike. Many people feel that it offers an alternative social model in a society that, after decades of war followed by a time of intense economic development, is searching for a more balanced development. When I was in Hanoi last year, I gave a public talk and an interview on GNH, and the national daily newspaper of the Communist Party published a detailed and very positive article on GNH, indicating that it could be a way forward for Vietnam. The Peaceful Bamboo Family has become for many a living example that GNH can be implemented in the real world and does not have to remain an abstract ideal.

When describing the various practices implemented in the Peaceful Bamboo Family, I believe that most Camphill communities would agree that it is very similar to their own way of living and functioning, yet there seems to be an opinion in some western countries that the functioning of the Camphill communities is outdated and needs to be adapted to 'modernity'. I would argue that the opposite is true: the so called 'modernity' based on neo-liberal economic ideology controlling all aspects of society, the regulation of the social field based on this ideology, and the marketisation of care, represents a completely obsolete model that has shown its own limits by creating the dire situation we are currently facing as a mankind. The time has come for new development models that address the challenges of our time: from transition towns[20] to caring economics[21], from eco villages[22] to sustainable cities.[23]

The Camphill Movement has shown over many decades and in many countries that innovative social forms are possible in living practice, and that people living with an intellectual disability can contribute to pioneering such social experiments.

Endnotes

[1] NGO: A non-governmental organisation is an organisation that is neither a part of a government nor a conventional for-profit business.

[2] Agent Orange: One of the herbicides and defoliants used by the US military as part of its herbicidal warfare programme.

[3] Scharmer, O. and Kaufer, K. (2013) *Leading from the Emerging Future: from eco-system to eco-system economics.* San Francisco: Berrett-Koehler.

[4] www.footprintnetwork.org/en/index.php/GFN/page/world_footprint/

[5] www.worldbank.org/en/topic/climatechange/publication/turn-down-the-heat

[6] Pickett, K. and Wilkinson, R. (2010) *The Spirit Level: Why equality is better for everyone.* London: Penguin.

[7] www.wfp.org/hunger/stats

[8] virtual-addiction.com/

[9] www.theguardian.com/environment/2015/dec/03/bhutan-has-most-ambitious-pledge-at-paris-climate-summit

[10] www.gnhcentrebhutan.org/what-is-gnh/four-pillars-and-nine-domains/ preservation-and-promotion-of-culture/

[11] www.resource-project.org/en/home.html

[12] www.casel.org/social-and-emotional-learning/

[13] www.mindfulnessinschools.org/

[14] www.themindfulnessinitiative.org.uk/

[15] www.weforum.org/videos/insights-experiencing-mindful-leadership

[16] sustainabledevelopment.un.org/index. php?page=view&type=400&nr=617&menu=35

[17] research.un.org/en/happiness

[18] www.theguardian.com/sustainable-business/2014/sep/23/genuine-progress-indicator-gdp-gpi-vermont-maryland

[19] Stiglitz, J., Sen, A. & Fitoussi, J-P. (2010) *Mismeasuring Our Lives: Why GDP doesn't add up.* New York: The New Press.

[20] www.transitionnetwork.org/

[21] www.caring-economics.org/

[22] gen.ecovillage.org/

[23] www.sustainablecities.eu/

Longing for
Virtuous Community

MICHAEL KENDRICK

'Community' as always ensuring wellbeing or as something more ambiguous

> We have all known the long loneliness, and we have found
> that the answer is community.
>
> *Dorothy Day (1983)*

A term that is constantly heard in regards to many matters related
to disability is the term 'community'. Most often community
is heralded as being a highly desirable, if not essential, element
of the good life for most people including those persons with
intellectual disabilities. It would seem for many that community
is perhaps even the *sine qua non* of a life lived well. In this regard,
community is clearly seen to be something that is highly associated
with personal wellbeing, such that the absence of 'community' in
one's life would be seen as constituting a form of deprivation or
perhaps something worse. Consequently, it is offered as an end
point for policy, practice and values. If 'community' in actuality is
an essential requirement of living and is not sufficiently present
for people, then the clear inference is that its lack will lead to
suffering and distress for those people affected by its absence in
their lives.

A lack of precision in how community is defined and interpreted
makes its assessment quite hard to specify, as much can be read into
the use of the term 'community' depending upon one's epistemology
and core assumptions. For instance, if the 'good life' is a life of one's
own choosing, how might one see the role of obligations to others

225

that limits one's choices? One could conceivably choose to have and raise children for the enjoyment and life satisfaction they might engender, yet place little importance on the parental duties and demands that raising children brings. This tension between self-centredness and responsibilities to others pervades the nature of 'community', as there are many potential benefits of 'community', but these might only be realised in reality if the people in a given community take on the responsibilities of upholding the ideals of that community. For instance, it is hard to imagine a commonwealth of any kind succeeding with equity when significant economic sectors of that society successfully evade their share of taxes while still benefitting from what those taxes generate in terms of community capacities (that is, a sanctioned 'free rider' in economic terms).

As has been said, the term 'community' can be used to suggest that being part of 'community' is integral to individual and collective wellbeing. Nonetheless, this very positive and benign notion of community presence and participation assumes that one's role(s) in community will always engender beneficial outcomes. However, the experience of many socially devalued groups within diverse communities seems to show the opposite, as the former suffer from prejudice, inequality, injustice and mistreatment, possibly for generations. The insistence that simply being in community is linked to inevitable beneficial outcomes may be predicated on the assumption that the individual is a valued and largely socially included member of the community and treated accordingly. Community as an automatic source of the 'good life' may be quite a wishful, if not naïve, understanding of how communities actually work. Hence, those people segregated and excluded from 'community' could be endangered in ways that have consequences that are potentially profound in their impacts on the inherent quality of those people's lives. One only has to look at the history of institutionalisation and its effects to realise that communities do indeed reject and banish people with dehumanising consequences for them.

Certainly, the long list of types of people who have been cast aside and marginalised in many societies is much too lengthy to dismiss as being some kind of rarity. Rather, human communities are quite problematic because of the very fact that the specific nature of communities is closely linked to how they operate and the kinds of values they embrace or fail to embrace. The miseries created in the lives of so many socially devalued people ought not to be seen as somehow divorced from 'community'. After all, these sufferings may arise from the essential character of a given community or society. For instance, when the life expectancy, health status, educational and employment prospects of socially devalued groups in a given community are much less than others in that same community, then that 'community' is culpable in tolerating that some people and classes of people will experience deprived lives and associated distress.

'Community' as a potential resource for a good life

A community is democratic only when the humblest and weakest person can enjoy the highest civil, economic, and social rights that the biggest and most powerful possess.

A. Philip Randolph (2015)

Though communities may not benefit people equally, it is striking how variable human societies are in terms of the benefits they provide to their members. If one considers various quality of life indices across societies, such as the UN Human Development Index, the OECD Better Life Index, the Gallup Global Wellbeing Index and the Social Progress Index, it is clear that societies differ considerably, notwithstanding the complexities of measuring something as difficult to define as human wellbeing. Obviously, the type of society will sizeably influence both what is possible for people's overall collective wellbeing as well as what may impact any given individual within that society.

The point not to lose sight of is that the character of a given society will have real consequences for the lives of people. Often these consequences are, on balance, quite beneficial, such as life expectancy, access to health care and education, freedom from crime and war, environmental quality, employment, etc. Though one could usefully dispute the precise importance of one factor of wellbeing over another, it would be unwise to doubt that the value choices of a society relative to its members are linked and so the key question is *what kind of community is it?* For instance, if one examines other societal indices of potentially advantageous or damaging impacts to the quality of community life such as the Corruption Perceptions Index, the World Crime Index and the World Democracy Index, we can see that if one is in a society that performs well on corruption, crime and democracy, there are real benefits to the population.

'Community' as a social movement 'meme'

> Cultures, along with the religions that shape and nurture
> them, are value systems, sets of traditions and habits
> clustered around one or several languages, producing
> meaning: for the self, for the here and now, for the
> community, for life.
>
> *Tariq Ramadan (2012)*

The term 'meme' is often not familiar to people. The Oxford Dictionary definition is 'an element of a culture or system of behaviour passed from one individual to another by imitation or other non-genetic means.' It would seem that 'community' is a cultural term in this sense. Not unsurprisingly, the claims put forward on the ostensible benefits of 'community' are many. What informs people's thinking may have components to it that reflect their own experience or perceptions of what they believe to be 'community' and also what others might say about their own experience of it. In other words, 'community' could well be a product of culture in the sense that it has become a 'meme' or core narrative of this period within what might be called the world of disability.

As many are aware, this sense of 'community' as being important owes a great deal of its prominence in the current era due to various interlinked social movements that have arisen in response to the past social devaluation and mistreatment of people with intellectual disabilities. Much of this abuse of people with intellectual disabilities had been specifically associated with the negative effects of residential institutions on people's lives. The subsequent dissent against such settings has revolved around how damaging the thinking and treatment of people with intellectual disabilities associated with that period has been and remains. Hence, the current prominence of 'community' owes a great deal to its explicit use as a central remedy or antidote to all manner of poor treatment of people with intellectual disabilities within society, including maltreatment which had happened within community itself rather than solely in segregated institutional settings.

At least on one level, 'community', like any potential cure-all or panacea, need not actually be in itself a remedy to the various evils it is meant to overcome. Its function as a 'meme' simply provides a common symbol that can help to rally and unite the diverse factions common to the heterogeneity of social movements. For instance, if one substituted the word 'hope' for 'community', one might find many supporters of 'hope' as long as it gave people a way to respond to human sufferings that had at least some promise in terms of making life better in the view of the proponents of 'hope'.

In this way, the term 'community' may, at the least, functionally provide a way for people to explicitly reject the realities that have brought about suffering and mistreatment of people as being oppressive, unjust, damaging and immoral. In this sense, it may move people to consider the necessity of abandoning key elements of a given social order even if they do not know what might conceivably replace these elements. Further, the conviction that 'something should be done' generates the search for what it is precisely that needs doing if things are to improve. Lastly, it forces people to examine and address what they perceive to be the sources of human wellbeing in both an individual and collective sense.

Given the social movement value of a shared analysis of what is wrong with the world and what might repair it, then the rise of a term like 'community' as a proposed end point to collectively aim for may make a great deal of sense as a socially unifying and collective ambition. In this version of its use it plays a symbolic and projective role rather than defining a specific eventual operational reality. This same unifying value in regards to other social movements can be seen in slogans such as freedom, democracy, justice, equality, rights, progress, etc. It is not the words *per se* that matter in a social movement, it is what people understand by and invest in those words.

Definitional ambiguities of what exactly 'community' is or might be

> We cannot seek achievement for ourselves and forget
> about progress and prosperity for our community...
> Our ambitions must be broad enough to include the
> aspirations and needs of others, for their sakes and for
> our own.
>
> *Richard Griswold del Castillo and Richard Garcia (1997)*

It is notable how many languages have a word for community yet does 'community' really mean the same thing from one language to another? Even within a given culture the term 'community' is used in quite varied and nuanced ways, so it is often very difficult to disentangle one shade of meaning from another, as the various versions of 'community' often overlap and are commonly used without any self-conscious attempts at precise definition. In fact, it may well be that too vigorous attempts to pin down what a specific slogan means may often produce schisms in social movements that arise from these conflicting interpretations. What follows are examples of the range of diverse meanings attributed to 'community'.

If we return to the Oxford Dictionary, we see that the origin of the term 'community' was the Latin word for 'common' i.e. *communitas* from *commis* and this evolved to Middle English *comunete*, from Anglo-French *communité*.

This same dictionary lists the following uses of the term:

1. a group of people living in the same place or having a particular characteristic in common;
2. a group of people living together and practising common ownership;

3. a particular area or place considered together with its inhabitants;
4. a body of nations or states unified by common interests
5. the people of a district or country considered collectively, especially in the context of social values and responsibilities.

It is evident that these formal definitions of 'community' do not specifically address the potential qualitative functions of 'community' as a source for supporting human life satisfaction and fulfilment that the social movement uses of the term tend to suggest. Rather, these dictionary definitions tend to speak to the types of relatively narrow commonalties between people that have clearly preceded the current era.

These resources embedded within communities may be assumed in some instances to be beneficial in nature, but clearly some communities may have abundant resources within them that do not equally benefit all members of that community. Hence, the use of the term 'community' may on occasion conflate the *potential* beneficial nature of community resources with some kind of universal access to them. Hence, there may be a presumption that communities will always be moral and ethical in their use of resources relative to those defined as community members. Such a use of the term 'community' may therefore operate from a wishful or romanticised view of communities *as many would prefer them to be*, rather than what they might actually be like in practice.

Consequently, one could evaluate communities as being variable in nature, not only in terms of the ethicality, equity and justice of their provision of 'community' resources to 'community' members, but also from other dimensions of 'community' functioning and resource distribution and its conceivable impact on the wellbeing of community members. For instance, some communities may favour certain classes over others, some may exploit some subgroups and not others, some communities may socially devalue some subgroups and exalt others, some may exclude some subgroups yet include others, and so on. Such an evaluation of communities as not being automatically beneficial in nature relative to community members is similar to the formulation in politics of *Realpolitik* to serve as a more discerning antidote, or at least counterweight, to highly idealistic or uncritically idealised views of politics as it is, rather than what many might want it to be.

Even so, this idea of 'realism without values' also has its difficulties, as an utterly practical and potentially ruthless approach to either community or politics risks the abandonment of beneficial morals and ethics and their enriching effects on community. For instance, many national communities have taken it to be axiomatic, for several generations at least, that all citizens without exception have reasonable access to health care, whereas a society such as the current United States has until recently enshrined inequitable access as normative and both morally and politically preferred. Clearly, this difference in principle and morality is not insignificant in terms of who suffers and who does not and thus has moral meaning as to the type of 'community' one can expect in that nation while that outlook persists.

'Community' is a term that is hard to divorce from its qualitative dimensions, as communities clearly can differ in terms of their comparative benefits to their overall members or subgroups of their members. Consequently, the tentative posing of 'community' as being an end point for human development and wellbeing, cannot be taken up as a question unless one is prepared to recognise that communities and their many features can vary in different ways as:

- both damaging and beneficial depending upon their specific impacts on the people in a given 'community';
- altered for the better or worse by the *de facto* value choices of that 'community';
- dynamic in nature and thus capable of change, evolution and decadence given what outlook on human wellbeing is in place;
- susceptible to being misunderstood by their members depending upon the ideologies present that shape public perception;
- driven by interests that may be unacknowledged, counter to popular assumptions and contrary to the stated values of given communities.

The vested interests of people with intellectual disabilities in the debate about the qualities of a more optimal 'community'

Community is a sign that love is possible in a materialistic world where people so often either ignore or fight each other. It is a sign that we don't need a lot of money to be happy – in fact, the opposite.

Jean Vanier (1989)

If decisions about the nature of 'community' and communities were proven to be inconsequential in terms of the wellbeing of the people in a given community, then promoting community changes for the better would be pointless. However, people with intellectual disabilities are never entirely apart from the collective decisions of communities even when they are segregated and excluded from that community, since such segregation itself derives from the roles such communities place people with intellectual disabilities in in the first place. Much as the privileged in a given community benefit from how that community is organised and what decisions it makes, it would be mistaken to assume that all decisions taken will invariably benefit community members equally. In fact, decisions taken not to require broad swaths of the community to ensure normative accessibility of people with intellectual disabilities to all of the major elements of community life will inevitably ensure that people with intellectual disabilities are deprived of the resources that others are able to enjoy almost without noticing.

There are many benefits of 'community' that people with intellectual disabilities have a significant interest in obtaining because these will impact on their overall wellbeing and quality of life. These include, but are not limited to, many normative aspects of community life that many others routinely can take for granted:

- obtaining an education, work and an income;
- having physical and social access to all public community events and locations;

233

- not being discriminated against due to negative stereotypes;
- obtaining the same variety of valued social roles available to other citizens that might personally interest them;
- having the varieties of relationships and 'community' group memberships that may be of personal interest to them;
- having the opportunity to contribute to 'community';
- having the same rights and opportunities as others enjoy;
- having the capacities and supports available to them to act and live with normative autonomy;
- obtaining a secure and appealing 'home of one's own';
- accessing financial and other pertinent resources sufficient to live autonomously within the 'community' without being involuntarily institutionalised;
- being assured of similar normative levels of safety and freedom from crime and abuse comparable to other citizens;
- being able to expect the same quality of public services as others.

The preceding are examples of significant ingredients of what many people might think of in terms of their own version of the 'good life'. However, their achievement is difficult if one is acting solely on one's own, as they are outcomes directly tied to how a given community or society functions collectively in practice for its members. In this regard they reflect the overall cultural character of a 'community' at a given point in time. It is most certainly the case that people with intellectual disabilities have a great deal riding on the question of the character of the communities in which they live as both the strengths and failings of a given 'community' can potentially have both beneficial and damaging impacts on their lives. Thus, the specific character of 'community' is intertwined with their wellbeing, just as it is with all other members of a 'community'.

'Community' as variable conditions of living

The wellbeing of a community of people working
together will be the greater, the less the individual claims
for himself the proceeds of his work, i.e. the more of
these proceeds he makes over to his fellow-workers, the
more his own needs are satisfied, not out of his own work
but out of the work done by others.

Rudolf Steiner (1927)

Interdependence with a 'community' is inevitable to a greater or
lesser degree, as most people's existence occurs within the context of
one or more communities. In reality, even those who intentionally
drop out of 'community' and live intentional solitary existences
apart from their former lives may not be entirely divorced from
'community', as much as being voluntarily withdrawn from the
life of community. Similarly, those persons who are involuntarily
removed from 'community' by the state because of their criminal
conduct still remain part of that 'community', but in a much more
restricted sense than previously. In fact, the extent and nature of
this exclusion from community for the same criminal acts varies
widely from one nation to another.

Given that many in the disability sector seem to portray
'community' as the essence of or key to the wellbeing of people
with intellectual disabilities, it is useful to distinguish whether
this hope that community will deliver wellbeing is justified.
First, given that not all communities are equal in terms of the
benefits they may bring to a given person's life, it is conceivable
that people with intellectual disabilities may be comparatively
disadvantaged by living in one community versus another, if
these communities differ substantively. For instance, it is striking
how different the rates of employment of people with intellectual
disabilities can be from one part of a country to another.

It is not unusual for a given person with a disability to have
a distinctly different life experience from another person with a
disability, even when they live in the same community. In this regard,
community life may have normative shared features in a collective

sense for its members, but that is distinct from the extensive variability evident in the lives of individual persons with intellectual disabilities. For instance, it is statistically true that people with intellectual disabilities are more likely to be victims of crime than the general population, but that still leaves the vast majority of people with intellectual disabilities not personally having experienced or being victimised by crime.

While the overall character of a given community creates many 'conditions on the ground' that might be advantageous or not to a given person and even broad groups of persons with a disability, this is not the same as saying that the character of 'community' somehow entirely controls the factors that might go into a given person's sense of wellbeing, as some personally important elements of wellbeing for a given person may exist despite the widespread oppressive constraints of a given community. For instance, many people with intellectual disabilities may find loving companions and marriage partners in life despite the fact that others who also would have sought this outcome ultimately find themselves without that element of wellbeing. This would also hold for non-disabled persons, as not all the potential benefits of communities are realised uniformly in people's lives.

The root of this mistaken conflation of 'community' with universal wellbeing seems to be the unwarranted perception that 'community' is the same as life itself, rather than the more warranted role of community as a key ingredient in shaping the conditions of life, but not as the source of life and wellbeing itself. Were it the source of all things good in life, then it would be a more reasonable expectation that simply accessing 'community' would somehow have an immediately existentially beneficial and even transcendent effect. In this sense, 'community' could equate somewhat to the terms 'deliverance' or 'salvation' in the secular sense, that is, 'preservation or deliverance from harm, ruin, or loss' (Oxford Dictionary). However, in the nonsecular Christian sense, deliverance could only be provided by God and clearly 'community' is not God, though the Christian concept of 'communion' presumes a shared spiritual link with God that potentially unites people with each other through the Divine. In this sense, 'community' may serve as an ideological proxy or even panacea for 'the good life', as has been indicated in the preceding remarks on its role as a social movement meme.

It is not hard to see why this mental linkage may have occurred given the brutal and damaging consequences of social devaluation experienced by many people with intellectual disabilities, both in institutional settings and in other largely segregated and deprived existences within 'community'. In both instances, such dehumanisation and degradation of people with intellectual disabilities occurred at the hands of 'community', so it would be puzzling on a logical level as to why 'community' is now somehow to be uncritically trusted as the way forward. Clearly, what the proponents of 'community' today are proposing is not the type of 'community' that led to the institutions, but rather a notably much improved 'community', that is, a transformed or redeemed 'community'.

In fact, the view that 'community' can, on occasion, be transformed for the better has certainly proved to be valid, as the life conditions and opportunities for people with intellectual disabilities within present day communities have clearly got better in many important ways in a comparative historical sense. However, given the many definitions of community that rest upon a sense of commonalities amongst people, even today's communities have not transcended human nature to the point of placing people with intellectual disabilities out of danger at the hands of their own 'community'. For example, it is often quoted that over 90-92 per cent of fetuses identified *in utero* as having Down's syndrome are aborted. More recent studies set this figure more at around 67 per cent, but that is without controlling for differences from culture to culture and differences within populations in the same culture. Obviously, the mere existence of offspring with Down's syndrome still remains devalued by a significant majority, since 'not getting born' most certainly irrevocably interferes with 'the good life'. Nonetheless, it is quite unlikely that such a number will remain the same given the plasticity of cultures and the attitudes embedded in them.

The recognition that 'community' can be changed for the better is quite real, as is the reality that community can also change for the worse. Further, both trends can be at work at the same time creating divergent tensions within the 'polity' of community. The overt mass killing of people with intellectual disabilities was public policy and lawful during the Nazi era, as was the involuntary sterilisation of people with intellectual disabilities in many countries up until very recently. Profound discrimination and abuse of people with intellectual disabilities persists into the present and yet simultaneously we also have the unprecedented UN Convention on the Rights of Persons with Disabilities. Paradoxically it would seem that 'community' is both the source of much of the sufferings of people with intellectual disabilities and yet also the source of much of their liberation from the oppressions of 'community'. Hence, what many reformers and activists might really mean by 'community' is not *community as it is*, but rather *community as it ought to be….and could be*, that is, a virtuous community.

The longing for 'community' as a search for moral conditions of life within community

> Although the world is full of suffering, it is full also of the overcoming of it.
>
> *Helen Keller (1903)*

Many might quite understandably see the longing for a virtuous community as somehow being a kind of misguided fantasy for naïve idealists who are unable to reconcile themselves to the realities of human existence. Often such critiques of various kinds of idealists as lacking realism are valid and compelling, as their wishful rather than discerning approach to changing communities leaves their efforts ineffectual. However, this critique itself becomes falsified when confronted with idealists who have few illusions about the potentially perverse nature of human beings and 'community', yet nonetheless refuse to accept the damaging and unjust conditions of community life as being somehow beyond challenge and eventual change. But simply wanting a better version of 'community' ought not to be confused with engaging personal resolve and commitment to bringing it about. Of course there is no assurance that the struggle will prevail so that people disadvantaged within a particular order of community life are treated ethically and honourably, but the very fact that people will make sacrifices so that this potential might come about brings with it moral force and resolve.

It is not an abstract 'community' that is most often sought, as the perception that a community could and should be better brings about the questioning of a community's shortcomings and begins the long process of changing that community and its ways. The resulting process may not be particularly orderly, but it can focus attention and consciousness on the question of the kinds of virtue that the community holds up as its ideals against which to measure its conduct and social institutions. In this way, the very nature of 'community' may be challenged and the search begun for what needs to be done to establish and maintain the virtues that are being sought.

People with intellectual disabilities are only one group in society and community who might stand to gain from the presence and embedding of worthwhile community ethics, values and principles that enable their lives to improve and thrive. We are all bound up in the universality of the human condition. Hence, notwithstanding the many imperfections of efforts to make life better for people, the struggle does create the possibility of communities standing for something and thus asking something of themselves relative to how people are treated within community. Where there is disinterest, disdain and hostility towards a community with virtue, then it can be expected that such attitudes will turn their back on those who are most weakly positioned to advance their own interests. Since there will always be people in this more vulnerable position, community values serve as one of the most fundamental safeguards for their ultimate wellbeing. This is why we must never lose our longing for a virtuous community, as all of us are endangered when people no longer care about what we are and what we have become.

References

Corruption Perceptions Index. https://www.transparency.org/cpi2014/results.

Day, D. (1983) *By Little and by Little: The selected writings of Dorothy Day.* New York: Alfred A. Knopf.

Gallup Global Wellbeing Index. http://info.healthways.com/hubfs/
WellbeingWellbeing_Index/2014_Data/Gallup-Healthways_State_of_Global_
WellbeingWellbeing_2014_Country_Rankings.pdf?t=1446762682108.

Griswold del Castillo, R. & Garcia, R. (1997) *Cesar Chavez: A triumph or spirit*
Norman: University of Oklahoma Press.

Keller, H. (1903) *Optimism, Part One: Optimism Within*. Boston:
The Merrymount Press.

OECD Better Life Index. http://www.oecdbetterlifeindex.org/#/11111111111.

Ramadan, T. (2012) 'Arabs and cultural emancipation', *Gulf News Thinkers*. http://
gulfnews.com/opinion/thinkers/arabs-and-cultural-emancipation-1.1003271.

Randolph, A., Kersten, A. & Lucander, D. (2015) *For Jobs and Freedom: The
selected speeches and writings of A. Philip Randolph*. Amherst: University of
Massachusetts Press.

Social Progress Index. http://www.socialprogressimperative.org/data/spi.

Steiner, R. (1927) *Reordering Society: The fundamental social law*. London:
The Anthroposophical Publishing Company.

UN Human Development Index. http://hdr.undp.org/en.

Vanier, J. (1989) *Community and Growth*. New York: Paulist Press.

World Crime Index. http://www.numbeo.com/crime/rankings_by_country.jsp.

World Democracy Index. http://knoema.com/atlas/topics/World-Rankings/
World-Rankings/Democracy-index.